In this book, an incisive and wide-ranging critique of ethnohistory and histori-cal anthropology, Michael Harkin develops an innovative approach to under-standing the profound cultural changes experienced during the past century by the Heiltsuks (Bella Bella), a Northwest Coast Indian group. Between 1880 and 1920, the Heiltsuks changed from one of the most traditional and aggressive groups on the Northwest Coast to paragons of Victorian virtues. Why and how did this dramatic transformation occur? These questions, Harkin contends, can best be answered by tracing the changing views the Heiltsuks had of themselves and of their past as they encountered colonial powers.

Rejecting many of the common methods and assumptions of eth-nohistorians as unwittingly Eurocentric or simplistic, Harkin argues that the multiple perspectives, motives, and events constituting the Heiltsuks' world and history can be productively conceived of as dialogues, ongoing series of culturally embedded communicative acts that presuppose previous acts and constrain future ones. Historical transformations in three of these dialogues, centering on the body, material goods, and concepts of the soul, are examined in detail. A valuable history of a little-known Northwest Coast Indian group and a highly original investigation into the dynamics of colonial encounters, the na-ture of cultural memory, and the processes of cultural stability and change, this provocative study sets the agenda for a new type of ethnohistory.

MICHAEL E. HARKIN is an associate professor of anthropology at the University of Wyoming. This is his first book.

STUDIES
IN THE ANTHROPOLOGY OF
NORTH AMERICAN INDIANS

Editors
Raymond J. DeMallie
Douglas R. Parks

THE HEILTSUKS

Dialogues of Culture and History
on the Northwest Coast

Michael E. Harkin

Published by the University of Nebraska Press
Lincoln and London

In cooperation with the American Indian Studies Research
Institute, Indian University, Bloomington

The paper in this book meets the minimum requirements of American
National Standard for Information Sciences—Permanence of Paper for
Printed Library Materials ANSI Z38.48-1984.
Library of Congress Cataloging-in-Publication Data
Harkin, Michael Eugene, 1958–
The Heiltsuks: dialogues of culture and history on the Northwest
Coast/Michael E. Harkin.   p.   cm.–(Studies in the anthropology
of North American Indians) Includes bibliographical references
and index. ISBN 0-8032-2379-X (cl: alk. paper)
1. Heiltsuk Indians—History—Sources.   2. Heiltsuk Indians—
Social life and customs.   3. Heiltsuk Indians—Missions.
4. Ethnohistory—British Columbia.   5. British Columbia—
History—Sources.   I. Title.   II. Series.   E99.H45H37   1996
971.1′004979—dc20   95-46842   CIP

1001639640

Contents

Maps

following page 22

Preface

Dialogues of History

This book attempts, in an experimental way, to fashion a new ethnohistory. I have tried to move beyond some older versions of ethnohistory, such as the use of oral sources within a traditional, Eurocentric historiography, or the reification of concepts such as acculturation and revitalization. Although initially drawn by the siren's cry of "the native's point of view," I have since found that goal to be desirable but too often elusive. Through the eyes of *which* natives are we to view the processes of radical culture change? How can we account for the radical changes this perspective would itself have undergone, assuming the native was not singularly obtuse? In the end we have many perspectives, a plethora of voices stretching over a century and a half, each of which is positioned, interested, and pragmatically engaged in the history it describes.

Is the task of the ethnohistorian, then, simply to record these voices, noting the biases of each? The reason it is not is that these voices, for all their diversity, are mediated by culture. They are spoken in the language of their place and time, constrained by the symbolic and social structures of their respective cultures. Thus, we might expect more than passing similarity among contemporary Heiltsuk voices or among contemporary Eurocanadian voices. We are caught, in a sense, between the Scylla of reifying culture, as the "classic" ethnographers of an earlier era did, and the Charybdis of reducing collective levels of reality to the individual. As an anthropologist, if I err, I err in the former direction.

But there are ways out of this impasse. My theoretical focus on *dialogues* is one. The dialogic perspective accepts the collective and symbolic qualities of culture as a given, but it places them in a framework of communication. This reminds us of the pragmatic dimensions of culture, which structuralism has been rightly criticized for leaving out of the picture, and helps us to see how culture is always open to the possibility of change. This dialogism, borrowed from the Russian semiotician Mikhail Bakhtin, is especially appropriate for ethnohistory. We see that, for the Heiltsuks, the constantly changing cultural milieu was the result of the interaction of two distinct cultural traditions, the Eurocanadian and the Heiltsuk.

That interaction was a process of negotiation of meanings, presentation and representation of self and other. Its currency included speech acts, symbolic actions, material exchange, violence, marriage, imitation, legislation, and witchcraft. Each such *utterance* transformed the dialogue and, to a greater or lesser degree, the lifeworlds of the interlocutors. Rather than to attempt to stick our fingers in the spokes of history, so that we can perceive discrete cultural-historical states, we shall follow the dialogues themselves, viewed against the backgrounds of their constituting cultural traditions.

The concept of dialogue has become increasingly common in anthropological discourse. Since the initial writing of this work, it has become almost a cliché, to the point where I believe it is necessary to justify and explain my use of the concept. Dialogue is often used as a shorthand for a set of concerns in cultural anthropology also identified as postmodern. Drawing, as I do, on the work of Bakhtin, many anthropologists have criticized the conventions of their professional discourse as *monologic,* a condition in which relations of meaning and therefore power are controlled by the Western observer. Thus, an interpretive anthropologist such as Clifford Geertz is criticized for his imposition of an external set of meanings on a fluid, Balinese tableau (Crapanzano 1986; see Geertz 1973:360–411). In response to this "crisis of representation," many members of the generation who did their main fieldwork in the 1970s have adopted representational strategies designed to overcome these limitations and to subvert the conventions from which they arose.

On the level of praxis, there is a serious concern with the inherently unequal relations of fieldwork and anthropological writing. The field-worker, in stark contrast to the informant, is a representative of metropolitan Western culture. He or she has access to institutions that give him the ability to create *discourse* in the sense of a serious, official, professionally authorized speech. Against that backdrop Vincent Crapanzano (1980) gives his subject Tuhami, an illiterate and mentally disturbed Moroccan tile maker, the voice to speak directly to the reading public. In this experimental work, Crapanzano attempts to relinquish authorial control over the production of an ethnographic text. Of course, such relinquishment can be at most partial, since even the selection of Tuhami's words is an authorial decision. Quoted speech and behavior are still used to illustrate authorial points. His strategy is not different in type from

Geertz's "thick description" (1988:91-101). Moreover, though Geertz may be criticized for drawing on images and symbols taken from popular American culture (sexual double entendre, Mickey Spillane realism), Crapanzano draws on a rarefied, *normalien* cultural milieu, in which Racine, Flaubert, and other French literary figures provide a representational framework (Crapanzano 1986). The attempt to carve out a discursive space for the *other,* which is by no means confined to the present era in anthropology, is always limited by the very nature of the enterprise.

It should be clear that my use of dialogue is somewhat different from previous anthropological appropriations of the concept. Although at one level the dialogue between anthropologist and consultant has shaped the present work, and its status as a text constitutes a further utterance in that dialogue, I am less interested in textual hermeneutics than in objective cultural and historical conditions. I do not mean *objective* in the Marxist sense. These conditions are extremely complex and include internal cultural dynamics as well as historical processes. I take it as a given that they are culturally and socially constituted. They are embedded in representational practices, many of which mediate between cultures. This is one important sense of an ethnohistorical dialogue. In addition I take the term to include, broadly, the interplay among action and reaction, event and interpretation, structure and praxis, memory and representation, domination and resistance, that characterizes the postcontact histories of tribal peoples.

What has become clear to me in working through some of the issues discussed in this volume is that they are at base questions of communication. That seems especially appropriate in considering the Heiltsuks, who were never engaged or defeated militarily and who brought about their own transformation in the context of specific domains of discourse. Not all communication is linguistic; I look at other important modes of communication between the Heiltsuks and Europeans, such as material exchange and bodily representation, and their impact upon the Heiltsuks.

The Heiltsuks

The Heiltsuks present a particularly interesting case for study. In addition to being among the least known of Northwest Coast peoples, they experienced perhaps the most rapid historical transformation. Like other groups, the Heiltsuks were subject to almost unimaginable destructive forces. Despite the magnitude and frequency of these forces—disease being the greatest—the Heiltsuks attempted to control their own destiny. This resulted in rapid, self-directed change, such as the invitation to the Methodist Church to establish a mission in the village of Bella Bella.

It was in the postmissionary period, from about 1880 onward, that Heiltsuk culture underwent the most rapid and profound change. The half century after 1880 is the central focus of this study. The Heiltsuks transformed themselves from the most feared First Nation on the British Columbia coast to paragons of the Victorian virtues of hard work, prosperity, and progress. And yet, looks can be deceiving. Under this placid surface lay subtle strategies of resistance; in the end the dialogues were about power.

In the first four chapters I attempt to describe Heiltsuk cultural contexts, both traditional and modern. I also look at narrative as a way of understanding historical processes. I am particularly interested in Heiltsuk narratives about their own history. In chapters 5-8 I look at the substantive transformations of the Heiltsuks. These are the dialogues that make up their history.

One of the two basic aims of this book is to demonstrate the usefulness of such a dialogic approach to ethnohistory. The other is, of course, to recapture some of the history and historical culture of the Heiltsuks. This is certainly an improvement upon the traditional "treaties and battles" approach in ethnohistory and, I hope, a contribution to the growing body of interesting and innovative work in ethnohistory (Blu 1980; Kan 1989; Cruikshank 1990).

Sources of Data

The research upon which this work is based consisted in part of twelve months of fieldwork conducted during the period 1985-87. Field research was primarily directed at eliciting historical narratives, but it came increasingly to involve the elicitation of ethnographic and some linguistic data. Formal interviews with fifteen native consultants provided the bulk of data collected. These interviews were conducted mainly in English but, with certain consultants, increasingly in Heiltsuk as time went by.

The data collected can be generally classified into several categories. My first area of interest was ethnohistorical data, particularly historical narratives expressing a Heiltsuk perspective on Heiltsuk history. As a class of data, this had largely been ignored by anthropologists who had worked earlier with the Heiltsuks. I found, however, that these narratives are an important component of the Heiltsuk narrative tradition and reflect Heiltsuk culture in historically dynamic contexts.

Other types of data supplemented material collected by Franz Boas, Philip Drucker, and Ronald Olson. I collected data on kinship, political and economic organization, religion and ritual, mythology, sickness and healing, art, and notions of personhood. In general, I considered these data as supplemental to, rather than opposed to, data collected in the first half of this century. I believe I am justified in doing so for several reasons. Of course, the consultants with whom I worked were among the oldest and often most traditional in the community. They were alive and many were adults at the time of Boas's and George Hunt's 1923 fieldwork. The topic of our conversations was always explicitly Heiltsuk *tradition* as remembered from their early lives. The practices and events discussed were recalled from this previous world. But there is also a theoretical and methodological point here. From one perspective, culture can be viewed as a persisting tradition—an authenticating structure by which a community invents and reinvents itself—rather than simply as an abstraction of observed behavior at a particular point in time. This perspective is increasingly important in the late twentieth century. Moreover, the Heiltsuks, like many other peoples, take this aspect of culture, as authenticating tradition, to be paramount. There is certainly a sense within the Heiltsuk community of continuity between Heiltsuk culture as currently enacted or remembered and traditional culture.

Of course, that is not to say that there has not been massive change in the Heiltsuk world in the last half century. Indeed, the place of traditional culture itself within Heiltsuk life has changed greatly; it has become more compartmentalized and dissociated from other aspects of daily life. Fewer people speak the language or remember the specifics of the potlatch or the dance series. Other cultural influences, for example American television, urban lifestyles, and popular music, compete with traditional ways of looking at the world. At the time of my first fieldwork, the community had only recently been connected to a satellite-cable television link. It led to confusion and, in many cases, to intergenerational conflict. Despite this—perhaps because of this—the importance of Heiltsuk culture as authenticating tradition appears to be increasing. The recent revival of Heiltsuk dances and the potlatch is one clear example of this development. In stressing the continuities as well as the discontinuities of Heiltsuk cultural tradition, I believe that I am following the lead of the Heiltsuks themselves.

I conducted the usual formal and informal interviews, but I was also graciously permitted to participate in public celebrations: potlatches, feasts, and other happenings. Again, in these public contexts of shared meaning, the relationship of the living community to the Heiltsuk tradition was the explicit theme of the events. Volumes of eloquent Heiltsuk narrative were spoken on the necessity of maintaining access to tradition. Reconstructed dances performed in some of these situations provide such access. Obviously, they are not exactly the same dances as performed in aboriginal culture, but they are continuous with them, and they are authentic. They are in fact a mode of giving authenticity to events, persons, and meanings.

In addition to field research, I carried out extensive archival research at eight locations across Canada from 1985 to 1993. In particular, I concentrated on the archives of the United Church of Canada, the National Archives of Canada, and the Hudson's Bay Company, owing to their superior collections of available material. Some text citations include abbreviated forms of such manuscript sources. These abbreviations are listed at the beginning of the reference section. Finally, I surveyed the ethnographic field notes of Franz Boas, George Hunt, Philip Drucker, and Ronald Olson as they concern the Heiltsuks.

My concern from the beginning was to synthesize data from these various sources and to produce an ethnohistory that would take into account a range of data traditionally ignored by both anthropologists and historians. I wished to focus especially on the role of the Heiltsuks in shaping, as well as narrating, their own history.

Earlier versions of chapters 4 and 7 appeared in *Ethnohistory* (Harkin 1988, 1993) and chapter 6 appeared in the *American Ethnologist* (Harkin 1994a).

Acknowledgments

Few books are truly the product of a single author. They are conceived in an intellectual milieu informed by the writing and teaching of others. In general, I owe a debt to the anthropology department of the University of Chicago where an earlier version was written. In particular, the following people have given advice, encouragement, suggestions, and so forth, based on reading all or part of the work in its earlier incarnations: Raymond Fogelson, Manning Nash, Shepard Krech, Sergei Kan, Jean Comaroff, Bruce Knauft, Donald L. Brenneis, John C. Rath, and Judith Berman.

Research was supported in part by grants from the American Philosophical Society, the Whatcom Museum, the Canadian Embassy, and the Heiltsuk Band Council. I am grateful. I owe a special debt to the Heiltsuk people, which I hope this book can begin to pay back. Especially, I would like to thank the Heiltsuk Cultural Education Centre and its director, Jennifer Carpenter, as well as its staff, Chief Clarence Martin, Dr. John Rath, and Evelyn Walkus Windsor. There is not space enough to thank all the Heiltsuk people who helped me with my research or who showed me kindness, but I would mention the following people: former chief councillor Cecil Reid, Gordon Reid, Sr., Moses Humchitt, and the late Mrs. Esther Lawson. Finally, I must thank my wife, Alison Harkin, without whose moral support this book would not have been possible.

Heiltsuk Language and Orthography

Heiltsuk is an Upper North Wakashan language, as are Oowekyala and Haisla. These languages are transcribed phonemically, not phonetically, and possess a virtually identical inventory of phonemes. The orthography used here is an adaptation of one created by the linguist John C. Rath (1981), of the Heiltsuk Cultural Education Centre in Waglisla (Bella Bella), British Columbia. All pre-1981 quotations of Heiltsuk words are presented as they appear. I use a preceding asterisk to mark reconstructed lexical items. For a detailed account of Heiltsuk phonemes, and a grammar, see Rath (1981).

SYMBOL	PRONUNCIATION
'	glottalization
c	alveolar affricate (*ts*)
e	vocalization of following resonant (*schwa*)
ḷ	vocalic *l*
λ	voiced alveolar laterally released affricate (*dl*)
ł, lh (in older sources)	voiceless alveolar fricative (like Welsh *ll*)
x	palato-velar fricative (like *ch* in German *ich*)
x̌	uvular fricative (like *ch* in German *ach*)
ʷ	rounding of previous consonant

1

The Nineteenth-Century Heiltsuks

The ethnological significance of the Heiltsuks is just about inversely proportional to their renown among anthropologists. Unlike their cousins the Kwaguls (Kwakiutls), who are among the most famous of all anthropological specimens, little has been published on the Heiltsuks (formerly known as the Bella Bellas), and they are virtually unknown outside Northwest Coast circles, despite the fact that they were, before and just after European contact, located at the geographical and cultural center of the entire region.

The Heiltsuks were the dynamic center of diffusion of masks, dances, myths, and other elements of culture. Of course, Northwest Coast cultures borrowed freely from one another, but the Heiltsuks were more frequently and significantly the donors. Winter Ceremonial dances diffused from the Heiltsuks in all directions. Haidas, Tsimshians, Nuu-chah-nulths (Nootkas) all borrowed extensively from the Heiltsuks. Much of the ceremonial repertoire of the Bella Coolas was Heiltsuk in origin. The most important dance complex of the Kwagul Winter Ceremonial, the *hámáċa* 'trying to bite' or Cannibal Dance was, according to both Boas and Curtis, Heiltsuk in origin (Curtis 1915:220-21; Boas 1966:258, 402).[1] Oral traditions of neighbors on all sides point to the Heiltsuks as originators of many important ideas, beliefs, titles, and practices (Swanton 1905:156; Boas 1916:546; Garfield 1939:184, 293). It is perhaps not an exaggeration to say that the Heiltsuks invented, on the Northwest Coast, the idea of the Winter Ceremonial as a dramatic opposition between cosmos and chaos, although the evidence for such a claim is admittedly circumstantial (see Drucker 1940:227; Kolstee 1988:85-95).[2]

This diffusion represented an artistic as well as a theological creativity on the part of the Heiltsuks. A great variety of fine masks were collected in Bella Bella in the late nineteenth and early twentieth centuries, including many with movable parts (Black 1988). The Heiltsuks were master carpenters as well, building large canoes that were displayed in London, New York, and elsewhere, including the seventy-five-foot war canoe still displayed at the American Museum of Natural History (Black 1988:129).

In the 1790s the earliest European observers commented upon the Heiltsuks' physical appearance, which was startling to European eyes. The Heiltsuks wore labrets, some as large as three and a half inches in diameter, and practiced cranial deformation (R. Brown 1866; Vancouver 1967:280; Hilton 1990:315). The Heiltsuks also appeared as one of the least friendly coastal tribes (R. Brown 1866; Vancouver 1967:272). Such first impressions colored the white perception of the Heiltsuks for most of the next century. The Heiltsuks gained a reputation as a vital and (from the white perspective) fierce tribe, second to none. Although couched in the language of racism, such statements reflect the practical knowledge that traders and administrators had of the Heiltsuks and bespeak a grudging respect for them (Lamb 1943: 117). They also feared the Heiltsuks, who had a reputation for violence and were implicated in the murder, in 1873, of survivors of the wreck of the *George S. Wright* (Gough 1984:200). The Heiltsuks were also much feared by neighboring First Nations because of the ferociousness with which they were willing to protect their honor against usually friendly groups and be-cause of the cold-blooded way in which they dealt with enemies, such as the Haidas and the Kwaguls (R. Brown 1866; Curtis 1915:112-13; McIlwraith 1921-24:373; Harkin 1985-87). Even neighboring groups, such as the Oowekeenos, were the victims of Heiltsuk massacres (Poutlass 1907).

The great Heiltsuk paradox is that this group, although not the first to receive missionaries, was among the first to take the evangelical message to heart and probably experienced the most rapid cultural transformation of any tribal group in the history of Western colonialism. This paradox inspired the present project, while making its execution more difficult.

One can only fantasize how the Heiltsuks would have appeared before sustained white contact. Claude Lévi-Strauss (1977:33-34), in his anthro-pological memoir, *Tristes Tropiques,* expresses in the form of a metahistori-cal parable the double bind implicit in the wish to encounter the truly other. Lévi-Strauss wishes that he had been present in Brazil at an earlier period, when more Indian cultures were more untouched, providing better and purer data for the anthropologist; but had he been alive at some earlier period, he would have lacked, to the degree of temporal removal from the modern age, the very intellectual and ethical perspective that would have allowed him to make his study. Like Lévi-Strauss's Brazilians, the chimerical image of the traditional Heiltsuks, always receding, that we can never possess, is alluring. The philosophical sophistication of Heiltsuk culture is apparent even in the refracted voices we can hear through walls of time and text.

The best we can hope for is an anthropological reconstruction of traditional Heiltsuk society and culture as it might have appeared in the early to middle 1800s, prior to the massive changes effected by plague, missionaries, and incorporation by Eurocanadian society. Of course, such a picture is an abstraction under the best of circumstances, and in the present case the data for many aspects of Heiltsuk culture are sketchy. Apart from problems of sources, the very project of representing cultures in static, monumental terms has come under considerable criticism from within anthropology itself (Clifford and Marcus 1986). Although certain elements of these critiques are valid, others, such as the complete rejection of objective language in ethnography, threaten to undermine cultural anthropology as a discipline.

In the present case it is taken for granted that the picture I present of Heiltsuk culture is an artifact. A real person's life in the early to middle 1800s would certainly not be fully or accurately portrayed by such a representation. Heiltsuk culture itself was no doubt always open to change and always, to some degree, more flexible and dynamic than we can know or say. Indeed, it is my very interest in attempting to describe the dynamics of postcontact Heiltsuk culture that makes a presentation of aboriginal Heiltsuk culture—however artificial that is—necessary. We must engage in that admittedly suspect project of cultural reconstruction less as a baseline against which to measure change (as archaeologists do) than as a template within which to understand processes of change.

Traditional Social Structure

The Heiltsuks were central in many senses. In terms of social organization, they were located between the northern coast region of matrilineal tribes and the central coast region of cognatic groups. Like the Kwaguls, they were faced with the problem of constructing a corporate group in a cognatic society. Unlike the Kwaguls, they had available to them the clear model of matrilineal descent. Their groups did not have quite so complex principles of recruitment as the Kwagul *numaym,* but neither were they as crystalline as northern matrilineages (Berman 1991:58–116).

The basic social unit of the traditional Heiltsuks was the *house* (*núyem-gíwa* 'carrying forth a mythical narrative'), a local group whose legitimation derived from its access to ceremonial names, privileges, and stories (Olson 1955:324; Boas 1966:37). It is useful to think of the house, like the Kwagul *numaym,* as primarily a set of names. Traditionally, only men held the highest names that were associated with the political control of clans and houses, although noblewomen *(wúṁaqs)* did hold high names. Women were also the preferred medium of transfer for certain masculine chiefly names (Olson 1955:324).

Matrilineal primogeniture was the basic principle of succession, although competing models existed, especially in postcolonial times. Strict matrilineal inheritance was found among the northerly Heiltsuks, the *x̌íx̌ís* (Drucker 1936–37). For most Heiltsuks, names could be passed down in several ways. Chiefly male names usually were inherited from the maternal grandfather or the mother's brother. Among chiefs, bilineal primogeniture—in which eldest sons inherit from fathers and eldest daughters from mothers—seems to have been common (Olson 1949, 6:58). However, in the case of the former, sons had to be adopted into the father's clan. Clan affiliation was primarily matri-lineal, and names were associated with clans (Olson 1949, 6:59).[3] A third mode was fraternal inheritance by birth order (Olson 1935, 5:24). Finally, in addition to rules of inheritance, the feelings of the name holder and the heir's ability to afford the maintenance of a high name were taken into account.

In considering Heiltsuk inheritance, it is useful to keep in mind that there was not one path but many. A chief would be both the benefactor and the legatee with respect to numerous names and privileges in the course of his life. Which path these items traveled on depended upon various factors and cannot necessarily be described by rules. Such a system left a great deal of room for strategy, which became particularly evident in the late nineteenth century, after population loss created a surplus of names and privileges and the influx of capital created new measures and means of value (Olson 1966).

Heiltsuk kinship terminology is completely bilateral. This was the case among all Heiltsuk-speaking groups. For example, the term for father's sister and mother's sister are the same: *ḣenís.* Likewise, the term for mother's brother or father's brother is *x̌ʷłém;* for cousin, nephew, or niece traced through either mother or father, *λúel;* for maternal or paternal grandparent (either sex), *gágém.* Clearly, this terminological system facilitated and complemented a flexible system of inheritance. On the other hand, birth order in both sibling and child terminology is highly marked.

The house was similar in many respects to European noble houses (Lévi-Strauss 1982:163–87). That is, it consisted in an abiding corporate group possessing a real, named house or houses, controlling real property, and possessing one or more permanent titles. Recruitment to houses was not automatic, however, but involved social processes, such as naming an heir, marriage, and adoption. In certain ritual contexts the chief was considered to be the instantiation of the lineage-founding ancestor. He also controlled the resources belonging to the house through his own labor and that of his kinsmen. Kinsmen were mobilized through the efforts of the chief himself and through the offices of the chief's lieutenant or *own man,* who served as a work foreman in the collection of food resources.

The social organization of the Heiltsuks and other central coastal groups has been described by the notion of the *conical clan,* a nonexogamous, ambilateral lineage in which the members are qualified as to degree of membership by rank (Kirchoff 1955:7; cf. Davenport 1959). Endogamy was practiced frequently by the nobility in order to keep privileges within the immediate family, although for most people exogamy was the rule (Olson 1935, 5:33).

Such systems are characteristically segmentary. That is, it is a system of hierarchically linked units, the largest of which (the *tribe;* see below) is constituted according to the same hierarchical principles as lower-level units (e.g., houses [Boas 1966:37; cf. Lévi-Strauss 1982:174]). This nested, segmentary system is constructed according to principles of opposition and incorporation. The oppositional nature of the relation between two units on the same level can be seen in the marriage ceremony. Marriage, called *wíná* 'war', was always conducted in the style of a war party, with the men of the house of the bridegroom arriving by canoe, feigning attack, and finally engaging in a semiserious battle (R. G. Large 1968). Interestingly, this was the case even when the couple were from the same village. Even then the bridegroom's party arrived by canoe, thus maintaining the oppositional fiction.

The units of this system were subject to both fission and fusion. Fission is common in myth and no doubt resulted from population expansion in certain ecologically productive areas (e.g., Boas 1932:82–85; Olson 1955:

323). Fusion of groups was very common in the period after contact, when population loss and the attraction of white forms of wealth and power altered the social landscape (Pierce 1881; Drucker 1950:159).

On a level both higher and more abstract than the house, the entire Heiltsuk society (and beyond) was organized into a system of four clans (geṁínúx̌ʷ): Raven, Eagle, Killerwhale (Blackfish), and Wolf. Although the Wolf clan had no chiefly titles associated with it, the other three contained titles and privileges, in some cases referring to transformations and instantiations of the clan ancestor. The names within each clan were strictly and permanently ranked, as were the clans themselves (in the order presented) (Olson 1955:326). An extant narrative explains this rank order in terms of a "great race" around an inlet between Raven, Eagle, and Killerwhale. The birds are allowed only to glide, and Raven wins the contest as the result of a ruse: he places props underneath his wings to allow him to soar without becoming tired (Harkin 1985-87).

There was an ideology of clan exogamy, although in postcolonial times this is hard to find in practice (Drucker 1936-37). Clans, even more than houses, were organizations of titles or "standing places," as Boas phrased it, rather than of individuals (see Boas 1966:50-52). The clans counted names as members, rather than persons. Since high-ranking individuals often had access to names in more than one clan, a career might involve being adopted into a new clan. Such adoption was a strategy pursued by chiefs who desired to extend or consolidate their power (see Seguin 1985:94).

The distinction between the clan and the house is not always clear and has been frequently confused in the literature. It is necessary to keep in mind the historical processes that led to the current situation in which clan and house are clearly separate. Aboriginally, winter villages were dispersed throughout Heiltsuk territory and consisted of only two or three houses, each house being the only local representative of one of the four clans. As such they had clan alliances to houses in other villages. However, with the increasing centripetal pressures in population movement of the postcontact period, houses came to have clan affiliation with other houses within their village, giving rise to an institutionalization of the clan relationship (see Pomeroy 1980:71-72). Prior to this, the intervillage clan relationship was simply an aspect of the relationship between houses (Drucker 1936-37).

Ecology and Residence Patterns

Local winter villages were the major unit of ritual association. It was the village that put on feasts and potlatches for outsiders. At other times of the year, however, houses set up resource camps in outlying areas. The very boards of the house were moved, to be reassembled on house posts at the resource area (Tolmie 1963:275). The winter village was then either vacant or sparsely and intermittently populated for most of the year. Only between November and January was the entire population in residence at the village. Beginning in late winter, the typical seasonal cycle started with mink trapping. In spring people gathered herring eggs and jigged for halibut and red cod, which were preserved by drying. Then, in late spring, a beach camp was used for gathering seaweed and catching halibut. Next, clams were gathered and dried. During the summer and early fall, the people caught salmon and dried them at riverine camps. In the fall, especially preceding major potlatches, certain men went out on the order of the chief to hunt deer and mountain goats. This began the sacred ceremonial season.

The period of residence in the winter village was the focus of the annual cycle. All validation of social status, marking of change, and contact with powerful superhuman forces took place within the winter village and, whenever possible, during the winter. The "secular" activities of resource gathering were, in large part, directed at accumulation of food and wealth (primarily furs) to be used in the potlatches and feasts that accompanied all ritual activity.

Winter villages had contact with one another, of course, and not only adjacent ones. The winter ceremonial and feasting season was a time for forging or strengthening alliances with distant groups. As a rule, the greater the potlatch, the farther afield a chief would send for guests. Certainly in some cases potlatching transcended ethnic and linguistic boundaries. Interaction was most intense, however, among neighboring villages. A sense of common identity existed among nearby villages, which was designated linguistically by the addition of the suffix *tx̌ʷ* 'people of' to a regional designation. The contemporary Bella Bella Heiltsuks recognize four such major divisions (now called tribes): *uyalitx̌ʷ* 'Outside People'; *uẃẃít'litx̌ʷ* 'People of the Inlet,' that is, Roscoe Inlet; *q̓ʷúq̓ʷayaítx̌ʷ* 'Calm Water People'; and *ísdaítx̌ʷ* 'People of *ísdaí*'. The *x̌íx̌ís* 'northerly' now primarily live in the Heiltsuk-Tsimshian village of Klemtu. A historic group, the *yáláλayitx̌ʷ*, lived on Goose Island but merged with the other groups around

1835 (Olson 1955:320; Mitchell 1981). Another historic group, the *uwígal-idox̌*, lived on Calvert Island but either merged with other groups or died out (Olson 1955:320). Boas (1923:32–33) lists three additional groups: áLeq!wídExᵘ, K!wálhgnagimix, and NúlaᴱwídExᵘ, each referring to known winter villages in the eastern and southern parts of Heiltsuk territory. These regional groupings, in addition to having more frequent face-to-face encounters, shared certain characteristics. In particular, a preponderance of one or two of the clans was common within them. Subtle distinctions in economic activity, dialect, and culture also contributed to regional distinctiveness. The Heiltsuk territory varied both ecologically and culturally along the east-west axis, from mountainous fiords to low coastal islands. Contact and intermarriage with non-Heiltsuk neighbors by several of the groups resulted in distinctive identities. For instance, the *ísdaitx̌ʷ* were frequently in contact with the Bella Coolas and thus provided a link for the diffusion of culture traits (McIlwraith 1948, 1:19–22). Finally, certain common origin myths belong to the tribes. These divisions were brought into the foreground in the postcolonial period as a single group, the *uyalitx̌ʷ*, came to dominate the fur trade, and the population center of the Heiltsuks later came to be in *uyalitx̌ʷ* territory (Tolmie 1963:272). Today in the village of Bella Bella these tribal divisions are quite prominent. It is clear that they were significant aboriginally as the highest level of social organization, with the exception of organized, pan-Heiltsuk war parties (Tolmie 1963:275–76, 293–94).

Names and Rank

The basis of the entire social system was title names. The status of any group—house, clan, village, or even tribe—could be seen as a function of the status of its chief or chiefs, whose power and stature were demonstrated in the context of potlatches. Chiefly names were associated with particular personal characteristics and imparted responsibilities, especially to distribute property (Olson 1935, 2:24, 5:32).

The possession of a chiefly title, which would be inherited in early middle age, implied control of resources and thus the ability, as well as the right, to distribute wealth. Successfully discharging these duties required political skill and moral authority, for although the office of the chief was held in great respect, it was rather lacking in enforcement powers. Chiefs cajoled and persuaded their kinsmen and clansmen to work toward a potlatch or a feast, which would in turn add to the chief's prestige and authority.

A chiefly career began at the age of ten months with the first title. Ten months was the culturally defined period of human gestation. Naming represented a second, social birth. A normal career consisted of five or more names, for each of which at least one potlatch would be required (Olson 1935, 5:31–32). The proper way to "fasten on" a name required that four successive annual potlatches be given by the holder, although this rule was often honored in the breach. The flexibility of inheritance meant that a career was rarely written in stone at birth. Rather, political ability and successful potlatch and dance performances, in addition to ascribed status, were necessary components of the chiefly career.

Beneath the level of chiefs (including the *gálák̓a*,[4] or head chief, and the three or four top-ranking names in clans) was a nobility (confusingly, often also called chiefs). This group may be defined pragmatically as those who might sponsor a potlatch on their own. It consisted of past and future chiefs, as well as close relatives of chiefs. Most of what has been said about chiefs held for nobles, but to a lesser degree.

The lower ranks of named persons, commoners, participated in potlatches and made individual distributions, but generally their distributions entailed a very small amount of goods (Olson 1955:326). Likewise, although these persons would receive something in any distribution, it was a mere token and was generally the same for all members of the class (Olson 1955:328). Thus, commoners were not excluded from the cycle of distribution, but they were usually excluded from direct participation in it. Similarly, commoners participated in the central religious drama, the *ćaíqa* 'shamans' dance series of the Winter Ceremonial, but were often excluded from the higher, more powerful, dances. Because these names were not highly valued, as compared with chiefly and noble titles, the system of inheritance for the commoners was more regular and tended to be matrilineal (Olson 1955:329).

A class existed that had no names at all, known as *x̌ámála* 'orphan' (Boas 1925:330). It included outright slaves and war captives, as well as unadopted orphans and anyone else who lacked access to titles and resources (Olson 1949, 6:60). Such individuals might also be called *pk̓ʷs*, meaning 'uninitiated' and referring as well to a humanoid creature, such as a Sasquatch, that was thought to live in the bush, devoid of culture. Not merely persons of low status, *pk̓ʷs* were in a real sense outside the social order altogether. They were barred from participating in, or for the most part even from seeing, the Winter Ceremonial on pain of death (Olson 1949, 3:109).

Formal marriage was impossible, as it required the exchange of names and named property (Olson 1935, 5:102). Most aspects of life in the winter village were closed to the $pk^w s$. It is indeed not an exaggeration to say that they were excluded from Heiltsuk symbolic life almost completely and so constituted a class of virtual nonpersons.

Heiltsuk society thus clearly included notions of class as well as rank, to address an old concern (McFeat 1966:134–79). However, it seems clear that the ranked order of names, especially chiefly names, was of paramount interest to the Heiltsuks. Each name referred to a unique mythical origin and set of privileges. In a sense the complete set of noble and chiefly names comprised a paradigm of all possible socially positive human qualities, present from creation. The duties of a chief or a noble in living up to a name thus went beyond considerations of prestige or political power. Through his person these qualities were kept alive and passed on. It is as if, in our culture, one person were responsible for manifesting in a paradigmatic way, say, the cleverness of Odysseus or the bravery of Achilles.

The Winter Ceremonial

In addition to the potlatch, the focus of Heiltsuk public life was the two dance societies of the Winter Ceremonial, the *λúeɬáx̌a* and the *c̓aíqa*.[5] The former was based on the system of chiefly and noble names and perfectly reflected the ranked order of society. The *c̓aíqa*, however, involved an overturning of the secular order in favor of a series of possession dramas[6] involving spiritual entities representing negative elemental forces such as hunger, death, insanity, and sickness. The ranked order of those participating in the *c̓aíqa* did not necessarily coincide with the secular rankings. In some ways (although more in terms of religious themes than social organization) the *c̓aíqa* represented an overturning of the established order of things (see Harkin 1996). As the Kwaguls did, the Heiltsuks considered the *c̓aíqa* to be a time when the world was turned upside down and when supernatural beings preyed upon humans, as humans preyed upon salmon during the rest of the year (Berman 1991:686).

The *λúeɬáx̌a* was held in late winter, after the *c̓aíqa*, and could be held at other times of the year. As the timing suggests, the *λúeɬáx̌a* represented a restoration and reassertion of the established order, which was based on the relationship of living chiefs to an empyrean realm and the ancestral spirits who dwelt there. It marked the beginning of the *bák^wenx̌* 'secular season', the spring and summer time of bountiful salmon runs and ordinary, practical concerns.

A chiefly career was integrally connected with the *λúeḷáx̌a* series. Names entailed the right and duty to perform particular dances and displays. Thus, soon after the inheritance of a name the recipient would perform the necessary dance and put on the attendant potlatch. Generally, the food and material goods were donated by relatives of the initiand, often including the one who had given him the name, such as the father, the grandfather, or the uncle. The fundamental rights and obligations of the name consisted in the dances and crest display and the distribution of goods.

The progression of names from low to high thus went along with the progression of dances in the *λúeḷáx̌a*. Unfortunately, little is known of the specific dances in the *λúeḷáx̌a* (Drucker 1940:210-11). A list can be reconstructed with difficulty from the published and unpublished work of the ethnographers Philip Drucker and Ronald Olson, who worked in the 1930s and 1940s, and from contemporary sources (Olson 1935, 1949, 1955; Drucker 1936-37, 1940; Harkin 1985-87). Beginning with the lowest, we have *q̓axuk,* a child's dance, said to involve the accidental inspiration by some heavenly spirit (either unspecified or forgotten). Next was the *hílakwíyus,* about which nothing is known, save that the initiand was carried away by the inspiring spirit, as was the case with all the higher *λúeḷáx̌a* dances. Etymologically, the word has something to do with healing, however, and may be related to the healing dance mentioned below. Next was the *wáwínalał,* or War Dance (ranked as the highest dance by the Oowekeenos), in which the novice was inspired by the War Spirit. The novice flew away and then returned, destroying property. This was an extremely expensive dance, as the dancer had to pay for all the property destroyed.

The next dance,[7] Inspired by Heavenly Spirits, was also called *mítla* ('to miss', which can be used for the series as a whole) and involved the disappearance of the initiand for four days, during which he was said to be in heaven. He returned displaying a mask representing the heavenly spirit that carried him away. The high-ranking dance *λúgwela* 'finding a supernatural treasure' was very similar in outline but involved inspiration by the War Spirit. The dancer returned after four days, during which time he was said to be transported around the world by the War Spirit. He appeared on a shore across the water from the village. A party including the master of ceremonies *(alk^w)* and a healer *(hailíkila)* "captured" him.[8] He was transported across to the village on a raft, upon which he danced. He displayed a war lance—a memento of his inspiration—and several masks. Finally his inspiration was removed by the healer. This dance, interestingly, provided the only explicit link between the two dance series. Performing it was tantamount to announcing the dancer's intention to become a Cannibal Dancer (of the *ċaíqa* series) later. Other *λúeḷáx̌a* dances owned by the Heiltsuks include Sea Monster Dance (*q̓úmuq̌ʷemł*), Ogress Dance (*zúnuq̓ʷa*), Wild Man of the Woods Dance (*pk̓ʷs*), and Blackfish Dance (Harkin 1985–87). However, it is not clear where in the larger order these dances fitted.

Two figures in the *λúeḷáx̌a* are worth looking at in more detail because they illustrate important principles that link this series to the *ċaíqa* and thus reveal important elements of Heiltsuk religious thought. One such figure was the *hailíkila*[9] (see Berman 1991:653) . Apparently this position was obtained simply by performing a certain number of dances. The term *healer* referred to his ability to remove (as well as to induce) inspiration in any of the dancers. He came and went at will and was generally exempt from the taboos and regulations of the *λúeḷáx̌a* series (Drucker 1940:211). In particular, the *hailíkila* had the ability to overcome the power of the War Spirit, the most powerful inspiring spirit of the *λúeḷáx̌a*. In present-day Bella Bella it is remembered and performed as the most important dance of this series; this coincides more or less with what Drucker (1940:205) notes for the Oowekeenos. In this dance the highest chiefs moved in a stately fashion, wearing frontlets ringed with copper spikes sticking upward, reminiscent of the northern shaman's headgear (Drucker 1940:211). Eagle down was placed on the crown of the frontlet and released in the course of the dance by a jerking of the head. Eagle down represents heaven, inspiration, harmony, and order. These qualities and the implied relationship between heaven and earth constituted chiefly authority.

The War Spirit was analogous to the Cannibal Spirit of the *ċaíqa*, the foremost of the destructive forces in the entire Winter Ceremonial. Not only did inspiration by the War Spirit imply later possession by the Cannibal Spirit, but the dances inspired by the two are also strikingly similar in character. In both cases the initiand ran amok, seemingly at random, in the one case destroying property, in the other biting people. The initiand had to make reparations when he recovered from his possession. The War Dancer, clearly, was much milder, in keeping with the nature of the *λúeḷáx̌a* series as relatively benevolent "inspiration" rather than the dangerous possession of the *ċaíqa*. However, Drucker called the War Dancer "the only dangerous dancer in the *λúe̲láẋa,*" indicating that there is here a problem of the same type as in the *ċaíqa* (Drucker 1940:206). Namely, the problem is one of "taming" the initiand and bringing him back into society.

One dance was intermediate between the *ċaíqa* and the *λúe̲láẋa:* the *nuḷam,* or Dog Eating Dance. This was at one time a separate series, which was seemingly eclipsed by the more powerful Cannibal Dance (Drucker 1940:211, 221). Among the northern Heiltsuks (*ẋíẋís*), this dance was part of the *λúe̲láẋa* series (Drucker 1936–37).

In the *ċaíqa* series all dances entailed possession by spirits representing negative elemental forces, especially death, destruction, hunger, and consumption. Each possession was a serious business, in which society itself was placed at risk (see T. Turner 1977:58). One way in which the *ċaíqa* series as a whole threatened society was by overturning the social order based on the authority represented in the *λúe̲láẋa.* Thus, chiefly titles were replaced by *ċaíqa* names, which were often humorous or obscene (Boas 1923; Olson 1935). The order of chiefly authority was temporarily replaced by the regimentation imposed by spirits. Society was threatened in more specific ways as well, opening it up to dangerous and terrifying forces, instantiated by the individual dancers.

Persons undergoing initiation into the higher dances in the *ċaíqa* society were said to be killed when they were taken away by the spirits prior to the performance, to the "house of *báẋʷbakʷáláʱusiwa.*" Among the Oowekeenos, initiands were said to have fallen into a crevasse while hunting mountain goats (Curtis 1915:219). When they returned they were ritually reborn. The Cannibal Dancer crawled, naked, on first returning from his isolation. Gradually he learned to stand upright and to walk. This process of rebirth gave initiands direct contact with the forces of life itself, which were also the forces of death and destruction (Kolstee 1988:102). What actually went on during the period of isolation from the village we do not know, except that the initiands camped with those already initiated, practicing dances, composing songs, bathing in cold water, and fasting (Drucker 1936–37; Kolstee 1988:102). The musicologist Anton Kolstee (1988:103) speculates that at least the Cannibal Dance initiands used hallucinogenic mushrooms, such as *Anamita muscarea,* which are common on the Northwest Coast. This is certainly possible and is consistent with the altered psychological state associated with the Cannibal Dancers.

In the most spectacular and highest-ranking dance of the *ċaíqa,*[10] the Cannibal Dance, an initiand was said to bring in a prepared corpse of a recognizable deceased and eat all or part of it.[11] He ran amok biting spectators, and finally, after four days, was tamed and purged with salt water. During his possession he was usually tethered to a special "cannibal pole." He climbed the pole periodically and passed out of the house through the smoke hole. The cannibal was accompanied by four masked dancers, anthropophagous birds, who stood at the four corners of the house. Their movable wooden beaks made clacking sounds that evoked the crushing of human bones.[12] When finally tamed, the cannibal wore cedar bark rings around his head and neck, with wooden replicas of skulls hanging from the former. He displayed his tamed state to the village at large, which fact was later verified in a potlatch (Drucker 1940:204, 208-10). During this liminal period he was forbidden from sexual relations and from the food production and preparation process (Olson 1935, 2:86; 1954:235). This avoidance of the dimension of fertility, broadly writ, seems to have been the case, to some degree, for all of the *čaíqa* dance initiands.

The Cannibal Dance represented the culmination of Heiltsuk metaphysical thought, in which the fundamental quality of negativity and nonbeing was recognized. In some sense use of the term *cannibal* is incorrect here, for the individuals who enacted real or feigned anthropophagy were controlled by the spirit of *báxʷbakʷáláhusiwa,* who was decidedly not human, but rather a sort of predator upon humans (see Berman 1991:686). This theme is reinforced by anthropophagous birds, whose voracity for human flesh, bones, and skulls is a reflection of Raven's mythical omnivorous hunger. As Martine Reid (1981:104-5) points out, birds are a useful symbol not merely for their hunger, but also because of their practice of feeding their young by regurgitation. Vomiting is, as has been pointed out by several authors, a pregnant symbol of the productivity of social relations of giving and receiving and of the analogous cosmological relations of death and rebirth (Boas 1966:193; Goldman 1975:247; Reid 1981:102-4).

The *čaíqa* is at its base a productive inversion of the structures of human society. The most important sense of inversion in the *čaíqa* is this transformation of humans from hunters into prey, establishing at a symbolic level a reciprocity between humans and the nonhuman world, which Westerners would subdivide into natural and supernatural. Such a division makes no sense from a Heiltsuk perspective, since the supernatural beings are integrally related to (and sometimes identical with) natural beings (Berman 1991:92).

The established social order celebrated in the *λúeḷáx̌a* dances was here seen to be founded on the control and manipulation of negativity and elemental negative forces. This system was not dualistic in a Manichean sense. That is, it did not posit a static opposition between good and evil. Rather, it entailed a dialectical understanding of the terms of existence in which the negation of the established order was a necessary condition of its existence. The central drama of the Cannibal Dance was the transformation of this pure negation of culture into its opposite, which has been glossed as 'taming' the cannibal. This taming was carried out by women called *háyáłilaqs,* a cognate of *hailíkila* (see Drucker 1940:204). The general process of restoration of the social order that we saw in the *λúeḷáx̌a* was carried out in detail here.

Possession by an exogenous spirit and subsequent taming of the initiand were the common characteristics of the *ċaíqa* series from top to bottom. This entailed the disappearance of the initiand from the village and his reappearance and "capture" some days later in a state of possession. Our data on the Heiltsuk *ċaíqa* are rather sketchy. According to one list, beneath the Cannibal Dance was the Fire Thrower, or Fool Dance (*nuénłcísta* 'foolish ones') (Drucker 1940). The Fool Dancer accompanied the Cannibal Dancer during much of the latter's possession. He was said to be afraid of fire and thus illogically tried to extinguish the fire by dispersing it (Curtis 1915:160). While the *hámáċa* was biting, the Fool Dancer ran about scattering fire—potentially a great threat in cedar houses! Like the Cannibal Dancer, he was tamed over a period of days.

Ranked beneath the Fool Dancer was the **qinkulatla* ('leaning against [the *hámáċa*]'), who likewise went through a possession, about which little is known except that the dancer accompanied the Cannibal Dancer (Curtis 1915:156; Drucker 1940:209–10). Also, this dancer displayed a trick, such as magically raising a rock from the floor (Boas 1923:260). Among the Kwaguls this figure was a female relative of the Cannibal Dancer who acted as an attendant responsible for obtaining corpses (Boas 1897:438–42).

Ranked after the *qinkulatla* was the Ghost Dance *(lúłáł)*.[13] This dance involved the disappearance of the initiand into the underworld. He reappeared across the bay from the village and was captured by sham combat. His dance costume included an apron adorned with human long bones and a headdress decorated with a human skull. On the fourth night of dancing, the initiand sank into a hole in the floor and returned to the underworld. A particular woman had the right to call him up from the underworld. The dancer made the supernatural journey several times before being tamed (Drucker 1940:210).

Ranked next was the *atlaqim* 'forest spirits', which entailed simply a stay of four nights in a cave. The initiand obtained some type of power—determining his future career in the *ćaíqa*—and displayed a mask or a "magic trick" (Drucker 1940:210). Beneath this dance was the *qʷúaminúaks* 'Skull Dance', about which we have little information except that the dancer wore a mask or headdress decorated with skulls and disappeared with the Cannibal Dancer (Olson 1954:242). Curtis identified this dancer as a large female attendant of the Cannibal Dancer, who accompanied him to be initiated by the cannibal monster *báxʷbakʷáláhusiwa*. She returned bloodied, having been attacked by the monster (Boas 1897:462; Curtis 1915:160).

Finally, the *úlala* was apparently the lowest of the *ćaíqa* dances.[14] The initiand did not disappear but merely became "excited." He was isolated in a special room, like other *ćaíqa* dancers. He did obtain and display some spirit power *(náwálakʷ)*. He was "healed" by the *hailíkila*, who drove the power from his hands by blowing on them (Drucker 1938, 1940:210).

Several other dances are mentioned by Olson (1955:337) and by contemporary Heiltsuk consultants. The gilúḱlalaL 'Thieving Dance' caused the Cannibal Dancer to be afraid and tempered his excitement. The *gámatsalákula* 'lying on the *hámáća*' was an attendant of the Cannibal Dancer. The dancer of the gwígwaslaL 'on one side' uttered a cry of *wewahaí*, of which the Cannibal Dancer was greatly afraid.[15] Another *ćaíqa* dance was the *maqaxšúklaxi* 'clearing of throat', 'snoring' (?), which involved the power of making people go to sleep (Harkin 1985-87).[16] This was probably a low-ranking dance. Other *ćaíqa* dances, for which the names have been forgotten, existed as well. One relatively high-ranking dance consisted in the dancer "breaking" and "stretching" the arm and then returning it to its normal state. This dance was generally performed by women (Harkin 1985-87).

Archival evidence exists for a *ćaíqa* performance called *xa'ápi* 'Cradle' Dance. Unfortunately, the details of this performance and its rank within the *ćaíqa* are not known. The figure represented is not actually an infant, although it is in a cradle, but rather a pubescent girl. Menarche was considered the most dangerous time in the human life cycle and was analogous to *ćaíqa*, in that both involved a similar process of "healing." This performance may be related to the figure of *pḱʷs*, or Wild Man of the Woods, because the parents are said to dwell in the woods.[17]

With the exception of the Cannibal Dance, *ćaíqa* dances were masked, emphasizing possession. The performances all employed a whistle—often secreted as a mouthpiece in the mask itself, said to be the "breath" of the possessing spirit. Although the stagecraft was elaborate, the songs of the *ćaíqa* performance generally simply consisted in the low-toned repetition of a single word or nonsense syllables, implying that the initiand had "lost his mind." The Cannibal Dancer most frequently hummed, in a kind of droning repetition of the lexical item *hám* 'eating'. This contrasts with the coherent and specific statements of privilege presented in the *λúeḷáẋa* songs and oratory (see Boas 1897:628-31). Altogether, the performative aesthetics of the *ćaíqa* underscored the idea of possession by inhuman and destructive forces. Its object was the display of *náwálak*^{w} (which means 'spirit power,' particularly as manifested by masks and ceremonial objects), not the presentation of an idealized vision of persons or society.

A further opposition between the two series was color symbolism: *ćaíqa* masks were black, whereas *λúeḷáẋa* masks could be painted any color (Boas 1923:60; see Berman 1991:576). In postcontact times, since the advent of button blankets in the two dance series, blankets were worn reversed—with the black side out—during the *ćaíqa* and red side out, with the crest design visible, during the *λúeḷáẋa*.

This simple opposition of black and red has connotations of death as opposed to life. Thus red *(tláq*^{w}*a)* is symbolically associated with blood. *tláq*^{w}*a* also refers to copper, the most highly valued substance. Contrariwise, black *(ćúḷa)* refers, among other things, to the blackening of the food that one feeds to ghosts (Boas 1932:143).[18] Likewise, black facial paint was used at funerals. This opposition of black to red and black to all colors (the Heiltsuks minimally had words for yellow-green and white in addition to black and red) symbolized the basic reversal that the *ćaíqa* entails.

This may be seen as a temporary reversal of the Heiltsuk lifeworld. The model for such a world reversal can be found in the notion of the land of the dead *(wénqábuis)*. According to traditional belief, the land of the dead is a world in which ghosts live, in certain respects like the living—for example, in villages—but fundamentally reversed. Thus, it is night there when it is daytime on earth, the sacred season there when it is the secular season on earth, and so forth. Fire, instead of destroying, creates positive things; salmon is black rather than red; speech consists of yawning without sound (Olson 1935, 3:4). This is not to say that the *ćaíqa* represented simply an overturning of the world of the living in favor of the world of the dead, although the dead did play an important role in the *ćaíqa*. Rather, the *ćaíqa* entailed the overturning of the ordered world in favor of the free play of elemental forces, responsible not only for death but for all forms of negativity: hunger, death, sleep, illness, fire, foolishness.

These negative terms represent, however, the conditions of possibility for human life. On one level the *ćaíqa* is about reciprocity. Human life is dependent upon treating other species, especially salmon, as prey, visiting upon their communities the hunger and death that the Cannibal Dancer promises to humans. Indeed, the entire universe, human and nonhuman, is characterized by alimentary requirements, which are both complementary and cross-cutting. Not only humans and animals, but different classes of humans, noble and non-noble, are possessed of distinctive appetites. In the human case these appetites do not conflict but refer to different species of food and different parts of fish and sea mammals (Reid 1981:86–87). In a sense this permits society to function smoothly under normal circumstances. Ritual, as the enactment of the abnormal, allows human society to articulate, or better, to establish social relations with, realms of existence and classes of beings whose interests do not obviously mesh with those of humans.

It is significant to note here that the land of the dead (which is relatively underrepresented in Heiltsuk myth) is not the only realm to be reversed from the human world. Indeed, all other cosmographic realms, especially the forest and the sea, are seen as inversions of human worlds. Thus, the salmon are having their *ćaíqa* when the humans experience *bák**enx̌*. Berman (1991:686) views this concept of reciprocity with animals to be the central theme of the Kwagul Winter Ceremonial. For the Heiltsuks I think it is clear that such reciprocity involves not only animals, but the human dead. Death is integral to life and makes possible the reincarnation upon which human society is thought to be founded (Harkin 1994b). The *ćaíqa* is a point of communication among these otherwise separate realms.

Marriage

Heiltsuk marriage was closely tied to the Winter Ceremonial and the system of names connected with it. Among the chiefly class, marriage was primarily a means of obtaining status through the transfer of names and the distribution of property. Chiefly marriages were generally held in conjunction with a performance of a high dance in either the *ćaíqa* or the *λúeḷáx̌a* series, for instance the *hámáċa* or the *ṁítla* (Drucker 1940:208). This type of marriage was called *q̓*ílág*'iɫ*, containing the word *q̓*ík** 'heavy', referring to the "heaviness" of the bride, that is, her wealth in both material and symbolic property. *q̓*ílág*'iɫ* was always arranged by the parents and kinsmen of the couple and was frequently between close kin and frequently endogamous (Drucker 1936–37). Postmarital residence apparently was flexible, because there are examples of both virilocal and uxorilocal residence.

q̓ʷílágu'íɫ was contrasted with *túbaút* 'walking the plank', in which the couple's wishes were the primary consideration. This type of marriage was thought less important than *q̓ʷílágu'íɫ*, although more permanent. Certainly, less wealth was transferred in this case. It seems likely that *túbaút* was primarily practiced by commoners.

Arranged marriage, especially juvenile marriage, was an important step in the career of a chiefly woman. This status was particularly associated with the return payment, or "buying out" (Drucker 1936–37). In all chiefly marriage an initial bride price *(ngʷúlém)* was doubled by the woman's parents, exclusive of her dowry. This was a means of raising capital on the part of the groom and status on the part of the bride. Over the course of a woman's career, the amounts of wealth and prestige involved increased with each successive marriage; that is, she became "heavier." Obviously, then, the basic strategy for a chiefly woman was to have arranged as many marriages as possible, to the highest-status persons, in the course of her life. Given the preference for matrilineal descent, the practice of arranged marriage made possible the concentration of both material and symbolic wealth in certain families and houses. It is not an exaggeration to say that it was the sociological basis of the Heiltsuk institution of chiefdom.

Mortuary Practices

Heiltsuk mortuary practices were concerned with the management of pollution and negative forces and the disposition of the elements that made up a person.[19] The proper disposition of the enduring soul *(pk̓ʷái)*, the appropriate disposal of the body, the reincarnation of the deceased, the passing down of names and privileges, and the purification of those close to the deceased were among the main functions of the mortuary process. The mortuary process was tripartite, corresponding to Hertz's categories of rites of separation, intermediate period, and secondary burial (Hertz 1960).

The mourning period began even before the moment of death. If a person was ill and his consciousness failed, it was thought that his soul had already taken leave. Immediately upon physical death, the corpse was removed (Tolmie 1963:308–10). The body was washed, and ceremonial objects from the Winter Ceremonial were placed in the coffin (Curtis 1915:55). The body lay in state for four days. Female relatives wailed and sang 'cry songs' ($\acute{q}^w\acute{a}y\acute{a}yu$) and cut and scratched themselves with shells and knives; a little later they would have their hair pulled out by male relatives (Charles M. Tate 1884a:111; Boas 1890:840). Food was blackened in the fire to transport it to the underworld. The deceased's possessions were burned for the same purpose.

The period of four days immediately following death was one of high taboo. Those closest to the deceased, especially female relatives, and even more the widow or widower, bore the brunt of these taboos. The widow or widower was considered, for social purposes, to be dead. Widows, especially, were thought to be so much on "the other side" that they had supernatural, and dangerous, powers akin to the powers of the čaíqa (Boas 1890:839).[20]

Many taboos applied to the widow for ten months following death. Especially pronounced was the avoidance of food production and preparation (Olson 1949, 4:78). She ate old desiccated salmon caught at low tide—maximally removed from its vital source—served by an old woman and eaten with utensils belonging to the deceased (Boas 1890:839). Most significantly, she could not remarry until the mortuary potlatch released her from all taboos (Boas 1890:840).

This regimen closely resembled the seclusion of a young woman after menarche. Both were in fact called by the same term: híkelá.[21] In both cases the subject was removed from society and particularly from the food production process. Failure to adhere to this regimen brought not only bad luck to her, but also disaster to the entire group.

On the fifth day following the death, the body was buried and the funeral feast held. This was the culmination of the initial period of mourning. Mourning or "cry" songs were sung, and the greatness of the deceased was praised (Olson 1954:234). At this point the heir was named. The title was not assumed, however, until the mortuary potlatch, which took place at least ten months hence (Olson 1955:329).[22] A second function of the funeral feast was to repay those who rendered services in the preparation and burial of the body. This could be done only with outside assistance, because "no chief dies with anything," having given it all away during his life (Olson 1949, 4:93).

After the burial and the funeral feast, a slight easing of taboo took place. So began the process of reintegration of the widow into society. The final lifting of taboo occurred at the mortuary potlatch, at least ten months postmortem. It sometimes took considerably longer than this for the deceased's house to gather the resources and wealth required (Olson 1955:329). The two main functions of the mortuary potlatch were the succession to the deceased's title and the erection of a pole or, later, a tombstone. Finally, it offered a last occasion to mourn the deceased, whose cry song was sung for the last time (Boas 1890:840; McIlwraith 1948, 1:472). Indeed, all potlatches began with cry songs belonging to all the groups present, because a central function of the potlatch was, and continues to be, the commemoration of the dead (Harkin 1985–87; Kolstee 1988:150).

A highlight of the potlatch was the breaking of a copper. A masked figure representing the clan ancestor, as well as the deceased, brought in a copper, which was then broken. The heir distributed the pieces, called "the bones of the deceased" (McIlwraith 1948, 1:472; Drucker 1950:292). The presence of the masked figure was an authorization of the use of the deceased's symbolic property in the subsequent potlatch. After the final singing of the mourning songs, he departed; the matter of the death was said to be "swept away."

The mortuary potlatch performed the functions of "deliver[ing the deceased] from the isolation in which he was plunged since his death," and replacing feelings of disgust with "feelings of reverent confidence" toward the deceased. In short, the deceased became an ancestor. In Hertz's model this transformation can be achieved only by a type of sacrifice. Interestingly, we have such a sacrifice here in the breaking and distribution of the copper as "the bones of the deceased" (Hertz 1960:55, 63). Coppers were an extremely complex symbol in Heiltsuk and Northwest Coast culture. It suffices here to state that they were symbolically associated with the human body (they have "heads," "eyes," "ribs," and "backbones," as well as names). When destroyed, they were "killed" in a manner reminiscent of human sacrifice (Boas 1897:564; Goldman 1975:155–58). Significantly, on this particular occasion the distribution of the pieces of copper incurred no debt (Drucker 1950:293). Through this act of sacrifice the deceased was introduced into the society of the dead, as the heir was introduced (in his new capacity) to the society of the living (see Mauss and Hubert 1964:97).

For the widow the mortuary potlatch represented liberation from taboo and pollution. The widow, like the deceased and the heir, was (re)introduced into human society (Hertz 1960:64). Most important, she was allowed to remarry and thus to become once again a full-fledged participant in the life of society.

Although the resolution of the mortuary cycle was positive, it would be mistaken to assume that Heiltsuk attitudes toward death were likewise positive. As in the *ċaíqa,* powerfully dangerous forces were active in the mortuary cycle. It was a victory of the social order to reestablish a normal state at the end. As in the *λúeḷáx̌a,* the mortuary potlatch was an expression of the positive structure of the society. External forces were uncontrolled and dangerous but also potentially tamable. The victory over death achieved through reincarnation, commemoration, and inheritance was but one aspect of the larger dialectic between cosmos and chaos.

This theme of the dialectical relationship between external, uncontrolled, negative forces and internal, structured power is one that will be developed further in later chapters. It is clear that it has implications for Heiltsuk relations to the outside world, a world that came to include the white man.

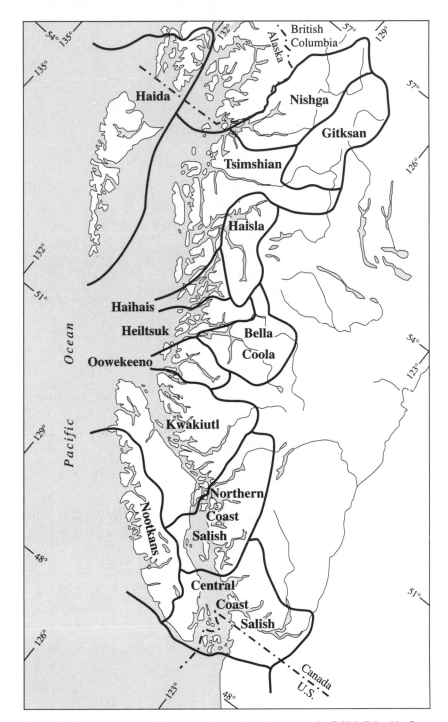

Map 1. Traditional territories of Northwest Coast cultures in present-day British Columbia. Redrawn from *Northwest Coast*, ed. Wayne Suttles, vol. 7 of *Handbook of North American Indians*, ed. William C. Sturtevant (Washington DC: Simthsonian Institute, 1990), ix. Maps are for reference purposes only, and are not intended to refer to questions of sovereignty or to continuing land claims.

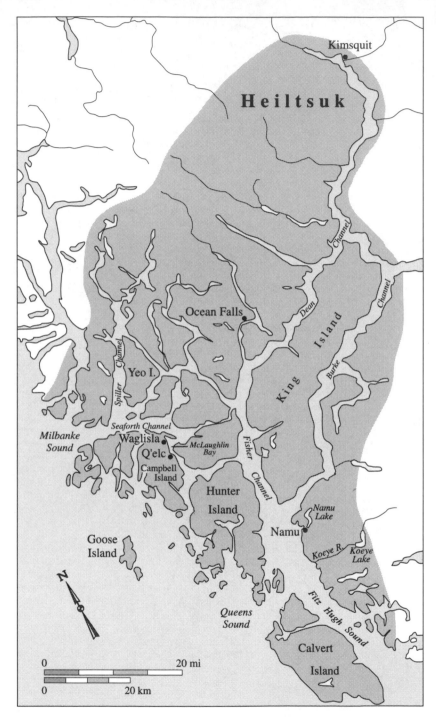

Map 2. Traditional Heiltsuk territory. Redrawn from *Northwest Coast*, ed. Wayne Suttles, vol. 7 of *Handbook of North American Indians*, ed. William C. Sturtevant (Washington DC: Smithsonian Institute, 1990), 313.

2

Contemporary Heiltsuk Contexts

The contemporary descendants of the nineteenth-century Heiltsuks are thoroughly modern. Their village is indistinguishable from white settlements in northern and insular British Columbia. They possess all the material amenities of modern life. They are connected to the outside world through air and ferry service, satellite dishes, Canadian Broadcasting Company (CBC) radio, and telephones. As I will discuss in later chapters, this modernity is integral to Heiltsuk identity. At the same time, here as elsewhere, the Heiltsuks are striving to forge links with the past through the revival of tradition, the preservation of the language, and, as Heiltsuk support of the current work attests, the documentation of their history.

The Heiltsuks with whom I studied live in the village of Bella Bella or, in recent times, Waglisla 'Stream Emptying onto a Sandy Beach', located on the eastern shore of Campbell Island (52° 10′ north latitude, 128° 10′ west longitude), on the central coast of British Columbia. The village is situated on the Bella Bella Indian Reserve Number 1. Altogether, the Heiltsuks have title to only twelve small parcels of land scattered throughout their traditional territories. At present the Campbell Island Reserve alone is permanently inhabited, although others are still used for resource gathering and recreation, especially during the summer. Most Heiltsuks are affiliated with the Bella Bella band, although a certain number of Heiltsuks live along with some Tsimshians in the village of Klemtu and together constitute the Kitasoo band.

The village of Waglisla has a population of approximately thirteen hundred. Of these, roughly a thousand are status Indians, those whose names are on the rolls of the band and who qualify for government benefits available exclusively to native Indians, such as exemption from income taxes. The remainder of the population falls into three categories: nonstatus Indians, non-Indian permanent residents, and professionals, including school administrators and teachers, a linguist, doctors, nurses, a dentist, Royal Canadian Mounted Police officers, a band administrator, construction workers, and others. This tends to be a transient population, although certain individuals become permanent or semipermanent residents.

Moving in the opposite direction is an out-migration of Heiltsuk individuals and families to the lower mainland of British Columbia, especially to Vancouver and the surrounding communities. A Heiltsuk diaspora of several hundred live in the Vancouver area. A major reason for the out-migration is the lack of employment and training opportunities available in Bella Bella. There is indeed a strong two-way path between Bella Bella and Vancouver. A Heiltsuk-owned airline provides twice-daily direct service between Vancouver and Bella Bella. Trips into Vancouver for the purpose of paying visits to friends and relatives, shopping, and entertainment are very common among those who can afford the airfare. Conversely, Heiltsuks residing in Vancouver return to Bella Bella, especially during the winter months, for Christmas and potlatch celebrations, as well as for extraordinary events such as funerals and weddings.

Vancouver is the primary geographical point of contact between the Heiltsuks and the outside world and, as such, plays an important symbolic role in the Heiltsuk worldview. It is the commercial and media center of the province and the center for native arts. Many Bella Bella residents visit Vancouver regularly. Despite the isolation of their community, these residents have a broad perspective on their province. Vancouver is an effective stage for achieving national recognition of native political issues. As I describe in chapter 6, the Heiltsuks made their presence known during the 1986 World's Fair that took place in Vancouver.

Apart from Vancouver, other, more local, points are important to the Heiltsuks as well. Many people take advantage of weekly ferry service to travel to Port Hardy on the northern end of Vancouver Island. A shopping mall there is a major attraction. Closer to Bella Bella, there is contact with the native villages of Klemtu, Bella Coola, and Rivers Inlet, owing to ties of kinship and friendship, although none of these places offers anything not available in Bella Bella. Moreover, all represent considerable trips by boat and, except for Klemtu, cannot be reached otherwise. Finally, in the immediate vicinity of Bella Bella is the white community of Shearwater or East Bella Bella, on neighboring Denny Island, which exists primarily as a fishing resort. People expressed resentment that whites were making money by exploiting Heiltsuk resources in this way. Despite that feeling, there is considerable exchange between the two communities, linked by regular "sea bus" service.

Bella Bella is thus by most standards fairly isolated, particularly during the winter, when weather can cut off air service for days at a time. However, the village is on a major sea route and is visited by a weekly supply boat and a ferry. A community satellite television service constitutes a very important link with North American culture. A range of American and Canadian television stations are available to the overwhelming majority of Heiltsuks, who own television sets. The effects of this fairly recent innovation are noticeable particularly among the young, who are geared to the latest fashions in clothing, hair style, and music (MTV is among the channels available). The strong influence of this powerful medium was decried on several occasions by traditionalists, including younger ones in early middle age. Indeed, their point seems to be correct: that feelings of isolation among the young are thereby increased, not decreased.

Young people bear the brunt of the many social problems that plague the contemporary community. High rates of alcoholism, violence, and suicide are especially troubling. Dropping out of high school before graduation is the norm. Out-of-wedlock pregnancy is extremely common. Taken together, these disturbing social facts connect Bella Bella with other isolated rural communities in the north and, more broadly, with communities on the peripheries of the capitalist world system, inner city communities as well as remote villages (MacDonald 1994). The "culture of poverty," as Oscar Lewis (1966:xlii) called it, constitutes a large part of contemporary Heiltsuk social reality. This is not the whole story, however, and the Heiltsuks have unique resources to deal with these problems, especially the cultural knowledge of the elders.

Most households consist of nuclear families, although it is not uncommon for three generations to live under the same roof. An elderly grandparent or a child's child may be added to the basic nuclear unit. Likewise, the tendency for postmarital residence is neolocal. However, a shortage of available housing on occasion causes married children to live with parents temporarily. It is not uncommon to see overcrowded conditions in old, inadequate houses, although this problem is being addressed by a program to build new houses. Many Bella Bella residents live in these new, large houses, built with the assistance of low-interest, long-term mortgages from the federal government. Considerable construction and expansion of the village have been carried out in recent years. New subdivisions of these fine houses may be seen where there was previously only bush. Nevertheless, the expanding population of the village means that a housing shortage persists. Many people still live in older, smaller, and less-well-built houses. This is a factor contributing to the migration of young people to the suburbs of Vancouver, where solidly middle-class housing is available.

Economics and Employment

A striking feature of Bella Bella is its high unemployment rate, which was well over 50 percent in the mid-1980s. It has a variety of causes: Bella Bella's relative isolation, its lack of locally generated commerce and industry, and the decline of the commercial fishing industry. Commercial fishing still is one of the two main sources of employment (the other is the band council itself). However, fishing has greatly declined since the 1960s, when it provided a general prosperity. Several factors—increasing costs of fuel and capital equipment, radically fluctuating markets, overcapitalization by some operators, and competition from Japanese "factory" ships—led to its decline in the last decade. A handful of remaining boat owners prosper, but they are unable to provide general employment or greatly stimulate the local economy. Moreover, this work is seasonal, leading to even greater seasonal unemployment rates.

The second main source of employment, the band council, provides service jobs. The band council operates two commercial enterprises, a band store and a hotel and lounge. In addition, the board of education and a certain amount of local enterprise offer some employment opportunities. Several small stores and a bakery are run by Heiltsuk people. Local artists and artisans produce some fine pieces, which are sold both locally and in Vancouver and elsewhere. Finally, government transfer payments, especially unemployment insurance and welfare, supplement incomes.

Reliance on local resources greatly contributes to the food supplies available to the Heiltsuk household. Although the land is unsuited for agriculture—and therefore all fresh vegetables must be imported—a range of sea-based resources provide a steady supply of a variety of foods. Of course, fish—especially salmon, halibut, and cod—is abundant. In contrast to the few who are involved in commercial fishing, many of the Heiltsuk households possess small boats suitable for subsistence fishing. During the summer and early fall, catches of salmon are so abundant that they are shared liberally throughout the village, even with non-Heiltsuks. This generosity is a point of pride with the Heiltsuks. It demonstrates both the great wealth of their traditional resources and the altruism that is so highly valued in Heiltsuk culture.

Fish comes in such quantities that its preservation is as important as the catching of it. Women cooperate with friends and relatives to maximize the efficiency of the cleaning and storing process. Traditional methods of preservation—smoking and drying—are still practiced but have been overtaken by the more convenient method of freezing. Fresh salmon is often prepared by the traditional method, barbecuing on a wooden frame on a fire on the beach.

Other traditional seafood, such as seaweed and herring eggs, is common as well and adds nutritional variety to the Heiltsuk diet. Herring eggs are gathered during the spring and preserved by drying. Hunted meat plays a much less important role in the Heiltsuk diet, although deer is hunted during the fall and constitutes an important food in public feasts and potlatches. Fowl, particularly grouse, is hunted also. Altogether, traditional food resources are very important to the Heiltsuks from both economic and nutritional points of view and for the connection they provide to traditional Heiltsuk lifeways. Not only do they supplement the common Heiltsuk diet of rice, potatoes, and imported meats and vegetables, but they also represent important markers of ethnic identity. This point was stressed especially by the elders with whom I spoke. Clearly, it is not merely the type of food per se— seafood and local land food versus imported and processed agricultural products—but also the entire social process enveloping the production and consumption of these traditional foods that is significant to the Heiltsuks.

Politics

Politics on the local level is focused on the band council, an elected body that administers local government. It is led by an elected chief councillor and an assistant chief councillor, who act as administrative heads and represent the band to the outside world. There is some correlation between elected office and high rank in the traditional name system, but one does not guarantee the other. Councillors come especially from powerful and high-ranking families.

Political rivalry tends to follow tribal group divisions as well as family lines. Influence within the community as a whole is based not simply on partisan politics, but also on inherited rank and public actions, particularly the holding of feasts and potlatches (see "Public Culture," below).

The Heiltsuks take an active interest in provincial and national politics. On one level that interest is expressed by support for candidates of the socialist New Democratic Party, which forms the principal opposition to the right-wing Social Credit Party in the British Columbia parliament. Successive Social Credit governments have been far more insensitive to the legitimate demands of native people even than has the Canadian government.[1] Their intransigence was demonstrated by the proposed clear-cutting of Meares Island, traditional property of the Clayoquot people, a move opposed by the federal government and by a range of environmental and native-rights activists. This issue was discussed in the United Nations General Assembly, among other places.

The government policy of ignoring native rights was also demonstrated by the less-celebrated logging of Mount Hand on Campbell Island, despite prior government assurances to the contrary, an action that has proved ecologically disastrous by, among other things, degrading the quality of Bella Bella drinking water taken from runoff from this same mountain. On top of all this, the provincial government has proved unwilling to discuss seriously with the Heiltsuks the issue of native land claims, and thereby to regularize a situation that has remained legally undefined for well over a century. Clearly, no successful attempt to overcome current economic problems can be made without titular rights to at least a fraction of traditional lands and resources.

A recent civil case between the Heiltsuks and the Ministry of Fisheries illustrates the resistance the Heiltsuks encounter in attempting to claim even a portion of their traditional resources (*Vancouver Sun,* 4 Dec. 1991). The ministry claims that the Heiltsuks did not gather herring roe aboriginally but developed it as a resource only after Japanese commercial demand made it profitable to do so. This is absurd. It is well known that the Heiltsuks not only used herring roe but cultivated it by placing cedar branches in protected waters to attract the spawning herring (Charles M. Tate 1884b). The branches were later removed, replete with roe. Obviously, the ministry is merely forcing the burden of legal proof onto the Heiltsuk band. Although ethnological and ethnohistorical data clearly offer such proof, the Heiltsuk suit relating to this matter was dismissed (*Vancouver Sun,* 4 Dec. 1991).

Public Culture

Several main contexts exist for public symbolic action, which can be seen most generally as the creation of shared, public meaning. These include ordinary church services, the rituals of marriage and death, the celebration of Christmas, and special events involving the distribution of goods, specifically feasts and potlatches.

Two denominations maintain a permanent presence in Bella Bella, the United Church and the Pentecostalist Church. The United Church is the descendent of the Methodist mission. It is still the "official" church of the community, and most of the older and higher-ranking persons maintain ties with it. Moreover, it plays a central part in many public events, for instance, Christmas celebrations. The United Church minister has a prominent role in public events held outside the church. For example, he is called upon to say grace before feasts held at the community hall. Physically, the church is central to the village, and its steeple dominates the view from the water. However, regular attendance is relatively low. Resentments remain against the United Church for what is perceived to have been its ambiguous role in Heiltsuk history. Unlike white society in general, it was honestly concerned with the welfare of the Heiltsuks but, nevertheless, acted in many respects as an agent of oppression (see chapter 7).

The Pentecostalist Church appeared more recently on the scene, having been established in the 1960s. The emotional intensity of this charismatic evangelism appeals to many people in Bella Bella, as elsewhere. Even certain community-wide public services held at the United Church are marked by forms of Pentecostalist worship, such as public testimonial and emotional prayer. It seems to be particularly effective among those who feel a need for self-reform. This was a central message in the Pentecostalist preaching and testifying at which I was present. The spread of television evangelism constitutes a new, external source of evangelical charismatic Christianity that resonates with, and contributes to, the local forms. Pentecostalism was traditionally intolerant of traditional Heiltsuk ritual practices and initially opposed the resumption of potlatching in the 1970s. Since that time, however, individual members have resolved neotraditional practices with their Christian beliefs, so that feasts and potlatches enjoy general support among the community's elders.

Funerals and weddings are public, often community-wide, events that involve one or both of the churches. Funerals are not single events but are extended over a period of four days following the death. They retain many features of the traditional mortuary cycle. Shortly after the death, relatives and close friends gather at the house of the deceased, to comfort the family. A vigil is maintained. Signs of mourning, such as public weeping, are seen in the village. Some possessions of the deceased are burned. For four successive evenings following the death, memorial services are held, usually at the United Church. Each service involves a sermon, hymn singing, and speeches by relatives and friends of the deceased, testifying to his or her good qualities and addressing the question of death, generally in Christian terms. Anyone in attendance may make such a speech, but in the cases I witnessed, no one except those close to the family did so. On the fifth day following the death, the actual funeral takes place. It is held in the late morning and is characterized by a much greater formality than are the memorial services. Mourners wear swatches of black fabric pinned to their left shoulders; pallbearers wear ribbons of the same fabric across their chests. Black flags are placed next to the casket, as is a large white cross with the deceased's names and dates written on it. Floral arrangements are placed around the casket as well as, in certain cases, prized possessions of the deceased, such as trophies and ribbons.

The service begins according to a standard liturgy, accompanied by music and singing. Specific persons are invited to give prepared presentations of speeches, songs, and a eulogy. Leather-bound Bibles are presented to the principal mourners by the minister. A procession is then begun, led by three pallbearers carrying the black flags and the cross. The casket is taken in procession down to the wharf, where it is placed in a large fishing boat or, on occasion, two boats lashed together. It is then taken, accompanied by the mourners closest to the family, to a nearby grave island to be buried.

On the evening of the burial, a funeral feast is held in the community hall, and the entire village is invited. Money is paid on behalf of the deceased's family to those who provided help and comfort, especially to the widow. Numerous speeches are made stressing the importance of comforting and taking care of the survivors. The family of the deceased (if he was a married adult male) gives a relatively small amount of material goods (fabric, dry goods, etc.) to the widow, ostensibly to compensate her for the possessions of the deceased that she has burned. The final item of business is to name the heir, who will take the deceased's name at a future potlatch.

Because the funeral feast is a public event at which goods are given away, and public meaning is thereby created, a tendency exists for other items of business to be handled at the same time. Names unconnected to the deceased are often taken by persons close to the deceased's family. Also, it is common for women to be "bought out" by their natal families at the funeral feast. In particular, daughters-in-law of the widow or widower are often thus bought out, with the practical effect of bringing money into the bereaved family at a needed time. Whereas historically buying out signified the formal dissolution of the marriage, it now signifies respect between the woman and her husband's family, to paraphrase a contemporary spokesman. In general, mortuary practices exhibit greater continuities with nineteenth-century practice than any other contemporary beliefs or ceremonies.

Weddings are generally performed in the churches according to the standard liturgies, although there have recently been attempts at revival of traditional ritual forms, incorporated within the wedding ceremony itself. In the more common mode, a reception is held after the wedding service in the community hall, with refreshments provided by the family of the bride, music and dancing, and a variety of parlor games, mostly involving mixed couples in competitions and races. These games, a custom begun during Edwardian times, were introduced by one of the missionaries. A consultant told me, half-jokingly, that this was actually the traditional Heiltsuk style of wedding, in contrast to the revived tradition.

Another important public event is the celebration of Christmas. This, of course, dates back to the very early days of the Bella Bella mission. Formerly, Christmas was celebrated almost entirely in public. Now it is mainly a domestic affair, very similar to the North American Protestant norm. Certain vestiges remain of the former practice, however. The missionary and his wife traditionally erected a tree under which lay a gift for every child in the village. This is still done, but it is organized through the school, with a child's family placing a present for him or her under the tree. The custom of giving feasts at Christmas time—also the season of the Winter Ceremonial—persists. The feasts are hosted by a chiefly family in a public space, such as the United Church. They are not open to the public at large, but usually only to a hundred or so people with kinship, tribal group, or friendship ties to the host. Speeches are made stressing altruistic themes appropriate to the season. Money is often raised for specific causes, such as a family in need or a person requiring money for expensive surgery. On these occasions the moral authority of the traditional chief is strongly felt and is effective in marshaling the resources of the people. This sort of organized altruism is strongly felt to be an important part of Heiltsuk cultural identity, recalling the traditional role of the chief in organizing ceremonial distribution.

At times other than Christmas, chiefs give feasts that involve the entire village. Like potlatches, they are held in the cavernous gymnasium, centrally located in the community. Folding tables are set out on the floor, with seating generally by family and rank. Complete dinners of roasted salmon, turkey, venison, and a variety of traditional and nontraditional foods are served. Seating is relatively marked, with the chiefs and chiefly families sitting at the head of a long set of folding tables. Beneath the position of the chiefs, space is generally not highly marked, although among elders and traditionalists there is a feeling that persons of the same clan and tribal group should sit together "beneath" the chief. This is complicated, however, by the great number of younger, nontraditional Heiltsuks and the many non-Heiltsuks present at such events. Certain persons are appointed as marshals to regulate behavior and to help seat people, but the rule is less strict than some traditionalists would have it.

The host employs a master of ceremonies, among other functionaries. The master of ceremonies, speaking for the host, makes general statements about the purpose of the feast (to maintain Heiltsuk culture and respect for tradition), the state of the village, the importance of people coming together in a formal context, and so forth. The main business of the feast is for the host formally to give names to his heirs. This is accompanied by speeches, made by the master of ceremonies on behalf of the host, explaining the purpose of giving names: it is not to elevate the status of the recipient, but simply to announce the names that he or she will receive, as a sign of the mutual respect between the donor and the recipient. In particular, the theme of filial duty and respect is often stressed (see Kan 1989). Persons other than the host may use the occasion to announce the transfer of their own names. In this case the host is paid for the privilege. In addition, the host makes payments to all the individuals who helped with the feast. Each payment—the amount, the reason, and the recipient—is announced by the host himself. But these are only the internal economics of the feast; the larger business is the distribution of goods to everyone in attendance. Fabrics, dry goods, plastic kitchen items, and money are given away to the guests. Of course, chiefs and higher-ranking people receive the best gifts and receive them first. However, everyone receives something, even if only plastic kitchen utensils and dollar bills.

Another function of the feast is the presentation of traditional dances. A revival has occurred in the last decade and a half of various types of dances.

An organized troupe of children perform very professionally a range of dances, mostly considered to be "play" dances, such as a paddle dance. Most of these dances are not connected with the dance series. Others of the dances derive from the lower levels of the two dance series, skillfully reconstructed through the study of texts and through contact with the earlier revival among the Kwaguls, as well as from the memories of Heiltsuk elders (Kolstee 1988: 92). Elders and chiefs sing traditional songs and beat time on a log drum placed at the head of the room. Behind them is a screen painted with the crest of the host, and behind that is the green room, where the dancers prepare themselves.

Serious dances are performed as well. In particular, the *hailíkila* and other *λúeḷáx̌a* dances are danced by the ranking chiefs of the village. These modern performances have a similar significance to that of performances in the traditional past, that is, to manifest and display the hierarchical structure of authority. The dances are often associated with the display of the host's crest, in the form of a large carved mask representing the crest animal. Both elected and hereditary chiefs participate. The audience is generally silent and respectful during this phase, in marked contrast to the air of informal enjoyment present at other points in the feast.

The potlatch differs from the feast primarily in scale. All the elements of the feast are contained in a potlatch. A potlatch lasts several days and is a sort of omnibus public ceremony, in which a large range of matters are dealt with. Potlatches are characterized particularly by the dedication of tombstones of persons deceased for at least a year, and sometimes as many as ten or more years. This is the first item of business, a very somber affair, in which usually several persons are thus commemorated. There is wailing and the singing of mourning songs. The matter is then, in the Heiltsuk idiom, "swept away" to allow for other, happier, business.

A broader range of dances are performed at potlatches than at feasts, including some of the important dances of the *ċaíqa* series. The sponsors of a potlatch are frequently several related persons, rather than a single person. Needless to say, the cost of a potlatch would be prohibitive for most individuals. At one potlatch I attended, I would estimate around twenty thousand dollars (Canadian) was spent on gifts in cash and in kind, food, and transportation for guests. The sponsors and their children or younger relatives are the ones who are thus initiated by dancing *ċaíqa* dances such as the *hámáċa*. Obviously, the performances are modernized versions of the dances; they are much shorter and completely nonviolent. Although the ideology of possession is not maintained, the performance of such a dance is considered to be quite significant in the life of the initiate. For these dances Kwagul ritual experts are hired, who coach the dancers on their performance. Few now remember these dances being performed in Bella Bella in early times; hence, there are no local experts. Some of the oldest members of the community are concerned by the performance of even sanitized versions of such powerful dances as the *hámáća,* but most of those in attendance view them as a good, if serious, form of entertainment.

Potlatches, like feasts, have as their main focus the transfer and announcing of names. Many names indeed are handled at a typical potlatch. In addition to the hosts, others may use the opportunity to announce names of their own. There are relatively few public occasions on which this can be done. Because the expense of putting on a full-scale potlatch is prohibitive for most families, any potlatch is a valuable opportunity to keep family names "alive." The host is concerned above all with the taking or affirmation of names that may transform his social identity. The host may have rights to high names that have not been publicly proclaimed for several generations. Perhaps the name itself derives from a distant place. Although the host may feel himself affectively to be fully a member of the community, there remains a sense of being on the outside if one does not possess a recognized name. Similarly, those who have moved away may want to sponsor a potlatch in order to reaffirm their place within the community, their identity as Heiltsuks who may wish to return at any time.

The recognized hereditary chief also feels a need to host potlatches and feasts. Of course, it is his responsibility to do so, a responsibility that is the defining quality of being a chief. More than this, there is a perceived need, especially on the part of the elders, to continue to provide contexts in which public meaning can be created, even if the meaning is one not always approved of by them.[2] Public meaning was, until recently, imposed upon the Heiltsuks by non-Heiltsuk authority, and so this need to create it is connected to the desire to maintain a Heiltsuk cultural identity and a sense of community. The relationship of the Heiltsuks to their own heritage and to the outside world is an important theme underlying all public culture.

Nowhere is this ideal of continuity with Heiltsuk heritage more clearly expressed than in the Heiltsuk Cultural Education Centre, founded in 1975 by the Heiltsuk band council. Physically located in the community school, the Heiltsuk Cultural Education Centre provides a point of contact among living elders, archival and artifactual materials, and younger generations of Heiltsuks. Its mission is ambitious and far-reaching, including the preservation and, where possible, revitalization of all aspects of the Heiltsuk heritage. A climate-controlled vault contains audio tapes, documents, and photographs that record crucially important data. The center has attempted, with the help of a professional linguist and other trained personnel, to record and preserve the Heiltsuk language. Sadly, this latter effort seems doomed to failure. As elsewhere on the coast, only older people speak the language fluently, and only some of the very oldest speak it as a first language. Children rarely learn more than a few words: the influence of English-only instruction, television, and other media would appear to be too great to overcome.

The Heiltsuk Cultural Education Centre is a testament to the renewed interest in historical culture that the Heiltsuks share with many native groups across the continent. Much of the planning and organization of potlatches, feasts, and funerals is undertaken with the cooperation of the culture center. Native artists use it as a resource center, and certainly the resurgence of Heiltsuk art is connected with the culture center's larger project of preserving historical Heiltsuk culture and providing resources for those who wish to investigate it. Under the auspices of the culture center, Heiltsuk elders have organized into the Iiilistis Society. A *hilístis* was a high-ranking woman who was redeemed by her family from a marriage within a year (Drucker 1936–37). The term has the connotation of returning from a trip within a day, that is, successfully (Harkin 1985–87). The society, affirming the high status of its elders within the community, hopes to guide the community on its own "journey."

One meaning of the multivalent term *dialogue* that I have borrowed for the present work is the relation of the contemporary society to its own past and traditions. The construction of tradition in the present historical period (which we might term the *neotraditional era*) is a rejection of the ideology of progress, with its radical separation of present and past. And yet, as I document below, that very ideology is a central feature of the real past. This paradox is a key element of contemporary Heiltsuk identity.

3

Narrative, Time, and the Lifeworld

In previous chapters I presented two starkly different views of Heiltsuk culture at two points in time separated by more than a century of historical change. In the simplest terms, the difference between the two states can be read as *history*. But how can that change be represented? In what sense have the enduring Heiltsuks been conscious of this disjunctive history? What we are really asking is how history becomes a part of culture, how the living live, not so much in the past, but in a present redolent with collective memories and representations of the past. After all, any society owes its existence to the past. Why things are one way and not another is understandable, if at all, only in light of that group's history.

The main form that such historical consciousness takes is narrative. This is probably a universal feature of human cultures, although some cultures are, admittedly, less interested in the past than others. Oral cultures are especially adept at using narrative as a repository of historical information, but as Ricoeur (1983) argues, we all do it. To understand Heiltsuk history, we must, first and foremost, look at the understandings contained in extant narratives. In this chapter and the following one, I set forth a model of historical narrative that attempts to address these issues, and I present Heiltsuk historical narratives. In so doing I suggest ways in which anthropology may be made more sensitive to historical processes and historical consciousness.

Much of cultural anthropology, especially of its "classic" period, is guilty of ignoring and devaluing history, despite the importance placed on it by those people anthropologists study. In recent years it has become fashionable to decry this antihistorical bias, more often than not in the name of some neo-Marxist theory of world history. It is not enough, however, to argue that anthropology should become somehow more historical. The task is more complex: what is needed is to ground a diachronic anthropology in an adequate theory of temporality and historicity, which can be applied to individual cases, incorporating culturally specific conceptions of time and history. Like other branches of cultural anthropology, that which deals explicitly with history must account for its dual status as both universal and culturally constituted.

History vs. "Real History"

Within the subdiscipline of ethnohistory, a question commonly asked of historical narratives concerns their relation to "real history." This is by no means a simple or simplistic question; rather it is one to which several sorts of answers suggest themselves. If by "real history" is meant European historical accounts, that is, European *historia rerum gestarum* (and this is indeed what is frequently meant), I would answer that there is no necessary reason for there to be a correspondence. I believe native accounts to be as inherently valid in their own way as any historical tradition. This is not simply a matter of principle. We must recognize that native historical accounts express fundamental truths about historical processes and therefore constitute an important expression of culture. Historical narratives are inherently inferior neither to European accounts nor to other traditional narrative forms, although they differ significantly from either.

If, however, the question is one of the relation to *res gestae* 'the events themselves', then we have entered more difficult philosophical territory. The problem is how to validate the relationship between *historia rerum gestarum* 'historical narratives' and *res gestae* (Ricoeur 1983:173–246). Logical positivists have made various attempts, through "covering laws" and other devices, to make history "scientific." These efforts were all doomed to failure for reasons rooted in the insurmountable space between the Cartesian subject and object. In particular, two species of epistemological atomism are present in positivistic historiography: that of the actor and that of the event. The individual, intentional actor is seen as the real historical subject; collective entities are merely abstractions or, especially in ethnohistory, rational actors writ large (Miller and Hamell 1986:313–15; Carr 1986:150). Thus, Bruce

Trigger attempts to account for the "behavior" of "Indian groups" in terms that are "logical and understandable," resolving the issue by pretending that societies act, and that they do so in accordance with utilitarian principles (Trigger 1975:55; Gadacz 1981).

I argue that we are dealing not with a methodological individualism but with a collective subject, which possesses something like a "social memory" (Connerton 1989). Its self-consciousness, its sense of time and action, and the conditions of its being are fundamentally collective (Carr 1986:149–66). Halbwachs argued that memory, even of personal events, is itself always dependent to a large degree on the group. The meanings of individual events must always be placed within a discourse, which is necessarily social (Halbwachs 1992:53). These special conditions require us to reject epistemologies and methodologies based on the individual subject.

A second positivist assumption is the atomism of the event. Apart from problems of observation, the positivist view of the event as a physical entity and a basic constituent of any system of historical knowledge ignores several epistemological issues. In particular, the specificity of the event is forgotten, that is, the notion that it is situated in a particular cultural and discursive context and is not merely a universal primitive to which a universal interpretation may be attached (Heidegger 1962:395; Ricoeur 1983:161). Furthermore, if an event is merely a term in a chain of cause and effect, what critical standards are there to state with *which* causes and effects it is embedded? Even if we assume narrated events to be "really real," they are still embedded in multiple discourses, among which it is impossible to choose "objectively." Indeed, it seems a more reasonable position to assume that narrated events owe their existence to the larger narratives of which they are a part. The fact that they seem somehow more real than other narrative elements is due to the "reality effect" produced by the narratives themselves (Barthes 1986:141–49).

Given these difficulties, it appears that only a naive positivism can proclaim an unproblematic relationship between narrative accounts and the events themselves. However, if we give up the atomistic assumption that events are the basic constitutive elements of history, it is possible to approach the question from a different angle. I draw on Heidegger's insights into the temporal nature of being. Just as Heidegger dissolves the "problem" of knowledge of the world by stating that we are as human beings already in the world and our knowledge of it is an aspect of this initial "thrownness," I hold that we are also already "in" history as an aspect of our being-in-time (Heidegger 1962:236–37). We are primally aware of, or "attuned" to, temporal states of being in which we find ourselves. These states of being are transformed or changed through the mediation of events. Thus, events can be defined in terms of the states of being to which they pertain, rather than vice versa. Our historical consciousness being attuned to a particular state of affairs, we are inclined to notice, and represent as events, changes to that world.[1] As David Carr has said, the significance of events lies in their "function of the *overall story* we tell . . . to each other about ourselves and what we are doing" (Carr 1986:167, emphasis added).

In a structuralist idiom, the problem of historical states and their transformation has been addressed before, in what we could call "theories of rupture." Henry Pachter describes an event as the juncture between two synchronic states of being, S and S', the difference between which can be seen as an implication of the event (1974:454). The event marks but does not in itself cause a "rupture" between synchronic states. This rupture is a function both of the deep structure of the states themselves and of their difference (Achard 1983:25). The event is a transformation of S into S' that mediates and likewise separates them (Pachter 1974:450). This model may be mapped onto a deep structure model, so that events can refer to states of varying levels of depth (Braudel 1969:46–51).

Being-in-Time and Historicity

Such a structuralism of the event is inadequate, however, for it fails, among other things, to take into account the fundamentally temporal quality of historical "states." The assumption of stasis impoverishes our understanding of historical consciousness. I shall argue several related points, drawn from Heidegger's analysis of being-in-time. The first and most basic point is that "states" of being are, as Heidegger says, fundamentally "ecstatic"; that is, the past and the future constantly impinge on them in distinct modalities, of which narrative history is, as Ricoeur shows, a very important one (Heidegger 1972:10–15; Ricoeur 1983). Thus, the fundamental quality of these temporal states is not stasis at all, but rather continuity and interpenetration of temporal modes. Structuralism accurately describes a moment in dynamic systems, but in order to appreciate their dynamism and other features that belie oppositional models, we must turn elsewhere (cf. Lévi-Strauss, Augé, and Godelier 1976; Haidu 1982:188–89).

Heidegger speaks of "Enpresenting" as a confluence of the three dimensions of time, which he takes to be a basic characteristic of human existence. Being is always occupied with both the future and the past, as well as the present. As Carr says, "The present is surrounded by or set off by the past and future horizons from which it stands out" (Carr 1986:168). I will argue that the mode of interpenetration of these dimensions of time, or simply the mode of temporality, is culture specific. Past history and future projects are organized into present being by cultural principles, in something like what Lucien Fèbvre called "temps vécu," or 'lived time' (Fèbvre 1942:431). Some cultures, such as that of the Maoris, may be concerned with repetitions of the mythic past, whereas others, such as that of the Italian Futurists, may be interested in the past and the present only insofar as they bring about a desired future (Sahlins 1985:54–72). Neither of these is truly ahistorical, and yet each represents a temporality radically different from that of humanistic historiography.

A second point involves the historicity of states of being, that is, their historical constitution by prior states of being and their limitedness with respect to future states. They are "set off" by their horizons (Carr 1986:168). In the most general sense, states of being are bounded not only with respect to antecedent and successive states, but to other historical possibilities as well (Heidegger 1962:385). That is, humans are thrown into a particular set of possibilities, within which still further limitations are enacted through the operation of contingency. At each juncture further limitations are introduced by projection into one of several possibilities. Communities are what they are because of irrevocable past events. This sense of possibilities enacted and lost seems especially strong in Northwest Coast mythical thought, as well as in the historical consciousness of the Heiltsuks (see Lévi-Strauss 1967).

A third, closely related, point involves the Heideggerean insight into negativity, an insight that I believe is central to Heiltsuk and Kwagul philosophy, as reflected in the ethnographic record. The boundedness of being, its relationship to a fundamental, negative otherness, is dialectically tied to the positive construction of being. This is seen, for instance, in the reversals of the Winter Ceremonial. This negative relationship defines as well otherness of another sort: that which pertains to the contingency of events and the presupposing nature of historical states of being (Heidegger 1962:194–95, 285, 385). Indeed, being is possible only against the background of its non-being, which, in Heidegger's metaphor, outlines and opens up space for being, in opposition to this otherness (Heidegger 1962:283, 354). Thus, on one level, other historical cultures are seen against the background of possibilities not taken, which amount to a historical and cultural other.

The relationship of all being to its negation involves certain prescribed cultural formulations, for instance, beliefs in a spirit world, an afterlife, parallel worlds, and so forth. Otherness is an essential category in Heiltsuk thought, and the relationship to this otherness is manifested in many aspects of Heiltsuk culture. These two levels of otherness—the temporal and the historical—are frequently merged in practice. Together they constitute the fundamental disposition toward otherness, which is viewed on the most general level as that which lies outside society.[2] To put it in simpler terms, different cultures and historical eras appear as possible other worlds. In this sense they are comparable to the posited other worlds of myth and religion.

Thus, when society opens itself up to the spirit world during the čaíqa, it is bringing in forces viewed from a narrow perspective as malevolent. And yet, from a broader perspective, it provides a representation of inverted worlds, which are oppositional forms of the human world. On one level this is the opposition between human and animal worlds. However, far from being a simple relation of interspecies dependency, as ecological biology would view it, the relationship is one of cosmological opposition. Numerous myths speak of how animals, including salmon, live in villages analogous to those of humans but experience the opposite season from the one humans are going through (e.g., Boas 1932:67-68; Walkus et al. 1982:150-54; see Berman 1991:109). Because the change of seasons was thought to result from the turning over of the world itself, animals were positioned as cosmological opposites.

This cosmological opposition is true also of the land of the dead. Although not well thematized in Heiltsuk thought, this region is also fundamentally opposed to the world of the living. The same sort of oppositions that pertain to animal realms pertain here, as well as, interestingly, a linguistic inversion, in which silence is a mode of speech (Boas 1932:142; see Harkin 1990a). What can be the meaning of the connection between these two realms, which also both happen to play a large role in the čaíqa?

Both realms, in their very negativity, provide the conditions of possibility of the human world. Animals must be on a different "ritual clock" from humans; that is why they are willing ritually to sacrifice themselves to humans. Humans, through their own ritual actions, ensure the resurrection of animals and the continuation of the species. Likewise, the land of the dead makes possible reincarnation and birth into spaces in human society vacated by the departed dead (Harkin 1994b). Although from a purely secular point of view, neither of these sets of relations is reciprocal, reciprocity is posited through human ritual actions.

Stories about the past are always also stories about the dead and so are representations of other cosmological realms. It would be a mistake to conflate such stories with ritual or mythic representations of other worlds, but it would be a graver mistake to ignore the similarities among different representations of cosmological otherness. Thus, stories of the past take place in worlds that are in some essential way different from the present. Moreover, the present can come into being only through the obliteration of those worlds. Hence, the analogy to representations of other species or states of existence is fairly complete.

A fourth point concerns the relation between past and present states of the world on one hand and the mediating status of the event on the other hand. As I have stated, the historicity of a being, individual or collective, consists in two aspects of its relation to temporality: continuity and discontinuity, or *horizonality*. By horizonality I mean the discontinuity inherent in individual and collective being. The continuity and self-identity of a being through a sequence of experiences is the most basic characteristic of a being as such (Heidegger 1962:390-91). Such continuities are always necessarily bounded by temporal and historical horizons, which delimit being but also define it. The historically constituted lifeworld in which a subject exists is constituted by its horizons.

If the historically situated world is thus constituted by its horizons, it follows that historical events are to a greater or lesser degree horizonal. That is to say, events that constitute a historically situated world also mark discontinuities between that world and other or previous worlds. Gadamer (1986: 269-70) stresses the necessity of attempting to reconstruct historical world-horizons in the process of interpreting historical events. That is, even with respect to one's own heritage, one must recognize that historical events took place in a different world from one's own. What then separates a world from its own antecedent? It is precisely the quality of events as horizons.

Heidegger, in his later writings, talks about events of Appropriation, or a bringing into presence. This is to be understood not as a physical occurrence in which something is created, but rather as an "extending" that "opens" a temporal and existential space (1972:14-20). The very character of being is thus to open up this negative space in time and history. Being is thus not a thing, but a temporal process (Gillespie 1984:151). He gives as an example of an event of Appropriation the founding of the European Community (Heidegger 1972:21). Commonsensically, we think of this as a good example of an occurrence in which something is created. For Heidegger, however, the creation is, as it were, a function of its horizon. It is in fact the horizon that is created, and this is done as part of an event that separates, in certain respects, a contemporary European world from its antecedent.

We need not limit ourselves to such an explicit and constructive act in considering the event as horizon. Rather, it is clear that all significant events constitute possible horizons, although this can be determined only from a post hoc perspective. Moreover, narrated events come to symbolize such horizons within the narrative tradition of bounded communities.

Horizonal Events in Historical Narratives

In native North American historical narratives, these discontinuities are usually particularly explicit and radical. What Fogelson terms "epitomizing events"—condensing, symbolic actions—in fact mediate between radically different yet consecutive worlds, whose conjuncture was, in terms of *res gestae,* more subtle and gradual; and yet, these epitomizing events provide meaningful cultural symbols and mnemonic devices for the discontinuities (Fogelson 1984:260). This agrees with Sapir's insight that condensational symbols are in practice blended with "referential symbols"; in other words, a single symbolic complex has both condensational and referential significance (Sapir 1934).

In our own culture, the fall of the Berlin Wall comes to mind as an example of an epitomizing event. Its dramatic quality stemmed from the fact that it was almost immediately perceived as an epitomizing event, embedded as it was in the central, and overripe, "metanarratives" of the twentieth century. In general, however, the tendency for narratives to epitomize increases with the age of the narrative. Beyond a certain period of time historical narratives take on special characteristics. They pass from the episodic to a level of greater coherence.[3] On the far side of Vansina's "floating gap," well beyond the span of a human life, they come to refer almost exclusively to epitomizing events (Vansina 1985:24). This temporal aspect reinforces the horizonal quality of such narrated events.

One conclusion resulting from these observations is that the fundamental character of the event is that of a symbol rather than that of a quasi-physical occurrence. Principles of selection, memory, and narration clearly place events within rather than outside the realm of culturally constituted reality. On the most basic level, the very pragmatic terms in which an event is situated—the actors, the setting—contain assumptions about the relevant social units involved. Indeed, certain events symbolize the constitution of new social units and so act as a charter for these very groups. It is important to recognize that the highest and most meaningful level at which narrated events and historical reality are mutually validating—that is, on which a historical narrative is "real"—is precisely that on which the historical narrative and a bounded social group merge to create a collective historical consciousness and practice (see Heidegger 1982:261–74; Ricoeur 1983:127–28). Through repetition within the community, narrated historical events become part of a common heritage, meaningful for those living after because of the intertwining of individual fate and collective destiny, to use Heidegger's terms (Heidegger 1962:384–86; Hoy 1978:341). Not only are particular historical moments of society contingent on these past events, but a culture's metahistorical conceptions, grounded in interpretations of past events, also feed back into destiny and determine the "directions" events can possibly take in the future (Heidegger 1962:395; Carr 1986:168).

Viewed from this perspective, both an event and a narrative description of an event can be seen as products of the same mytho-historical praxis. As de Laguna says for the Yakutat Tlingits, both they and various Europeans "acted and recorded their experiences in terms of what they perceived to be their origins, their national destinies, and their own human roles" (de Laguna 1972:211). It seems to me that narratives are bound to be "analytic" in the sense Renato Rosaldo (1980:89–90) defines, containing principles of analysis and interpretation of historical events, which reflect underlying cultural structures. Western narratives, with their generally linear and future-oriented structuring of time, space, and action, contain built-in analyses of the way history works. Further, historical interpretation and historical praxis are part of the same cultural framework.

For example, witness the mutual validation of Frederick Jackson Turner's "Frontier Thesis" and the peopling of various American "frontiers." Not only was it a narrative structure that resonated with recent American experience, but in its congruence with the ideology of Manifest Destiny it also provided an impetus for the exploitation of ever new frontiers, such as the Philippines.

This conclusion, that the event is a symbolic phenomenon embedded in a historical practice and reflects the temporal consciousness of members of a community, has several general implications for ethnohistorical analysis.[4] Historical narratives must be analyzed on their own terms, informed by the symbolic forms of the culture. In particular, notions of the person, time and space, life and death, the social unit, exchange, and inside versus outside should be considered (Fogelson 1984). Second, inasmuch as historical practice is culturally constituted and *res gestae* imply historical states, we must view the events themselves as culturally constituted. It is not merely a question of cultural "interpretations" placed on relatively transparent events, but rather a question of the conditions of possibility of the events themselves. Although subsequent discursive organization of events is an important issue, it must not be thought that such a "culturalist" approach is founded on an equivocation on meanings of *event* (or of *history*). It is indeed impossible to imagine human events (as opposed to natural events impinging on human society)—which in their most reduced form consist of actions and words—as being somehow outside the realm of culture, as things that simply happen to people.

If the events themselves are culturally constituted symbolic practices, then in cases involving relations between and among social groups, their basic character is dialogic. They involve the gradual clearing out of a space of shared meaning. Gadamer (1986:270) speaks of the dialogic quality of historical understanding as a function of the historical horizon. It is important to take account of the fact that horizons separate a historical world not only from its antecedent, but from other historical worlds as well. This gives such events a doubly horizonal quality. Events of culture contact, for instance, constitute new horizons with respect to both a culture's own past and the wider world represented by the contacting culture.

Contact Narratives on the Northwest Coast

It would be difficult to imagine a class of event more significant than contact with an alien culture. A famous Tlingit description tells of the encounter with the French navigator LaPérouse in Latuya Bay in 1786 (Emmons 1911:294-98; de Laguna 1972:259). The setting is a cove endowed with malevolent supernatural powers; in fact, four canoes of natives are drowned just before the arrival of the European ship. When they see it, they take it to be a great supernatural bird, Yehlh (Raven), with a flock of small dark crows. A war canoe sets out against the creature but is turned back by the fear of the warriors. Finally, a very old, nearly blind man boards the ship; but once aboard he still perceives the sailors to be crows. The rice they set before him he takes to be worms. He makes a small exchange with the sailors and returns with some goods and food. Finally, upon reflection, he realizes that these were merely people and not supernatural creatures and that it would be good to trade with them.

Several observations, relevant to my later analysis, can be made about this brief narrative (unfortunately, not reported verbatim by G. T. Emmons, who collected it in 1886). First, the initial setting is one of desolation and loss; this state is replaced by one of gain brought about by contact with the Europeans. Second, the Europeans are perceived initially as supernaturals. Third, the direct encounter is made by an old man, nearly blind, who was seen as expendable (Emmons 1911:298). Fourth, everything, even the white man's food, is unrecognizable. Finally, this lack of understanding is superseded by an ability to master the situation and to derive gain from it. That gain prefigures the network of exchange between Indians and Europeans that is the primary structure of culture change; on the most basic level, that is what this narrative is "about" (cf. Miller and Hamell 1986:320–21).

As a narrative, the Latuya Bay story organizes the conjunctural structures of the fur trade and intercultural communication. The background for the event of contact is an unsettled period of loss and foreboding, constituting a type of prophecy. The event itself is constructed as a horizon creating empty space to be filled with meaning. To pick only the most obvious analytical theme (to some degree these have been preselected by the recorder), a cognitive incommensurability is replaced by mutual understanding and advantage. It has almost the quality of a parable: of blindness being replaced by sight, of scales falling from one's eyes. It provides a type of answer to questions concerning the process of interethnic relations in the fur trade period. Further, that precisely would be its function: to be repeated within a bounded community over a period of several generations as a means of understanding an important aspect of a contemporary historically constituted world (Emmons 1911:294).

This double horizon separating historical worlds of radically different character is characteristic of the epitomizing event. The event mediates between the worlds preceding and following it, as well as between the native and the European worlds. It represents the initial clearing out of a cognitive and experiential space in which the two cultures come to establish structures of communication and exchange.

Gain and Loss in Northwest Coast History

The historical process of adoption of many—but by no means all—aspects of white culture by the Northwest Coast and other groups has traditionally been organized around the concept of *loss* in the anthropological literature, of acculturation as "*a*culturation" (Olson 1955:319; Codere 1961:513). Undoubtedly, this perspective has a certain validity; indeed, it is one theme of contemporary Heiltsuk reflections on their history. However, such an approach ignores several important points. The process of loss is generally seen as a corollary of native passivity, its possibility a function of the irrevocably static quality of native culture (Patterson 1972:28-29). Such a view coincides with an often romantic notion of the richness of a traditional past (i.e., of the Noble Savage) as well as a devaluation of the contemporary society (Blackman 1983:61-62). Moreover, it fails to address the question of how the native people themselves viewed the historical process: how they helped shape it with certain goals in mind. Finally, it ignores contemporary traditions that articulate just such a viewpoint.

In his "enrichment thesis," historian Robin Fisher suggests that contact produced an efflorescence of native culture. He insists on the need to look at British Columbia Indian participation in the maritime fur trade from the point of view of contemporary native motivation, rather than a posteriori readings by either white or native scholars. In many respects it was not a question of cultural loss but rather of cultural gain. For instance, plastic arts were given great stimulus with the influx of new tools and wealth (Fisher 1977:21). Not merely material gain, but the obtaining of certain types of symbolic property is arguably an equal component in this enrichment (Miller and Hamell 1986:314-18). However, this perspective is limited. As we examine the larger span of Heiltsuk history, we will find many examples of loss: loss of power, of knowledge, of population. For the time being we will focus on enrichment, which is the central theme of the Heiltsuk narrative presented in the next chapter.

4

Contact Narratives

Rare indeed are the opportunities the ethnohistorian has to hear "the native voice." Because it is primarily oral, native knowledge and testimony about historical events is rarely preserved. The recent concern in cultural anthropology with the airing of multiple voices is appropriate for both anthropology and ethnohistory, although it is more practicable in the former field. The advantage of employing anthropological methodology is that one has access to present-day testimony about past events. Of course, it would be extremely naive to equate this testimony either with a contemporary native perspective or with some sort of ultimate historical truth value. Such voices make extremely valuable contributions, however, to the complexity and validity of historical knowledge. This is especially so when, as in the present narrative, we have a story that has reached the level of a communal myth, told and retold in much the same form across generational and sociological boundaries. As a communal myth it presents the community's self-image and view of its own past in the clearest possible terms.

The Heiltsuk historical narrative quoted here[1] reflects two central issues that I have dealt with thus far: the event as horizon and the dialectical relation between controlled and uncontrolled, internal and external, forms of power. In the first instance this narrative presents a mythopoetic statement of the horizoning function of epitomizing events, the symbolic "appropriation" of a bounded temporality for a historical practice. Second, the narrative explains this historical crisis largely in terms of a central dialectic of power forms.

The First Schooner

I

A

A couple of old people of those days
when they used cedar bark clothes
a man and a woman—
    and the stone ax, not the ax we see today
a couple of old people went handlining codfish you know
    codfish in the pass here
and the first steamboat traveled through this pass—
    no steamboat before that—
    the first big steamboat traveling through
and they seen as it was coming that big thing on top
and they were just paralyzed, the two of them
And the captain went on the side of the canoe—
    picked him off,
    picked her off—
    set them at the table
and feed them just like you feed kids.
White people already had everything then—
clocks, lamps, cups and stuff and so forth—
and they feed them, they feed them just like they feed kids.

B

After they feed them they dress him up in this kind of clothes[2]
and dressed her with the women's clothes
And they lined up four gunnysacks full of stuff right up—hundred pound
gunnysack—they put that steel blade ax—
—they didn't even know it was an ax, either, steel ax—
and they got everything after they feed them,
they get all these sacks
and put them in the canoe,
put them back in
go home
When they landed at the beach there,
people went to meet them,
they wouldn't let them get off their canoe
till they changed their clothes back to bark clothes.

II

1

A

And then these people from Old Town, *q̓élc,*
they go to a place where they call *k̓élemt*
    that's Strom Bay,
'cause that's a reserve
and they go
    because everything's close by
    the halibut, pretty short distance,
and they get seals, seals and everything, mussels, clams close by—that's why
they go there in the summertime—
    and this big sailing ship landed there from
    South America.
And the crew of the sailing ship asked them to do everything—

B

they want a swimming race, swimming you know,
    'cause it's a nice beach
    It was Strom Bay
and the boys from there just walk away from them
    'cause that's all they do
    they swim all the time, see.

C

And after the swim race they want canoe racing:
    you know, paddle.
They just go right away from them:
    you know, canoe.

D

Boat race last thing they do.
They go right away from them.

2

A

And I say this to the people
    I tell this to the white people in Vancouver—

they must be a fine-looking people,
    and they call them Bella Bella

B

That's where the Bella Bella come from
    from South America
so that's a Latin word, you know
    from Latin

C

'beautiful beautiful',
    that's what it means
"Bella Bella"—
they named them "Bella Bella"—

D

that's where the Bella Bella comes from.

[Harkin 1985-87]

The text displays an obvious patterning based on counterpoint and parallelism. It can be divided into two- and four-part groupings based on repetition within a thematic unity. Thus, the lines dealing with the removal of the couple are punctuated by the repetition of "picked him off /picked her off." This pairing continues with "feed them . . . feed them," "dress him . . . clothes . . . dress her . . . clothes," "gunnysacks . . . gunnysack," and so forth. This patterning is based on traditional Heiltsuk narrative patterns (e.g., Boas 1928:104-5). As in Kwakw'ala narrative, the repetition of elements signals the division into independent clauses, or lines, which are in turn organized as "couplets" within "verses" (Hymes 1981:184-99; Berman 1983:10-14, 1991: 389-432). In addition, the repeated use of initial particles marks lines: "and" here, /wE/ in Kwakw'ala.

On the largest scale the poetic and logical structure of the narrative is bipartite. It consists of two episodes. Although they are interlocking, each tells of a separate event. The first episode is described in section I, the second in part 1 of section II. The final part of section II is separate in many respects from the rest of the narrative. I return to this problem below.

The two episodes differ with respect to setting, number, and modality. I shall argue that the first section is characterized by the logical principle of incorporation, the second by structural opposition. Further, these two modes are related serially, and as such participate in a relation fundamental to Northwest Coast culture.

The two episodes, like the smaller units, clearly exhibit these qualities of parallel construction and counterpoint. Thus, each describes a meeting with a European ship in Heiltsuk territorial waters, meetings that are unrequested and unexpected. People are engaged in activities characteristic of the time of year: fishing for cod in the winter, swimming and playing, with plenty of food close at hand, in the summer. Each episode describes a three-part process consisting of (1) this initial state of normal activity, (2) the encounter itself, and (3) a final fundamentally changed state, including a reminder of the encounter: the gunnysack of goods in the first episode and the name Bella Bella in the second. They describe similar events, in the sense of an irreversible change in the Heiltsuk world. Against the background of this structural parallelism the two sections are distinguished by counterpoint, which can be organized thematically under several categories.

Setting

In the first episode the events take place in the bay near $\dot{q}\acute{e}lc$, the central winter village of the late-nineteenth-century Heiltsuks and the place where the separate tribal villages came together.[3] The second episode occurs at $\acute{k}\acute{e}lemt$, a fishing and sealing resource area seaward of $\dot{q}\acute{e}lc$'. The opposition of land and sea is a significant factor. The sea is the source of wealth, life, and—in the context of the $\acute{c}a\acute{i}qa$ series of the Winter Ceremonial, as salt water—the power to overcome the destructive, consuming force of the $h\acute{a}m\acute{a}\acute{c}a$ (Goldman 1975:117; Furst 1989). Moreover, the sea is opposed to the land as summer is to winter. Indeed, it is winter in the first episode, summer in the second. Winter is, of course, the sacred season; winter villages themselves maintain a sacred character, whereas life in the fishing camps is largely secular. Finally, winter is characterized by relative scarcity, summer by relative abundance. Hence, the protagonists in the first episode are out in lonely laborious pursuit of a single food species, but in the second segment the people have "everything close by."

Modality

By *modality* I mean the manner in which the encounter occurs and the power relations between the two parties. In the first episode the protagonists are characterized by passivity, subordination, and ignorance of the situation in which they find themselves. They do not even know what an ax is used for. This is characteristic of crest acquisition myths, in which protagonists are unable to act as long as they are in the spirit realm (Berman 1991:562–67, 573–74). Contrariwise, the Heiltsuks of the second episode are masters of the situation. Rather than becoming "paralyzed," they "do everything." They are not helpless children, but rather prove more competent than their rivals at relevant tasks. They just "walk away from them" in the races. Not only the modalities of the relation in general, but also of the encounters themselves, are opposed. Rather than being plucked off a canoe and taken, passive, to their host's dwelling, they are themselves the hosts. The role of host is, of course, related to the question of abundance. The nice, sandy beach echoes the myths in which people encounter supernatural marine beings and are taken in by them, often by coming across a sandy beach far out to sea (Boas 1932:71, 113).

Finally, there is the question of levels of technology. In the first episode the Heiltsuks are paralyzed by fear of the steamer's smokestack. They are overawed by steel axes, clocks, and "everything" the white man has. In the second episode the ship is a sailboat—a schooner—sailing being a technology the natives easily adopted themselves. Moreover, the technological sequence of races provides an evolutionary sequence of nautical technology: the first level is zero technology (swimming), the second a canoe, the third a rowboat. (The oarlock, like the sail, was an important innovation quickly adopted by the Heiltsuks.)[4] Rather than being struck dumb by white technology, the protagonists of the second episode prove their mastery not only of the technology itself but of the technological series. I shall return to this point.

Number

In the first episode the number of protagonists is two; in the second it is indeterminate. The important point is that in the second episode the actors include the entire community residing at *kélemt*. Although it is true that only the young men race, the entire community is given the name Bella Bella. In the first episode the protagonists are a minimal pair, a small part (and also basic unit) of Heiltsuk society as a whole. This provides the clue for the larger interpretation that the narrative turns on the distinction between incorporation and opposition.

Modes of Encounter

I shall proceed by comparing these two episodes with respect to the distinction between incorporative and oppositional encounters. In general terms I mean here two modes in which the logical form is either one of inclusion of outside elements into a whole or of contrast and opposition among elements within a whole.

The first episode is pervasively incorporative. Thus, the man and the woman are a part of the whole of Heiltsuk society and are literally incorporated in the dwelling of the host. Conversely, structural opposition translates into competition at the level of social action. The young men, whose number is unspecified and who can be taken to be the entirety of this class, stand for the Heiltsuks as a whole. Just such a group would have represented it in warfare. They compete against their counterparts, the South American sailors.

The results of the two episodes also correspond to this distinction. In the first section the result of the encounter is a container (a gunnysack) of esoteric items; in the second it is a name that is exoteric. It comes from far away and is told even (and especially) to whites in Vancouver. The ethnonym contrasts with and opposes other names of the same type. This was the case with all public names, from low-ranking personal names to the highest chiefly titles.

In the context of Heiltsuk culture this opposition of incorporative, contained, and esoteric to oppositional, competitive, and exoteric was fundamental and central. I examine below the ways in which it was central and how it is possible to interpret the narrative in light of this analysis.

Opposition and Incorporation

We saw in a previous chapter how traditional Heiltsuk social organization was characterized by the model of the conical clan: a dynamic hierarchy in which segmentary units were related to one another either as smaller units to a larger whole, or as units of the same level, in opposition. Moreover, at times of flux the individual units of the system were rearranged and transformed through fusion or fission. That is, a new high-level unit may be created by merger, or two units may emerge out of a previously unitary whole.

This system is characterized by alternating principles of incorporation and opposition. Thus, the basic principle of the clan at any level was of incorporation of the population by the apical ancestor. In the case of the "house," this relation attained a high degree of visual explicitness. The physical house was carved and painted with emblems of the ancestor, and often the door was constructed as a mouth or a beak, through which one must pass to enter. The interior of the house was likewise coded as a body (Olson 1935, 5:20). In the Heiltsuk language, ideas of bodily boundaries, houses, and social position (as well as a settled order of any sort) are closely associated.

On the other hand, in cases of fission or of normal relations between social units of the same level, the mode of relation was oppositional. Thus, chiefs of houses faced each other as representatives of their respective founding ancestors; they addressed each other by the eponym. The relation between them was characterized by competition: structural opposition at the level of social action.

We can probe this question more deeply by examining the relation between two modalities of power, which I will distinguish as encounter/possession versus control/display. In the first modality supernatural power is obtained through an encounter with a supernatural being. These encounters always have the structure of a rite of passage, consisting of separation, liminality, and aggregation. In particular, the liminal state is stressed.

This modality of power is expressed in the ċaíqa series of the Winter Ceremonial, where the initiates were "captured" and sent to an uninhabited spot to spend up to two months in isolation, during which they were said to be dead (Olson 1935, 2:43, 86; Drucker 1940:203–4). As we have seen, ċaíqa initiates were in a dangerous state from which they must be "tamed," in order to be reintegrated into society.

The contrast between the ċaíqa and the λúeḷáx̌a can be formulated as one between incorporative and oppositional modalities of power. Essentially, the λúeḷáx̌a was a validation of the status of the chiefs and their rights to names, privileges, and stories. It was founded on the principle of inspiration, rather than possession, communication rather than liminality. The ordering principle of the λúeḷáx̌a was identical to that of society as a whole. It was explicitly

stated and based on exoteric principles rather than esoteric ones. The names
validated were those by which a chief was known publicly. On the contrary,
ćaíqa names were obscene and motivated by attributed sexual proclivities.
These would never, except in the case of powerful shamans, be used outside
the ćaíqa performance itself (Olson 1935, 3:109; Harkin 1985-87).

A further distinction can be made between syntagmatic and paradigmatic
relations. This point is enlightening here. Thus, the ćaíqa involved a "communion" (in the sense of commutation and consumption) between elements of
the same order, in a relation of predication (or predation). An initial actor, the
cannibal spirit báx^wbak^wáláhusiwa, consumed the initiate, who in turn consumed other members of the ćaíqa. This could go further, as some of the victims of the hámáċa would later become hámáċas themselves. Moreover, as
an emblem of this elemental force of hunger and consumption, the hámáċa
was connected to the larger cycle of predation/consumption of the world at
large (Goldman 1975:3). The λúeḷáx̌a, by contrast, represented the paradigmatic relation between two separate orders. That is, chief A is to chief B as
mythical founder A is to mythical founder B (cf. Lévi-Strauss 1963b:77).

Each modality of power was associated with a set of phenomenological
features proper to it. The incorporative modality was contingent, emergent,
and historical. The ćaíqa was distinguished by chance encounter, not only in
the mythology, but also in the practice of "kidnapping" the initiate (Olson
1935, 2:42). Moreover, the encounter was always with a chthonic or an
aquatic being, who represented a "new force" on the scene and in the world.
In the dance performance itself, this contingent quality was underscored by
the enforced "forgetting" of the dances from year to year. Any mention of the
ćaíqa during the year was taboo. Names in the ćaíqa were created anew
(Olson 1935, 2:47). Each time, the drama of taming the hámáċa was played
out in a real and serious way, as if the possibility existed that he would be
untamable. Finally, acquisition of power was historical and was always
placed in the "real" and often fairly recent past (Boas 1923:297). It was generally intertwined with movements of population from place to place and the
transformation of social units.

The oppositional modality of power was quite the reverse. It pointed to
the fixed order of forces that preceded the human world, prior to the division
of night and day; the differentiation of the species; and other primal events. It
was essentially unrecoverable and could be conceived of only metaphorically.
It had the a priori, constituted quality that may be called "facticity" (Heidegger 1962:82-83). Socially, it referred to a fixed order of units, ignoring their

potential for transformation. It was fundamentally static, whereas the *čaíqa* was fundamentally dynamic.

It is important to point out, however, that the static quality of the *λúeḷáx̌a* was not absolute, its opposition to dynamism and contingency not polar. Thus, change was encoded in the static order itself. Status was a direct function of the (temporal) priority of ancestors. The highest chiefs *(gáláx̌a)* were those whose mythical ancestors were the first to descend from heaven. The eternal order was not premised on a "denial of history," but rather on its appropriation (cf. Bloch and Parry 1982:11)

At this point we can understand the iconicity of dance movements of the two series: the regular, gentle movement of a chief, remaining in place within the larger pattern of chiefs in the *λúeḷáx̌a,* as opposed to the seemingly random thrusts of the *hámáča* into the crowd, mixing flesh with flesh, blood with blood. One is a *tableau vivant* of social order, the other an overturning of that order in favor of contingency.[5]

This distinction between contingency and timeless order constitutes a central contradiction in Northwest Coast narratives and culture. John W. Adams (1974:175), in his analysis of the Tsimshian narrative "The Story of Asdiwal," demonstrates that the contingent quality of acquired supernatural power creates a conflict with society that can be resolved only by means of expulsion and readmittance. In the liminal period the uncontrolled power must be transformed into food and wealth, which are fundamentally under control and follow the lines of distribution of the established social order. Moreover, this contradiction existed within society itself, between the timeless social units and names and the individuals who must acquire names within that order.

The two episodes of "The First Schooner" correspond to this opposition between the contingent and the timeless, the *čaíqa* and the *λúeḷáx̌a.* The entire sequence of action in the first episode recalls the initiation of a *čaíqa* novice. As with the *čaíqa,* this episode involves a liminal phase of isolation through which transformation is effected. The old couple are literally snatched away from their daily activity ("picked him off, picked her off") unexpectedly. They remain for a certain time in incorporated seclusion and return to the village with treasures concealed in a container. They are fed and clothed according to a foreign custom. Like the *čaíqa* initiates, they can be readmitted to society only when they shed the clothing that marks their liminal status. Or, rather, the shedding of these clothes signifies their reentry, even "rebirth," into society.

The man and woman are treated "just like kids," ironically, despite their advanced age. In part this refers to the passivity inherent in the role of recipient that pervades Northwest Coast thought, finding perhaps its most extreme expression in the grease feasts of the Heiltsuks and the Kwaguls, in which guests were expected to sit passively despite insults from the host and the real possibility of incineration (Olson 1935, 5:108; Boas 1966:96). As Goldman (1975:128) states, the role of recipient involves the temporary destruction of self (Mauss 1954). The protagonists suffer the temporary "death" of their social being: they lose whatever status and identity they had as Heiltsuks and become, in effect, European children. Furthermore, they are incorporated or "consumed" by the host. The affective aspect of this loss of self is the "paralysis" they experience upon seeing the steamship, which marks the liminal phase of the first episode. Van Gennep (1960:25–26) characterizes the liminal phase as like entering a house. This same aspect of incorporation applies to entering a steamship.

It is by these means that the power is acquired to fill a vacancy within the supernatural order. Precisely such a vacancy was created by the appearance of whites. Here was a type of power that had not yet been acquired. The white man, like other supernatural donors, temporarily incorporates in the process of donating power.

The second episode describes the control and display of this power. In it we have a well-fed, healthy population who are masters of the situation, unlike the first episode in which the protagonists must be fed "like they feed kids." Food facilitates the normalization of exogenous power within a fixed social order. This episode describes an encounter between rivals and is characterized by opposition and competition. The meeting is one between competitors who compete on terms similar to those of the potlatch. The Heiltsuks display the fact of their power in their health, indeed beauty, while at the same time demonstrating that they are worthy of it. (The functional connection between abundance, which is exhibited in the distribution of goods in the potlatch, and health and fitness is obvious.) What is behind this mastery is precisely the claims to legitimate and controlled power that are the subject of the *λúeɬáx̌a*. For this reason the greatest potlatches were always associated with the *λúeɬáx̌a* (Olson 1954:249).

The display and control of supernatural power and of the material bounty associated with it were indeed the function of the potlatch. Opposition was the dominant mode of the potlatch, which was appropriate to relations between social groups on the same level of organization. Present-day Heiltsuk potlatches, although largely lacking in explicit rivalry, nevertheless display a strongly oppositional logic. Gifts are always made to persons who are in some sense social alters to the host, as members of another community, another clan, another family, or as affinal relatives. The latter are often paid for services rendered in connection with the potlatch itself and so are both hosts and guests.

The progression of the narrative is not merely oppositional but dialectical. The first section describes the acquisition of supernatural power through incorporation, and the second describes the control and display of supernatural power through opposition.[6] This dialectical function of Northwest Coast narrative is well known. Hymes, in his analysis of a Clackamas Chinook myth, demonstrates a progression of dialectical terms, the intersection of which "drives" the action of the myth along to its conclusion (1981:274–308; cf. Lévi-Strauss 1963a:224).

This dialectical principle operates on several levels in "The First Schooner": not merely on the larger scale of logical modes, but on the microlevel as well. As noted above, the text is organized into pairs of lines, based partly on parallelism. If we look closely we can see that this parallel structure rests on a contrast of terms or of the signs of the terms. Thus:

> A couple of old people of those days
> when they used the cedar bark clothes
> a *man* and a *woman*—
> and the stone ax, not the ax we see today

Even the mention of cedar bark clothes contains an implicit contrast with the modern clothes mentioned at the beginning of section B, thus distinguishing the two sections of the first episode. This main set of contrasts, between the aboriginal material culture and that of the Europeans, is continued:

> and the first steamboat traveled through this pass—
> no steamboat before that.

The second episode, however, contains no such microlevel contrasts. Rather, it is contrasted as a whole with the first episode: summer versus winter, young men versus an old couple, plenty versus poverty, and so forth. This contrast reinforces its paradigmatic function. That is, both the action described and the description itself are paradigmatic.

The resolution of these two episodes is contained in the second section of part II, in which the narrator takes a perspective outside the action of the narrative itself and speaks of the effect of the narrative. From this commentative point of view, the dialectic is resolved in favor of the control/display aspect, which becomes the point of the narrative. ("They must be a fine-looking people.") The narrative as a whole is used as a *λúeḷáx̌a* narrative to justify current status with respect to a particular social matrix.

However, this contrast between the first and second episodes is not the complete picture. The second episode is more than a simple antithesis to the first. The dialectic of opposition versus incorporation is nested with respect to supernatural and social power and operates within the potlatch itself. Thus, there was always the threat of incorporation by a dominant chief or social group. The very act of donation contained within it the implication of such incorporation (Goldman 1975:128).

The name mediates between these two modes. It is at once the product of the incorporation and the foundation of the relation of complementarity within a fixed order. In order to obtain the name, one must be as recipient the one benefited and destroyed; as holder of the name one must engage in mutual display with other named beings. But this display stage itself entailed both opposition and incorporation. For the name to be validated, or "fastened on," the initial relation of incorporation was recapitulated in the context of the potlatch. Thus, a dominant image in these competitions was of oral consumption (see Walens 1981).

The name Bella Bella itself reveals two aspects. On the one hand it is the foundation of a social group, which stands for "a fine-looking people" and is told to the "white people in Vancouver." These "white people" are the contemporary neighbors of the Heiltsuks in the context of present-day British Columbia, just as in the past, lower-level units (e.g., houses) faced one another. The source of the name is, interestingly, not these whites, but whites from South (i.e., "Latin") America who spoke "Latin." The connotation of Latin as a means of communication with heaven is perhaps not too far-fetched. Certainly the fact that they came from a great distance and are no longer on the scene gives them an extraordinary quality. In this sense the name is static and oppositional. On the other hand the name needs periodically to be "fastened on." Furthermore, the social group to which it refers is itself an aggregation of smaller units cast adrift during the turmoil of the nineteenth century and so is dynamic and incorporative. The name refers to the ethnic group, which only became a relevant category in the nineteenth century.

Interestingly, the name Bella Bella shares a part of the semantic field of

the proper name for this group. *Heiltsuk,* like many North American ethno-
nyms, means 'native', 'of any place', or 'to speak one's own language': in
short, to be human. In a more restricted sense it means aboriginal person. Finally, in its most common sense, it refers to members of the Heiltsuk community. If one pursues the matter etymologically, however, it is clear that a
notion of beauty is central to this idea of humanity. Thus the root *hylh,* meaning 'right, proper, well', generates the word *hailhxs,* which means 'beautiful'
and 'without stage fright' (in the context of the Winter Ceremonial) as well as
hailíkila 'healing' (Lincoln and Rath 1980:388; Rath 1981, 1:289). This
"beauty" and lack of "stage fright"—that is, a disinclination to make mistakes
in public situations, but rather to demonstrate control—indicates mastery of
supernatural power and an ability to display it competently. A further meaning—'well' in the sense of "healthy" as well as "properly"— refers to the
ability to heal *(hailíkila):* specifically, to overcome an uncontrolled power.
Thus, the name Heiltsuk—and by extension Bella Bella—semantically includes the notion of control and display of power. In addition, the pragmatic
function of Bella Bella as a title-name indicates precisely this. This "translation" between languages and of an ethnonym into a collective privilege
historically coincides with the creation of a newly relevant social unit.

The Spirit of History

But what is the nature of this power that is obtained from the Europeans? In
order to examine that issue, it is useful to look at a European narrative
concerning the Heiltsuks and their first encounter with a steamship:

> They promised to construct a steamship on the model of the Beaver. We
> listened and shook our heads incredulously; but in a short time we found
> they had felled a large tree and were making the hull out of its scooped
> trunk. Some time after, this rude steamer appeared. She was from twenty
> to thirty feet long, all in one piece—a large tree hollowed out—re-
> sembling the model of our steamer. She was black, with painted ports;
> decked over and her paddles painted red, and Indians under cover to turn
> them round. The steersman was not seen. She was floated triumphantly,
> and went at a rate of three miles an hour. They thought they had nearly
> come up to the point of external structure; but the enginery baffled them;
> this, however, they thought they could imitate in time by perseverance
> and the helping illumination of the Great Spirit. [Walbran 1971:46-47]

This incident, which occurred in the 1830s, is interesting in several respects. Of course, it demonstrates great ingenuity and a desire to acquire new forms of power. In addition, the specific manner in which the craft was made indicates that it was definitely regarded as a type of supernatural power. Traditionally, performances of aquatic spirit "dances" in the ƛúeḷáx̌a involved the construction and operation of complex craft, expertly carved and painted and manned by hidden men. A widely known story tells of an incident in which several men were killed operating a Killerwhale device of that nature during a Winter Ceremonial performance (Olson 1935, 5:4; Cove 1987:258–59). This illustrates the process that we saw in the Latuya Bay narrative. From an initial condition of fear and misunderstanding, the natives are able finally to acquire something, in this case the very spirit power of the steamship.

Of course, this is not just any power. Normally, the power is either "wild" to begin with and must be "tamed" or is already tamed but must be controlled. In this case, however, it is an element of a powerful cultural system, one that was increasingly to encompass the Heiltsuk universe. Semantic value was built in as the external world appeared more and more as a completed sign system. The ability to incorporate exogenous forms of power was exceeded by the determining power of those forms. Nevertheless, the continued attempt to incorporate them within a distinctively Heiltsuk structure represents an important persistence of Heiltsuk culture, in the midst of the change wrought by them.

But it is arguably not a type of technology per se that the Heiltsuks acquire—either axes and European clothes or the steamship—but in fact a new historicity. One way in which this can be imagined is in terms of spatial-temporal configuration. Two such configurations—"chronotopes," to use Bakhtin's concept (Bakhtin 1981)—are represented in the narrative. First, we have an essentially cyclic chronotope that describes the everyday world of the Heiltsuks. Their spatial world is bounded in all directions: by mountains, forest, sea, and foreign territory. They move through these territories in annual cycles. We see the subjects in the two episodes in different arcs of this cycle. Outside the circle lay uncontrollable human and superhuman forces: in the sea, the underworld, the mountains, the sky, north and south. Long-range (linear) travel by canoe was technically possible but infrequent and fraught with danger.

As we have seen, these external forces were the subject of the ċaíqa dances. In a sense the incorporation of these forces creates the center. It is for the *ćaíqa* that people return to the winter village and so create this centripetal space, the epicenter of which was the cannibal pole erected for the occasion.

Returning to the question posed earlier of the setting of the narrative, we can see now the full significance of the setting of the first part of the narrative in winter and near the old winter village of *q̓élc*. The power of the whites is brought into the very center of the Heiltsuk universe, as a form of power in the *ćaíqa* of the Winter Ceremonial. The white man is thus a supernatural donor. This much is fairly plain.

As an epitomizing event, however, this narrative condenses more than the fact that Europeans were suppliers of exogenous forms of power. It reflects as well the longer-term centripetal movement of the Heiltsuk population. From a traditional territorial settlement including dozens of winter villages, the Heiltsuks were by the early twentieth century mainly living in Bella Bella (the twentieth-century successor to *q̓élc*). That movement was the result both of depopulation and of the increasing importance of the fur trade and European trade goods. Both of these conditions predisposed the Heiltsuks to view the Europeans as possessors of supernatural or exogenous powers. Surely the fact that the point of contact with them was a winter (i.e., sacred) village contributed to this perception. Furthermore, *q̓élc* was not merely a winter village; it was the newly created center of the Heiltsuk world, a centripetal space of greater concentration and importance than ever before. More people lived there, and for a greater portion of the year, than had lived before in a Heiltsuk winter village. This new residence pattern at once reflected the creation of a new social unit and determined certain aspects of the subsequent relations to the Europeans, namely, the tendency to sacralize European forms of power.

The chronotope of the whites is, on the other hand, linear. Steamships are agents not merely of linear movement, but of historical change as well. (They are not called "liners" for nothing.) This is a chronotope that is most fundamentally open to the outside and driven by the notion of progress. Time itself is seen to be one-dimensional (Heidegger 1982:257–64). It is interesting to note, recalling the aquatic races, that within a period of forty-four years the maritime technology with which whites appeared to the Heiltsuks changed radically. Thus, when Mackenzie appeared in 1793, it was in a canoe (Sheppe 1962:235–39). Numerous fur-trading schooners appeared thereafter, and by 1837 the Hudson's Bay Company steamship *Beaver* was on the scene, serving Fort McLoughlin, which was located precisely in the place where the first episode of "The First Schooner" is set (Rich 1941:272).

Time and History

"The First Schooner" is a Heiltsuk account of the Heiltsuks' own history. Of course, this narrative purports to describe historical events that account for the present state of the world (cf. Boas 1932:x). Not only is the subject historical, but the mode of explanation is as well. The white man not only is seen as different, but different in a temporal sense: he "*already* had everything then.*" Thus, the technological gradations of the aquatic races, and of the European appearance to the Heiltsuks, have a temporal, indeed developmental, significance. The ability of the Heiltsuks in the second episode to master the sequence of nautical technology demonstrates also their mastery of linear history, which is the most fundamental identity of the supernatural power acquired in the first episode. It is surely significant that clocks are the first items mentioned in the list of white possessions in the first episode. It is, of course, true that clocks have an aspect of circularity as well as of linearity, which refers to the inescapably circular aspect of time. However, clocks are the objectification of "everyday time," which is the temporal basis of linear history. Clocks also relate in concrete ways to the historical experience of the Heiltsuks. Without accurate chronometers, the calculation of longitude—and hence the carrying out of a radically linear space-time— was impossible. We will later consider the role of clocks in cultural domination of the Heiltsuks, as seen in the chronomania of Methodist missionaries and cannery bosses.

On this fundamental level, the function of "The First Schooner" is to relate two distinct historicities, which correspond to linear and cyclic chronotopes. The narrative relates these two distinct modes of being in time and space. This opposition is expressed early by the inability even to recognize a steel ax, although it is not dissimilar from native woodworking tools. The historicity of the whites is so alien that nothing can be recognized. As in the Latuya Bay narrative, this incommensurability is replaced by understanding, in this case even mastery.

The event of contact involves the clearing out of a space of mutual understanding in which the Heiltsuks can come to terms with novelty in something analogous to the traditional method. Thus the "old timers" of the first episode cannot comprehend what the youths of the second master. This notion of progress resonates with the self-image of the village of Bella Bella in the early twentieth century, which took great pride in its position as the most "progressive" Indian village on the Central Coast (Canada 1907). The difference between the traditional and the progressive is cognitive and phenomenological. The youths live in a radically different world from their elders. This reveals the horizoning nature of the events described in the narrative.

Indeed, the alien historicity is ritually appropriated. As in other cases of ritual appropriation, a name adheres to the appropriator. That name in turn places the Bella Bellas in the context of other named social groups, against whom they must constantly assert their right to the name and their worthiness as rivals. Hence to the "white people in Vancouver" (and is not "Vancouver" a type of eponym?) the validating story must be told.

"The First Schooner" sets the stage for our analysis of archival sources on Heiltsuk history. The idea of progress permeates that history. Moreover, the sense of history as dialectical and dialogic, implicit in this and other Heiltsuk narratives, provides us with a useful framework in which to view the events of the colonial and missionary periods of Heiltsuk history, which I will characterize as dialogues of power.

5

Dialectic and Dialogue

Dialectics of Power

I have described a basic contradiction within Heiltsuk society, between un-controlled exogenous forces and the ordering principle of society, as a dialectic. It is necessary now to clarify the sense in which I am using that concept and to pursue further the question of its relation to historical change, which I have characterized as dialogic.

In speaking of dialectical systems and their relation to historical change, we may distinguish the *internal dialectic* of a cultural system from the *dialectic of articulation* with respect to the outside world. The internal dialectic refers to contradictions within the "traditional" system. In the case of the Barolongs, whom John L. Comaroff discusses (1982:146, 154), that contradiction is between individualism and egalitarianism, on the one hand, and aggregation and hierarchy on the other. In addition, Barolong society was constituted with respect to "lateral" relations between itself and the outside. Thus, traditional societies are not viewed as either purely reactive to external forces, as various "World Systems" approaches hold, nor as phenomeno-logical isolates, as neo-Boasian cultural anthropology holds. Questions of historical change can sensibly be seen as both conditioned by possible in-ternal transformations and responsive to external forces.

The internal dialectic, existing on the "grammatical" level of culture, gives rise to different possible "surface" formations, which are transformations of one another. Thus, the same cultural system can appear radically different, depending upon which side of the dialectic is ascendent. For the Heiltsuks, the appearance of society varied primarily according to season. The year was divided into two seasons, *báḵ*ʷ*enx̌,* the secular, resource-gathering season, and *ćúénx̌elá,* the season of the Winter Ceremonial. During the winter, population was concentrated in the villages, and a hierarchical political system prevailed. During the rest of the year population was dispersed, and social and political control was minimal (see Mauss 1979).

This dialectic is somewhat different from what I referred to in the previous chapter by that term, although the two are closely related and can be seen themselves as transformations of the same principles. On one level there is a system of relative sacredness that corresponds to centralization, hierarchy, and markedness. Thus, the "profane" life of the resource camps, on the periphery of Heiltsuk territory, went on relatively free from hierarchy and the centralization of power. According to one consultant, in the camps, status played no role in sleeping arrangements. The composition of the group itself was relatively loose, with individuals coming and going to take advantage of local variation of resources. Territory was controlled by particular houses but was often shared. Food was generally abundant and consociate groups were relatively small. Distribution and consumption were relatively unmarked.[1] This mode of existence can be characterized as praxis-oriented.

In contrast, during the sacred season, which began around mid-November and lasted for two to three months, society was highly structured and based on principles of hierarchy and centralization. The winter was said to begin at the end of the salmon drying season, when people were still in the camps. They would hear *báx*ʷ*bak*ʷ*áláhusiwa* (the spirit of the Cannibal Dance) outside and know that it was time to complete the fish drying and return to the village. The chief might himself be taken by the cannibal spirit (Boas 1923:7).

People resided in the winter village for the duration of the season. The village was highly marked spatially. Thus, for the uninitiated to be in the *ćaíqa* house was a fatal offense, whereas the *λúeḷáx̌a* and related potlatches were held in relatively public space (Olson 1935, 2:29, 86).[2] A range of taboos associated with the dance series reinforced this partitioning of physical, social, and moral space. The cannibal pole was the ritual center of Heiltsuk space; it was also the most forbidden space. Only the Cannibal Dancer and his attendants were allowed into the room built around the base of the pole, and only the Cannibal Dancer himself could climb the pole (Hunt

1933). Thus, spatial organization perfectly reflected social structure during the winter, both marking gradations of centrality (Durkheim 1965:25).

Food distribution became highly marked during the sacred season, thus employing the surplus created during the secular season and in a sense appropriating praxis itself. This reaffirmed the facts that resources were "owned" by the chiefs and that it was their supernatural power that made abundance possible.[3] We have seen how this marked distribution of food and property was based upon and reaffirmed the authority of the chief as instantiation of an ancestor and embodiment of the house.

From this perspective the system can be viewed as based on a familiar sacred-profane dichotomy, articulated with respect to the seasonal variation of economic activity (Durkheim 1965:52; Mauss 1979). Thus, the word for summer, *bák^{w}enx̌*, is related to *pk̓^{w}s,* meaning 'uninitiated'. They both derive from the root *bk̓^{w},* meaning essentially 'human'. That is, mere humanity unadorned with supernatural power is the essence of the secular. It stands in relation to empowered humanity roughly as individuals of a natural species relate to supernatural embodiments of that species (Reid 1976:154). The *bák^{w}enx̌* was, obviously, the time during which humans interacted with other natural species primarily as individuals and economic resources. Thus, *bák^{w}enx̌* can reasonably be translated as 'season for gathering and preserving food' (Rath 1981, 1:188).

But, the situation is more complicated than this. If we follow the axis of profane-sacred, unmarked-marked, we find a reversal *within* the opposition itself. On the profane side, we have the extreme of dispersed, praxis-oriented activity with unmarked space and distribution of food. As we move into the sacred season and the winter village, we find a relative and centripetal structure of markedness. Some spaces were only weakly marked, whereas the sanctum sanctorum of the Cannibal Dancer's chamber and pole was most strongly marked. Likewise, the distribution of all food and drink was most highly marked in the presence of the Cannibal Dancer, who was first in all matters of consumption, even the most trivial (Drucker 1940:206). The Cannibal Dancer, controlling the innermost centripetal space of the entire system, was the epitome of sacredness.

However, the way this sacredness was constituted contradicted the very notions of hierarchy, order, and centralization of power that characterized the sacred as viewed from the perspective of the *bák^{w}enx̌*. As we have seen, the Cannibal Dancer, and to a lesser degree the entire *ċaíqa* series, was premised upon the *uncontrolled* nature of supernatural power. Moreover, the origin of the *čaíqa* powers was not a centripetal space but a perfectly dispersed one. The ideology of the *čaíqa* stressed the contingent, "chance encounter" aspect of acquisition of *náwálak^w*, as in "true" shamanism. The mythical foundations of the dances were always thus. Four brothers just happen to be captured by *báx^wbak^wálánusiwa* while they were out mountain goat hunting, thus originally obtaining the rights to the Cannibal Dance (Boas 1928:48–65). Indeed, the spatiotemporal features of the acquisition of power are exactly those of the praxis-oriented activity of the sacred season. Some places are more favorable than others, but an encounter can occur anywhere and at any time.

The paradox of a state highly structured with respect to spatiotemporal, social, and power categories being founded on an unstructured, dispersed power represents an antistructural "turn" at the very heart of the system. This reversal parallels the foundation of the marked and hierarchical social organization of the sacred season upon the material base acquired through a dispersed praxis-oriented social form. The connection of the two in myth is quite strong. Thus, not only were supernatural powers obtained in ways very similar to hunting, and often indeed in the act of hunting, but also a result of the acquisition of *náwálak^w* was generally the radical increase in abundance of food and wealth and the subsequent increase in population (e.g., Boas 1928: 101).

I have spoken about the essential negativity that the *čaíqa* entailed: the negative elemental forces, especially death, that were portrayed, opened up a positive space in which human society could exist. This enabling negativity of death was closely related in Heiltsuk (and Kwagul) thought to the food species themselves. Thus, both the human underworld and the world of the salmon were reversed in every respect from the living human world. Significantly, during the winter the food species, animal and vegetable, for the most part disappeared. Human society was maximally removed from its source of regeneration. In the absence of this sustaining relationship, a reversed relationship in which humans themselves were prey to outside forces was enacted.

The negative identification between human society and the realm of animals and the human dead reflects the fundamental insight that human society is founded upon the death not only of food species, but also of humans. Because these two realms are virtual mirror images, human society provides the negative function with respect to this antiworld. Thus, communication between the two realms was characterized by death and regeneration. For example, when salmon bones were thrown into the water, or when human bones were properly disposed of, the antiworld increased, ensuring that, on one level, animals and humans were immortal (Reid 1976:154).

This immortal aspect of humans and animals was reflected in the *λúeḷáẋa,* where enduring names and attributes of animal/human ancestors were maintained. On the individual level, both humans and animals, of course, die. Communication between the two realms by individuals was always characterized by death, whether in hunting or in the *ċaíqa.* The *ċaíqa* symbolically objectified this relationship by making it reversible.

This fundamental paradox of the internal dialectic is, then, also a relationship between society and what lies outside it, physically and phenomenologically. In spatiotemporal terms, that relationship involved the acquisition of what is *most outside* society—in fact, its very negation—and internalizing it. The negativity of death and antistructure that made possible society as a whole was brought to the very center of that structured space. It was partitioned off and surrounded by a highly marked space, a sort of defense-in-depth that was never entirely secure.

External Dialectics

The dialectic of articulation can be seen to flow from this internal dialectic. Thus, relations with the outside were always characterized both by a recognition of danger and antistructure and by a desire to acquire exogenous powers. In normal conditions of dispersed, praxis-oriented activity, these relations were routinized and not especially problematic, involving the gathering of food and material resources.

In special circumstances, however, the antistructural problems were brought to the foreground, primarily, of course, in the *ċaíqa* and the question of acquisition of exogenous powers. In addition, relations with outside groups, even extremely closely related ones such as the Oowekeenos, were frequently predatory, reflecting this basic disposition. Raiding among neighboring ethnic groups was common, occurring most frequently in the period immediately following the *ċaíqa* during the season of intervillage potlatches.[4] Raiding parties on occasion used the cover of inviting neighboring groups to potlatches. This was the case in an incident in the 1850s known as "Slaughter Bay," when a group of Heiltsuks massacred a large number of Oowekeenos (Poutlass 1907; Harkin 1985-87). One goal of the raids was to obtain power from their victims (Boas 1966:114-16).[5] A second goal was the capture of persons to be used as slaves or sold for ransom. The prevalence of the state of war is attested to both by contemporary consultants and by narrative traditions (e.g., Boas 1928:124–46).

The dialectic of articulation and the internal dialectic are thus versions of the same basic disposition. The Heiltsuk cosmology posited a controlled, marked social space as opposed to a negative, uncontrolled external space. The essential operation upon which the social order was founded was the appropriation of exogenous negative powers and their incorporation into the most internal, structured social space. We have seen this relation of appropriation above in "The First Schooner," where the power of the white man is obtained from the outside and finally used to strengthen the social group.

Dialogic Forms of History

This, then, was the basic disposition of Heiltsuk culture toward external forces, which was linked as well to internal transformations. It speaks to the question of transformations within the existing traditional system. However, the question of change of the system itself is a different one. In previous chapters I spoke of the dialogic character of contact events as the clearing out of a space of mutual intelligibility. This can be seen as the primary context of cultural change, because the dialogic relationship involves the constant negotiation and change of the meaning elements in discourse (Bakhtin 1981:279). Dialogue contrasts with dialectic, which involves a set of reversible oppositions and transformations.

Contact events entail a special type of dialogic structure. Dialogic utterance requires common horizons of spatiotemporal, semantic, and valuative elements. Thus, on first encounter utterances are necessarily severely limited by the relatively small commonality of horizons (Todorov 1984:42). For this reason contact languages are quite simple, usually having a small vocabulary. In the contact events discussed earlier, this commonality of horizons was limited mainly to the spatiotemporal dimension. That is, the two parties happened to be at the same place at the same time. And yet, because of the horizoning quality of the event, the common semantic, valuative, and spatiotemporal elements increased. At the conclusion of "The First Schooner," the two groups shared largely common horizons, as different social subunits within a larger society (the people of Bella Bella and "the white people in Vancouver"). The increasing commonality of horizons within which dialogue occurs is nothing other than the change of the phenomenological world of the interlocutors. As Bakhtin states:

> Relations between A and B are in a permanent state of formation and transformation; they continue to alter in the very process of communication. Nor is there a ready-made message X. It takes form in the process of communication between A and B. Nor is it transmitted from the first to the second, but constructed between them, like an ideological bridge; it is constructed in the process of their interaction. [Medvedev 1978:204, quoted in Todorov 1984:55]

That is, the dialogue is not a neutral, purely formal structure for the transmission of a message, like a wire that conducts an electrical charge. Rather, it entails the negotiated change and creation of meaning elements, and further, it effects changes in the horizons of the lifeworld itself, in a feedback relationship (see Gadamer 1980; Swearingen 1990).

It is important to understand this dialogic relationship as a semiotic space, broadly writ, rather than an exclusively linguistic one in which two subjects, self and other, interact. Its "utterances" are symbolic actions (including linguistic ones) within a meaningful context (Volosinov 1973:9–11). Utterances are at once presupposing, as part of the established context, and unique (Todorov 1984:49–51).

In the changing discursive context of cultural contact, unique utterances were always innovative, changing and expanding the dialogic space. As the dialogic space expanded through increasingly shared horizons, it became the primary context of utterances. All utterances came to be shaped by the new other, either *in praesentia* or in absentia (Todorov 1984:77). The white man, by his mere existence, irreversibly changed the meaningful context of Heiltsuk lives.

Monologue and Colonialism

Although all discourse is fundamentally dialogic, subsidiary monologic forms exist as well, which deny the significance of the other: "Ultimately, monologism denies that there exists outside of it another consciousness with the same rights, and capable of responding on an equal footing, another and equal I (thou)" (Todorov 1984:107). Monologic discourse is characteristic of hierarchical and hegemonic political forms. It is the very language of colonialism, becoming increasingly common during the colonial period of British Columbia, when the forms and ideology of the British Empire replace the mercantile interests of the early postcontact period (see Fisher 1977:89–94). For instance, with respect to the central question of land rights, the chief commissioner of lands and works, Joseph Trutch, stated in 1867:

> The Indians really have no rights to the lands they claim, nor are they of any actual value or utility to them. . . . It seems to me, therefore, both just and politic that they should be confirmed in the possession of such extents of land only as are sufficient for their probable requirements for purposes of cultivation and pasturage, and that the remainder of the land now shut up in these reserves be thrown open to pre-emption. [quoted in Fisher 1977:164]

Clearly, this is an utterance that denies the rights of the other, and it pretends to be the last word. A question of vital importance to the continued existence of the British Columbia Indian is thus reduced to a pseudo-objective assessment of his "probable" needs, without taking into account any economic practice other than a narrowly defined English one based on agriculture and husbandry, even though these pursuits were impracticable among the coastal groups.[6] According to this view, it is not even necessary actually to speak to the Indians themselves, as was not done until a royal commission inquiry in 1913, a full three-quarters of a century after the question was opened.

Such monologic discourse contrasts with the dialogic discourse of the early fur-trading period, when the objective of the whites was to create grounds of mutual understanding. The Hudson's Bay Company factor William Fraser Tolmie provides a good example of the dialogic disposition: "Wacash's reply to the *query*—What is the use or purpose of the Tseetzaika [*čičaíqa*, pl. of *čaíqa*] I know not but it was the custom of our forefathers" (Tolmie 1963:319, emphasis added). In his diary Tolmie records a variety of ethnographic and linguistic data (with surprisingly accurate transcription) and exhibits an active curiosity and interest in understanding the other. Apparently at every opportunity he visited Indian villages, asking questions about customs and language. He even engaged in that classic ethnographic endeavor, census taking. Obviously, Tolmie was a gifted and extraordinary observer. Trained as a physician at Edinborough in the 1820s, he was heir to the best scientific traditions of his culture, as well as to the post-Enlightenment interest in cultural comparison. Nevertheless, it is exactly because he was a product of his age that he is of interest. His dialogism is not a unique

manifestation of genius, but rather an intelligent expression of existing cultural tendencies. Dialogism characterizes the early contact period in British
Columbia (Fisher 1977:80).

We can posit a basic pattern of discourse in the postcontact history of the
Heiltsuks. An initial dialogism is replaced by monologic discourse. The
Heiltsuks and their culture become objectified by the colonial authorities. Increasingly, the direction of communication, and thus of power, is one-way.
Monologue is not restricted to colonial authorities, but rather is always characteristic of hierarchical political structures. Certainly, indigenous monologic
forms existed in Heiltsuk culture. The $\lambda \acute{u}e\underset{.}{l}\acute{a}\check{x}a$ is the foremost example.
Speech acts in the $\lambda \acute{u}e\underset{.}{l}\acute{a}\check{x}a$ and in related potlatch rhetoric were centered discourse, from which noise and dialogue were eliminated, and redundancy was
fostered in the form of rhetorical tropes such as anaphora. Such speech pragmatically constituted authority, as I have argued elsewhere (Harkin in press).
However, in Heiltsuk culture this form of discourse was circumscribed by a
more fundamental dialogue, seen in the $\acute{c}a\acute{i}qa$.

The Construction of Dialogues

We have spent some time describing the formal qualities of the dialogue.
The next logical step is to describe the contents of the ethnohistorical
dialogues, which I do in the remaining chapters. An important feature of the
dialogic model is its merging of form and content within a communicational
practice. This quality is, indeed, the essence of its appropriateness to the
ethnohistorical problem. We shall see in the material to be analyzed in the
remaining chapters that the dialogues themselves are profound agents of
change in Heiltsuk ethnohistory.

Stated differently, at one point in this analysis I was faced with the
problem that the very things I was analyzing as the contents of dialogues—
economic exchange, the body, the soul—were themselves constituted in these
dialogues. The idea of a soul as the subject of an elaborately ethicized escha-
tology is impossible without Christianity or a similar religion. Likewise,
economic exchange as "disembedded" from other social relations is dependent upon the commercial economy that appeared in the postcontact era. Even
the body as a biophysical entity arises only as the subject of Western medicine. This built-in paradox—that we can only speak of these processes from
the post hoc perspective, in which they have been reified and institution-

alized—is acknowledged in my use of the model of dialogue.

I speak in the remainder of this work of three distinct if overlapping dialogues between the Heiltsuks and Eurocanadian others. First, I will discuss the corporeal dialogue, the dialogue with respect to the body; second, the evangelical dialogue, the dialogue of missionization; and finally the material dialogue. These categories are partly heuristic but reflect as well divisions of the phenomenological field itself. They are neither entirely institutional categories nor aspects of Heiltsuk categories of society and the person. They are in the end categories themselves, dialogically constituted at the intersection of institutional and reified divisions of Eurocanadian society and Heiltsuk categories. The discourse contained in these dialogues is fundamentally about power.

Perhaps it would be saying too much to state that these dialogues were discrete and real entities; certainly, there is at least an overlapping of boundaries among them. I believe, however, that there are persuasive reasons for organizing the data in this way. The process of postcontact history was for the Heiltsuks and all colonized people characterized by an increasing acceptance of Western cultural categories, reified into institutions and misplacedly concrete divisions of the person (i.e., mind and body). Acculturation was above all an enforced imposition of these reified Western categories upon indigenous people, through a monumental series of monologic discourses. Simply to reproduce those Western categories in a historical narrative (as is done by most historians and ethnohistorians) is to reproduce the same monologism. But neither is it acceptable to objectify indigenous cultures without regard to the reality of historical change: that would create a monologue of another, similar sort (Fabian 1983:28-35).

Instead, one must attempt to take into account the "guerilla" struggle against the imposition of these categories and against the monologic quality of discourse itself. Examples abound in Heiltsuk history of attempts to reassert the dialogic character of relations with the other. Thus, several extant historical narratives refer to the purported dialogic relationship between Heiltsuk chiefs and Queen Victoria, involving particularly the grant of title to land or the payment for alienated land. That tête-à-tête relationship was thought later to have been denied and suppressed by various officials (Harkin 1985-87). Such an assumption was noted frequently by officials in the nineteenth and early twentieth centuries (e.g., Canada 1882, 6:143).

Moreover, had the monologic discourse of colonial powers prevailed entirely, the indigenous Heiltsuk categories would have disappeared; clearly, this has not been the case. Sophisticated psychological and philosophical concepts persist, particularly among contemporary elders, drawing on the traditional holistic model of the person. Such holistic notions of health, sickness, and curing persist, as do other elements of the personal category. Thus, it can be concluded that the basic dialogic disposition was maintained as well to some degree.

I attempt in the remainder of this work to demonstrate the reality of these dialogues. I define them as dialogues primarily, rather than monologues, not merely because evidence of cultural persistence suggests that the monologic discourse was never entirely successful, but also because dialogue is always present as the foundation of discourse—a fact that monologues attempt to hide (Todorov 1984:62-63).

6

Bodies

The body is the field in which the dialogue of cultures between the Heiltsuks and the Europeans is most immediately and contentiously enacted. Domination, resistance, and cultural transformation are played out in bodily practices, beliefs, representations, and ways of being. Just as individual bodies mediate between self and other, so on the level of culture the meaningful and empowered body mediates cultural otherness. For this reason the body constitutes a highly contested cultural domain. In colonial discourse the non-Western body is the epitome of savagery; for victims of contact it is, literally, the embodiment of their threatened lifeworld.

In any cultural "borderland," such as a diaspora, the body is obviously an important arena of contestation, of the forging or transmuting of identity. But this is even more the case in the processes linked to European conquest and colonialism, especially in the Americas and Australia, because of two factors. Most obvious is the phenomenon of "virgin soil" epidemics that greatly reduced or even annihilated aboriginal populations, sometimes in advance of direct contact. Less obvious, but also significant, is the coincidence of the high tide of colonialism with the European development of discourses and technologies of the body, making bodily practices a conscious object of colonial and missionary policy.

The onslaught of pandemic disease has been perhaps the most significant set of events in the history of contact between the colonizing West and the colonized Rest. The most potent weapon in the armory of "ecological imperialism," pathogens defeated armies, opened land for resettlement, and

77

abetted imperialist fantasies and schemes that were dependent upon a "disappearing savage" (Berkhofer 1978:29; A. W. Crosby 1986).

The biomedical model of disease makes it seem natural to view illness as an impersonal force. This Western model essentially masks the underlying power relations, both of the disease itself and of therapeutic and hygienic interventions. Indigenous models, however, more frequently emphasize the personalistic aspects of illness. Narratives of illness based on these models have a moral dimension that recaptures the power relations of the original disease event (Harkin 1990b). I argue that this perspective is in the final analysis the more valid and that the colonial history of the Heiltsuks and other aboriginal groups can be understood only with reference to power as rooted in bodily experience.

The Heiltsuks see whites as active agents in the spread of illness, through magical malevolence. Indeed, we know that in some cases whites did intentionally spread disease by distributing infected blankets among uninfected Indians (an action that would be glossed as "witchcraft" in virtually all aboriginal conceptual systems). What is more, the initial impact of disease was a prelude to the imposition of a new power relationship based on systematic principles of discipline and control of the body—principles that are idealized and internalized and thus become hegemonic.[1] In North America, recent research suggests that mortality rates from introduced disease were much higher than previously thought, with deaths in the millions.[2] Robert T. Boyd (1985) has examined this issue for the Northwest Coast, with equally striking results. My own data suggest that the Heiltsuk population was reduced by 80 percent or more in the mid-nineteenth century, primarily because of several outbreaks of smallpox.

In human terms, suffering and death at this level are apocalyptic. They also constitute crucial events in the ethnohistories of groups, because they forcefully challenge the aboriginal cognitive system, laying the ground for radical change (Wallace 1970:189).

Power is the key term in this equation. Power is not simply coercion but involves cultural schemata of authority, efficacy, energy, purity, and so forth. Schemata of power are not uniform cross-culturally but do share a "family resemblance" in the Wittgensteinian sense (Fogelson and Adams 1977). What is at stake in the corporeal dialogue between colonizer and colonized is never simply the dynamics of raw force but the deployment and finally the imposition of structures that presuppose asymmetric relations of production, reproduction, legitimacy, and symbolization (see Jean Comaroff and John L. Comaroff 1992).

Michel Foucault has taught us to see the exercise of power in the domain of the body, even in the most ordinary of bodily practices. Foucault's insight will guide my examination of the Heiltsuk ethnohistory of the body. The study of nineteenth-century colonialism is especially amenable to such an approach; there we find the technologies of power fully fledged. The institutions that Foucault has studied, the clinic and the prison, are products of the modern age that reached a peak of efficiency at precisely the moment that Euroamericans began to colonize, rather than simply trade with, the natives of the Northwest Coast (see Loo 1992). For the Heiltsuks, this fearful efficiency, operating under the sign of humanitarianism, overwhelmed a cultural system that was always open to the outside.

Europeans deployed a three-part strategy of subjugation in the wake of pandemic disease. The three constituents were the biomedical clinic, the Protestant theology of discipline, and the carceral institutions, including the jail and the residential school. Each leg reinforced and augmented the others. The theology of discipline was spiritually "hygienic" and was enforced by the carceral institutions (see chapter 7). The clinic deployed quasi-theological concepts such as purity, filth, and redemption. Indeed, the three are homologous; each pursues a strategy of isolation and control that in its final stage is self-imposed.

Disease Events in Heiltsuk Ethnohistory

I heard about this—what happened years ago, before my time—what they called smallpox, whatever it was, in those days. People used to live in Denny Island there. . . . They were dying just like . . . I don't know how many deaths were there. And one old fellow, to get away from there, climbed a mountain to go right straight across to Hauyet. . . . And that's a reserve, because it's a salmon brook, you see. They used to go over there and dry fish, you know. . . . They couldn't tell how many people had died. Some women lay down dead, and the little baby was still sucking their tits, and she'd be dead. They'd tell me that story. [Harkin 1985–87]

Thus a Heiltsuk historical narrative describes the smallpox pandemic of 1862, which resulted in a mortality rate of 69 percent (Boyd 1990). The loss of population over thirty years was even more extreme. Approximately fifteen hundred people inhabited the area around the Hudson's Bay Company Fort McLoughlin in 1835; the population was two hundred or less in the 1880s (Canada 1889; ARMCC 1889-90:96; Tolmie 1963:320; R. G. Large 1968: 5).[3] Indians returning from Victoria brought the disease to the central coast (R. W. Large 1904). Even today this holocaust is remembered with considerable emotion.

The narrative quoted above stresses the lack of continuity the smallpox entailed. Most dramatically, dead mothers cannot provide breast milk for their doomed infants. The survivors could not even count the dead. This not only suggests the proportions of the disaster, but symbolizes as well an absolute breach between the living and the dead. The most important responsibility for a Heiltsuk person was, and continues to be, to provide proper commemoration for a kinsman when he dies (see Kan 1989:172). Here, the dead not only cannot be commemorated, but they cannot even be named. They cannot even be counted! Another consultant stresses the point that the dead were not buried but simply placed on the beach rolled up in a blanket (see Storie and Gould 1973:75-76). One tradition holds that canoes full of people set off from Vancouver, but they would have to stop from time to time to lay a corpse on the beach. By the end of the journey, only one person was left alive, to infect his village.

The Heiltsuk universe was founded on a continuity from generation to generation and exchange between human society and nonhuman realms, as explicitly seen in mortuary practices, notions of reincarnation, and the Winter Ceremonial. The entire set of relations entailed in social and biological reproduction was threatened. In addition, the direct causal effect of the smallpox on other historical developments, such as the consolidation of tribal groups around the village of Bella Bella and the loss of esoteric cultural knowledge, is clear (Olson 1935, 5:52).

Significantly, the narrator interjects into this narrative an explicit communal claim to land ("And that's a reserve").[4] The devastation of smallpox is associated in his mind with Eurocanadian threats to Heiltsuk land. He is not merely telling Heiltsuk history; he is commenting on it. He presents the narrative as one who heard it long ago—hence the narrative bracketing—and provides both a retelling and a commentary. This indigenous account, with its superficially curious juxtaposition of disease and economic resources, provides a telling insight into the historical processes of colonialism in British Columbia, in which the health of aboriginal peoples—rooted in, but not limited to, individual bodily states—and the appropriation of economic resources were inversely related.

Disease and Health in Heiltsuk Culture

Epidemic and pandemic outbreaks of disease were recurrent among the Heiltsuks in the nineteenth and early twentieth centuries. Like a series of aftershocks, fatal outbreaks of measles (1882), tuberculosis (recurrent), smallpox (recurrent), whooping cough (recurrent, especially in 1891 and 1905), and influenza (1919) devastated the Heiltsuks (Charles M. Tate 1883; Hopkins 1892:87; G. Darby 1919). According to a contemporary consultant, influenza killed some forty-seven people in Bella Bella. Every night someone died, sometimes two per night. No medicine was effective; the stronger you were, the faster it killed you. Again, there is the sense of helplessness and of some essential breach in the Heiltsuk world order. The particular inversion of influenza was that it seemed to kill primarily the young and healthy (G. Darby 1919).

For the Heiltsuks, disease was related to the larger moral state of the world. Affliction was "the dislocation of self and context" (Jean Comaroff 1980:644-45), in which a breach of the cosmic order was both cause and result. Such a breach could be considered either passive or active, an unwitting violation or a positive malevolence, producing minor or serious affliction, respectively. In the former case the transgression involved an unintentional or careless failure to discharge a responsibility necessary for the smooth functioning of the world, that is, proper relations between the human world and the worlds of the dead, of supernatural beings, and of natural species. For example, carelessness in hunting or mistreatment of game animals that resulted in their suffering inevitably led to illness and was considered a major cause thereof (R. W. Large 1905:115; see Hallowell 1976: 419). In the case of serious affliction, witchcraft or sorcery was implicated (R. W. Large 1905:115).

Two factors separated these pandemics and epidemics from normal affliction events. First, the diseases were of unprecedented virulence. Second, in the case of smallpox the disease struck the entire society. The virulence of the illness produced the view that an active malevolence was behind it. Because it struck virtually all Heiltsuk people, the malefactor was located *outside* society; in this case it was the Eurocanadian. Smallpox was called, in English, the "White Man's Sick" and was viewed as the product of witchcraft by hostile whites (R. W. Large 1904:130). One narrative, recorded in the 1960s, expresses this view:

> And the White People get tired of the Indians going over there [Victoria] and they try to chase them away. Well, sometimes they sneak around, and they have some disease with them, this smallpox disease. The Indians see them put something in the bow (of a canoe) and put it, put it way in. So when they are against the wind it blows right to the stern and everybody will catch it. [Storie and Gould 1973:75]

This idea of white culpability expresses the reality that the cause of the disease was external, that it originated with non-Indians in Victoria. More-over, whites living in Victoria indeed objected to the large number of Indians living in settlements around the city, including the Songhees reserve, which had been allocated to a local group of Salish people in 1850 (Kew 1990:162). In this sense pathogens clearly abetted the interests of colonists.[5]

The modus operandi, secreting the disease in a box, reflects Heiltsuk notions of corporeal causality. Witchcraft (*dásgiú*) was often performed by collecting bodily disjecta or an object that had been in contact with the body and hiding it in a box (Olson 1949, 6:49). Manipulation of the contents of the box introduced a foreign object into the victim's body, causing illness or death (R. W. Large 1903a:232). Interestingly, the technique in the case of smallpox was a combination of Heiltsuk and Western etiologies; the notion of an airborne substance flying into the bodies of the afflicted reflects the bio-medical perception of bacterial and viral disease.

In addition to viewing whites as potential witches, Heiltsuks frequently accused one another throughout the late nineteenth and early twentieth cen-turies, reflecting massive social and cultural dislocation (R. W. Large 1903a: 232; E. Darby 1922; Fougner 1931). The Heiltsuks believed that the death of a child was always the result of witchcraft (Boas 1923:284). Not surprisingly, the most serious internal accusations of witchcraft occurred around the time of the influenza epidemic, 1919 to 1920.

Affliction as Bodily Transformation

For the Heiltsuks, witchcraft was a marked, personalized form of disease in general. It involved transformation of the body according to certain general principles, which included the body as a container, incorporation, penetration and drawing out, secret versus public, and the efficacy of analogy. Such corporeal transformation had significance beyond the health or sickness of the individual, implicating the larger worlds of village and native society and their relationship to outside forces.

The body was the primary focus of the culturally constituted lifeworld, particularly the symbolic organization of space. The body created (and recreated) the spatial and symbolic categories of a culture, which were expressed in other symbolic series. For instance, the body was an especially good symbol for social groups (Ellen 1977:354–55, 357; Jean Comaroff 1981:368).

The most fundamental quality of the Heiltsuk body was containedness (see Fleisher 1981; Walens 1981; Seguin 1982). The essential social container, the house, was modeled on the human body. Traditional Heiltsuk houses had "mouths" through which one passed to enter. The interior was organized into a "head" and "sides." For the Heiltsuks the primary referent of the notion of right and left sides, as a measure of rank and value, was the human body (Olson 1935, 5:20; see Hertz 1960). Other specific house-body associations existed as well.

Like the house, which contained its members, the body was thought of as containing the soul or life force. Boas records for the Kwakiutls that the body was the "house of the soul" (1921:724). For the Heiltsuks the soul was housed in the body but could leave it (Boas 1923:18, 264). When the soul did leave the boundaries of the body, it was potentially in danger from witchcraft. Similarly, hostile forces threatened a member of a house when venturing abroad, especially outside the territory of the lineage. Heiltsuk narratives stress the dangers involved in leaving the structured space of the house, especially to hunt (Boas 1928:48–64).

Alternatively, outside forces could penetrate the container, placing the victim in grave danger. Witches and shamans killed and inflicted illness by projecting an object into the body (Olson 1935, 2:79) or by obtaining personal items and placing them in a new, natural or artificial container, which could then be penetrated and manipulated (G. Darby 1933; Olson 1949, 6:49). One such method was to make a model of a head with such items and then to pierce it with a sharp object such as a fish bone. Clearly, the notion of penetration of the body or corporeal object is central (R. W. Large 1904:135).

Healing, on the other hand, consisted of extracting objects from the body (R. W. Large 1908; G. Darby 1933). The power of shamanic curing was

called *gigeltk^wílá* 'lengthening of powers'. The shaman developed powers
that could extend through bodily boundaries. Without the aid of shamans, one
could extract or expel foreign objects by "purifying" the body through bathing, steam baths, and emetics (G. Darby 1933).

Special pools and hot springs were favored for the drawing out of foreign
objects. Young women particularly were in need of such purification; commonly a frog would appear, as the material form of the impurity. Frogs were
associated with illness and curing on the Northwest Coast; their attribute of
boundary-crossing, as neither terrestrial nor aquatic creatures, is perhaps
related to this (Lévi-Strauss 1982:120–22). Frogs are greedy, a trait associated with impurity (Boas 1932:4). Frogs are also, for the Heiltsuks, associated
with human fertility and pregnancy. Pregnant women wore button blankets
embroidered with a frog design. It was taboo for young women to kill frogs
(Boas 1923:281). The association of feminine fertility, pollution, and disease
is clear in the symbol of the frog. These notions all involve violation or
breaking down of the bodily boundary.

The openness of female bodies was a source of pollution but also of
power. A Heiltsuk myth tells of the destruction of a man-eating octopus
through the use of menstrual blood of a chief's daughter (Curtis 1915:298).
This act constituted the basis of a *λúeḷáx̌a* dance. Similarly, menstrual blood
was an ingredient in the paint used on some of the masks in the *ċaíqa*
(Harkin 1985–87). One *ċaíqa* performance, *x̌a'ápi* 'cradle', appropriates the
power of pubescent girls.

The bodily boundary is the epitome of other types of boundaries and
margins (Douglas 1966). The complex of practices associated with bodily
purification *(λáwásila)* clearly shows this. Purification was performed particularly in anticipation of hunting, that is, venturing out beyond the boundaries
of society into a nonhuman realm. Sexual and food abstinence and the use of
saltwater emetics served to close and fortify the boundaries of the body, to
eject any internal foreign objects, including animal meat, and then to close off
the orifices and strengthen the margins of the body. This allowed the hunter
to function purely as a human in the animal realm and thus to engage in the
fundamental exchange between humans and animal species in an unam-
biguous way. The appearance of those in an inherently marginal state, especially menstruation, pregnancy, and bereavement, in a food resource area
depleted the supply of that food species (see Harkin 1990a). The basic terms
of the exchange were destroyed.

The bodily condition associated with liminality reflects this lack of clear boundaries. Menstruating and pregnant women are not closed off and continent but open to the outside. Widows and those in mourning opened their bodies up to the outside by weeping and self-mutilation (Boas 1890: 839–40).

The liminal subject is in a dangerous and vulnerable state that has consequences for the entire social group. It was necessary, after the first stages of pollution and openness to the outside, to contain and control this danger, through a regimen called *híkelá,* consisting in the radical restriction of the subject. *híkelá* applied to widows and widowers, as well as to menstruating and pregnant women. A contemporary native gloss is 'to take care of, to keep away from danger.' It entailed the isolation of the subject, who was forbidden from participating in any daily activities of the household. A specific taboo existed on the handling of sharp objects, such as knives, that is, instruments capable of penetrating and opening up the container of the body and used in the production and preparation of food.

Concepts associated with the body clearly reveal the contradictions within the cultural order, such as between production and reproduction, social control and creative anarchy. Thus, the body in states of affliction constituted a crisis in the cultural organization of these contradictions (Jean Comaroff 1981:368–69). The Heiltsuk belief in witchcraft in connection with cases of epidemic illness called into question the category of the person as an integral and empowered being. In such a crisis of basic categories, affliction created the possibility for cultural change by foregrounding these normally implicit categories and the essential contradictions they entail. It was against this background of crisis that Western categories and technologies of the body appeared.

Affliction, Biomedicine, and Corporeal Reform

The Early Contact Period, 1800 to 1840

Heiltsuk perceptions of sickness[6] rested on the relationship between outside sources and internal forms of power. As in the Winter Ceremonial, the wielder of power, to harm or heal, depends upon his relationship with a nonhuman or sociologically distant donor. From the therapeutic perspective, the primary etiological maneuver was to specify this relationship in particular cases; this was the job of healing shamans. The initial appearance of whites on the scene radically altered both the internal and the external worlds. They appeared primarily in the role of malefactor, secondarily as potential healer.

One manifestation of the white man's power was the musket. The musket was iconic of the Heiltsuk notion of corporeal causality. It acts by penetration of the bodily container; it acts from afar and is connected with external sources of power. It provides a visible symptomatology exactly fitting with the Heiltsuk concept of sickness. The required intervention is clearly the removal from the sufferer's body of an embedded foreign object.[7] Moreover, the invisible etiology remained intact; accidental shootings came to be seen as one possible outcome of a particular witchcraft technique (R. W. Large 1903a:229). The musket, as a long, thin, death-dealing object, was associated with the Death Bringer, a common object of Northwest Coast mythology (Curtis 1915:114–15; Boas 1928:101).

From the beginning of the fur trade the musket was an important trade item, becoming even a generalized medium of exchange. Shootings, both accidental and intentional, became a common occurrence after the establishment of the Hudson's Bay Company Fort McLoughlin in 1833. The traders of the Hudson's Bay Company were not above using their superior firepower to further their perceived interests; in one skirmish several Heiltsuks were killed or injured by gunfire.[8] The arrival of the musket coincided with that of biomedicine. William Fraser Tolmie, the Hudson's Bay Company doctor posted at Fort McLoughlin, provided limited medical treatment, including the treatment of gunshot wounds. This evinced two aspects of the whites' power: the ability both to injure and to heal by essentially the same technique of penetration, analogous to, but qualitatively different from, the practice of shamans and witches. Tolmie's services were given sparingly, on the belief that he would be held responsible by kinsmen should he fail to treat the sufferer's complaint successfully (Tolmie 1963:301, 308). This resistance on the part of the potential benefactor accorded with the Heiltsuk perspective that Europeans, at least those with esoteric knowledge, were the possessors of a potent supernatural power.

The Heiltsuks found this withheld power all the more attractive, on the principle that the more difficult a type of power was to obtain, the greater its potency and value. Further, the Heiltsuks increasingly experienced a need for this aspect of the whites' power. The introduction of the musket and alcohol, as the two main trade items, greatly increased the frequency and devastation of incidents of intra- and interethnic violence.[9]

The second, far more devastating scourge of this period was, of course, the epidemic and pandemic diseases, in particular the first smallpox epidemic (1836 to 1838), which reduced the northern Heiltsuk population by 34 percent

(Boyd 1985).[10] If these plagues were manifestations of the white man's power, then the possibility of healing also lay with him, according to an equation implied in the Heiltsuk concept of sickness. Cause and cure were simply different modalities of the same power. Indeed, in 1837 the Hudson's Bay Company sent cowpox vaccine to Fort McLoughlin to treat the local populations, apparently with some success (Rich 1941:217; Tod n.d.).

For the Heiltsuks, the function of the healer was to articulate the external-internal relationship implicated in the particular sickness and to provide the mediation between sufferer and the larger world. Or, as the Heiltsuk metaphor succinctly puts it, healing *(hailíkila)* is exactly "setting things right." However, this setting right required the incorporation of white forms of power and the addressing of the discontinuities between the Heiltsuks and what came to be seen as a separate human society rather than (primarily as) a new manifestation of supernatural beings.

The Missionary Period, 1860 to 1920

In the 1860s and later the Heiltsuks were increasingly living among the whites, other non-Indians, and other Indians in the canneries that had been established in their own territory and in the city of Victoria. This provided access to manifest forms of power within Eurocanadian society, in particular those of the organized churches. Among the most approachable of these was the Methodist Church, which took as its primary responsibility the "lower orders" of British Columbia society: dockworkers, sailors, day laborers, and, of course, Indians (Charles M. Tate 1929:12; see Grant 1984:133). The development of missions is treated in greater detail in chapter 7, but several relevant points should be brought out here.

The second smallpox pandemic began around 1862 and spread up the coast of British Columbia from Victoria. In 1868 the Methodist missionary Thomas Crosby, although without benefit of medical training, followed in its wake administering smallpox vaccinations. There are no figures to indicate the scope of this vaccination, nor its effect. The mere fact of Crosby's action was certainly important. His experiences impressed him with the need for medical missions to be sponsored by the Methodist Church (Stephenson 1925:152–53). From the point of view of the Heiltsuks, the form this treatment took was familiar, if the direction was reversed from the usual. The hypodermic needle effects a bodily penetration, usually denoting the introduction of a dangerous foreign body. However, it could have been interpreted as a form of counterirritation, a traditional medical practice involving the cutting and puncturing of the skin in order to allow the escape of the malignant substance (G. Darby 1933).

This combination of a state of "dis-ease," as an inability to mediate an unknown external force and thus to "set right" the Heiltsuk world, and the increasing presence of a new, exogenous form of power manifested in the person of the Methodist missionary, led to an attempt to revitalize society by incorporating this new power (Grant 1984:245).[11]

The same situation presented itself to other British Columbia Indian groups, an immediate result of which was the beginnings of a religious "revival" in Victoria in 1870. This movement began from a rented barroom and was, significantly, led in part by native preachers. The culmination came in 1873 at a camp meeting in Chilliwack on the lower mainland, at which many northern Indians, including some Heiltsuks, were present (Grant 1984: 133; Goodfellow n.d.).

The message was taken back to Bella Bella and proclaimed by two native converts. After initial resistance, a missionary, Charles M. Tate, an Englishman with six years' experience, was asked for and provided to the community. Although it was not at first a medical mission, an important focus from the start was the physical health of the Indians. Tate visited the sick, even in outlying resource areas (Charles M. Tate 1929). He possessed some basic medical supplies but no medical training. Partly for this reason, but more importantly for ideological reasons, the thrust of the missionary's concern for the bodily state of his parishioners was bodily reform. Physical well-being and appearance were taken as symbols of one's spiritual state. "Cleanliness is next to Godliness" is a particularly Methodist maxim. Notions of dirt, disease, sexual license, "heathenism," and racial inferiority are condensed in the image of "darkness," employed frequently for decades by the missionaries, possessing multiple referents: not merely skin color and "unenlightened" souls, but a range of cultural practices such as face painting and even the lack of light in traditional houses (E. Darby 1922; see Grant 1984: 229). For example, during Tate's visit to Bella Coola in 1881, he stated: "These people are very dark. It seemed hard to make them understand anything. And the filthy state of their house, their clothing and their person is beyond expression" (Charles M. Tate 1881). One of the first actions of Tate as a missionary had been to teach the natives to make brooms out of cedar branches (Charles M. Tate 1929). Thomas Crosby, recalling a visit in the

early 1870s to the Heiltsuk village of q̓ʷúqʷaí, compared the Methodist
Gospel to a cleansing flood tide. He told a resistant chief: "You can't stop the
tide; it will come up all around your village here and wash away all the dirt
and bad into the great sea" (T. Crosby 1914:142). This rhetoric has its root in
the peculiar sacrificial, quasi-erotic imagery of the English Methodists of the
eighteenth century, in which Christ's blood is the divine but corporeal
purifying agent and sole legitimate object of desire (Thompson 1980:408-10).
The nature of this tide is to cleanse the saved, by separating out those
elements and persons who reject salvation. Thus, in a too-perfect example of
poetic justice, the resistant chief is soon afterward drowned while on his way
to a potlatch. Interestingly, the Heiltsuks considered drowning, along with
death by gunshot, to be the product of witchcraft (R. W. Large 1903a:229).
This implied great power on the part of the missionaries and made them akin
to the most powerful shamans and Cannibal Dancers, who could cause similar
deaths (Drucker 1936-37). For the missionaries, the chief's drowning was a
means for "opening the Gospel" among the Heiltsuks, because the Heiltsuks
themselves generally considered it a judgment against the chief (T. Crosby
1914:142).

The Heiltsuks were prepared to buy into the new ideology of bodily
purification, in part because disease created among them a psychological state
of shame, which was not far from the Methodist idea of the "dis-grace" of the
unsaved. The Methodists frequently invoked the idea of shame, with considerable effect. The sickness of a chief was especially humiliating for the
Heiltsuks, representing a state of collective weakness and vulnerability. In the
1850s a Heiltsuk chief was dying of tuberculosis. At a potlatch an Oowekeeno man performed a dance making fun of the dying chief, and the Heiltsuks retaliated by massacring a large number of Oowekeenos (McIlwraith
1921-24:373). Within the traditional ideological system, this was the most
efficacious way of overcoming shame.

The Methodists offered an ideology of bodily perfection that promised
less a means of overcoming disease (that would come later) than a new
technology of bodily control, which was simply the outer sign of an internal
state of grace. Again, this was not so far from certain indigenous ideas, such
as cold-water bathing and fasting, which bespoke purity and power. Of
course, for the missionaries such "pagan" practices in no way ameliorated the
Indians' state of dirt and darkness. The missionaries were especially concerned with bodily adornment in this connection. A widely circulated story

concerning the first Heiltsuk converts holds that they were rebuffed by the local chiefs, who "commanded the men to put on their blankets, paint their faces and return to the customs of the tribe" (Stephenson 1925:173–74).

Clothes were thought of as an index of civilization, which was directly related to the question of grace; one could not exist without the other (Grant 1984:223). The native missionary William H. Pierce makes an interesting comment in his memoirs to the effect that the immediate and visible result of his missionary activity in Bella Bella was the forswearing of traditional cedar bark clothes and the taking up, within a matter of weeks, of European clothing (Pierce 1933:42). Judging by the Hudson's Bay Company records, the change was not so sudden; neither did it occur after the arrival of the mission. Rather, the purchase of European clothes increased incrementally from the mid-1870s onward (Hudson's Bay Company 1876–77, 1877–82). Nevertheless, the change was indeed fairly sudden, with the increase in the importation of European clothing and other items increasing roughly geometrically for several years. Pierce's recollection may not be literally correct, but it is true in the manner of an epitomizing event, in which long-term processes are condensed into a single recalled or narrated event (Fogelson 1984).

Clothing marked, for the Heiltsuks, something approaching its meaning for the missionaries, an extension of an inner spiritual/bodily state. Marked forms of apparel, such as the cedar bark rings used in the Winter Ceremonial, expressed and to some degree extended power. Furthermore, clothing was an extension of the internal personal essence of an individual. To wear another's clothes, as occurred only in the case of a mourning spouse, was to be incorporated by the clothing's owner (Harkin 1990a). Cedar bark clothes (as opposed both to button blankets and European-style clothing) contained the bodily essence of the maker and wearer. The bark was chewed (by either the wearer or a female house member) to be made supple (Hudson's Bay Company 1834). Likewise, the wearer's perspiration was absorbed in the fiber. As they were permeated with this bodily substance, bits of clothing—even European clothing, to some degree—were potential objects for witchcraft (R. W. Large 1910b:918).

Almost as powerful an index of "heathenism" as clothes, facial painting was used in the important ritual contexts, specifically, mortuary rites and the Winter Ceremonial. In particular, black ("dark") paint was used on ritual occasions (Boas 1923:10). For the Heiltsuks facial paint represented an extraordinary spiritual state characteristic of liminality. For the missionaries it likewise represented a spiritual state, albeit a negatively valued one. Although temporary, and thus eminently reformable, facial paint was to the missionaries a mark of Satan. The missionary objection to facial paint thus epitomized opposition to ceremonial culture generally. It was, in their view, a diacritic of savagery.[12]

Heiltsuk mortuary practices were a primary focus of the missionary's horror in the nineteenth century (Caroline Tate 1883; T. Crosby 1914:191). One incident is particularly telling: A small girl was dying during an epidemic of measles. The medically untrained wife of the missionary visited the girl but left, because she believed nothing could be done to save the child's life. The missionary's wife returned several hours later, to find the female relatives of the child in mourning, having prepared a coffin and placed blankets and other items in it, along with the child, who was still breathing. The woman reacted with horror and literally struggled over the body of the child with the other women. Finally, she took the child back to the mission house, where the girl promptly died (Caroline Tate 1883). The woman's horror at the proceedings was due not to a disagreement between herself and the Heiltsuk women on the imminence of death. Death itself, especially the death of children, was actually welcomed by the missionary, as a "touching but triumphant" end. The missionary reported deaths in the village in the same contented terms as conversion; the two were morally equated (Calvert 1888).[13]

The conflict was over the relationship between outward bodily signs and the inward state of vitality of the soul (see Harkin 1990a). It was also over the details of burial: "I had some of them prepare a coffin which was very rudely constructed, as they have no idea how to make anything of the kind, their custom being to put a corpse into a deep box and in a sitting position" (Caroline Tate 1883). That one method of burial, flexed, in a square box, could be considered so inferior to prone burial in an oblong box demonstrates the close identification in the mind of the missionary between the possibility of salvation and bodily practices. The point is not simply that an entire range of cultural values and practices were intermixed and imposed on the Heiltsuks in the guise of Christian belief, but rather that the body itself was viewed, at least by the missionaries, as the objective field of struggle between opposing powers, powers of "savagery" versus those of "civilization."

The missionaries' special horror at these particular practices was therefore owing to the fact that they had as their main reference the body itself, which becomes the objectified form of the spiritual state. Thus, one missionary to the Heiltsuks, W. B. Cuyler, wrote in 1884:

A great work has been done for these poor people. They show upon their arms scars where in former days mouthfuls of flesh were torn off; and, comparing the past with the present, we conclude that the former days were not better than these. [T. Crosby 1914:191]

Unlike clothing and face paint, such bodily marks were indelible signs of "heathenism" and thus, by contrast, of progress. Indeed, this scarring was an icon of original sin. Just as each individual struggled to overcome the state of childhood depravity, with the help of stern disciplinarian parents and teachers, so the racial childhood represented by the Indian might be overcome but never forgotten (see Thompson 1980:414).

Scars were a reminder of the dangers of leaving the body to its own devices. Missionaries knew the biting of the *hámáċa* to be the ecstatic culmination of a religious festival, which bore a twofold resemblance to the Methodists' own cathartic rites. The horror at the "heathenish" practice of anthropophagy derives at least in part from its similarity to Methodist and Christian notions of the body of Christ; it was close enough to be considered a fiendish inversion of the latter (see Thompson 1980:408–10). Moreover, the tempo and psychodynamics of the Methodist chapel meetings were, to their mind, mocked by the "heathen" rites. The climactic emotionalism of each— for the Methodists a guilty secret that must be hidden in the hyperdiscipline of everyday life—suggested a commensurability of the two systems. Missionaries and natives recognized in each other's practices familiar forms, which constituted a basis for communication.

The main topic of this communication was discipline. Bodily discipline was the cornerstone of missionary practice; nineteenth-century missionaries perceived the Heiltsuk way of life as a whole, including its mode of production, as intolerable libertinism (Tod 1924; see Weber 1976:157–60; Grant 1984:225). The temporal dimension was especially stressed. The Methodists, missionaries and converts, began the day at 4:00 A.M. and studied scripture for several hours before taking breakfast and beginning work, ideally physically demanding and tedious work (Charles M. Tate 1929; Thompson 1967: 87–88; see Weber 1976:160–61). The Methodist worker became "his own slave driver" (Thompson 1980:393). All aspects of corporeal life were subject to the structures of Methodist discipline. One photograph from the 1890s shows several converted Heiltsuks, who had formed an Epworth League, dressed in constraining black uniforms; here the Methodist virtues of uniformity and physical discomfort were combined in the body covering.[14]

The missionary control over bodily practices extended beyond productive labor. Practices associated with female sexuality were especially targeted. The traditional institution of arranged adolescent betrothal was considered a major peril. The mission immediately began taking in young girls faced with this prospect, in order to "save" them. The practices associated with *hîkelá,* or ritual seclusion at menarche and other life crises, quickly became a point of contention. The concern on the part of parents that the young girls maintain aspects of ritual seclusion and inactivity was branded "superstition" and not in keeping with Methodist discipline (Caroline Tate 1881). For the Methodist, physical inactivity, even for the purpose of religious study or meditation, was morally inferior to organized, disciplined labor (Weber 1976:158).

To this end, women were organized into a Ladies Aid Society to furnish and maintain the interior of the church and school; this work took the form of organized sewing sessions, with the product sold for the profit of the church. These were combined with scriptural study and lessons under the direction of the missionary's wife (Kissack 1903; I. Large 1905:592). The goal was to "teach the Indians to be systematic" and to accomplish things in a disciplined rather than a "spasmodic" fashion (R. W. Large 1910a:518; see Thompson 1967).

Missionaries concerned themselves with consumption, as well as production and reproduction. One of the most serious threats to corporeal discipline was seen to be the use of alcohol. Among other things, alcoholism was seen to be a basic cause of intermittent work rhythms (R. W. Large 1900; Thompson 1967:76). A temperance society was established, aimed primarily at Indian men (Charles M. Tate 1881). Missionaries thought liquor to be not only a source of moral backsliding, but also a direct cause of infectious disease (G. Darby 1919:53). Dr. Richard W. Large, medical missionary from 1898 to 1911, imposed "public-health" ordinances against alcohol, as well as against behavior such as public spitting, in order to stem tuberculosis and other infectious diseases. He brought home his point in frequent public lectures, with the aid of a chart showing "the effects of alcohol on the body" (Stephenson 1925:201).

Food, as well as alcohol, was contested. Many traditional foods were disfavored by the missionary, to the point where they nearly disappeared from the diet. Culinary ethnocentrism explains part of the missionary resistance to exotic foods, such as oolichan grease, a fermented fish oil. It was really the production of traditional food, however, to which the missionaries objected.

The logic of time discipline was perfectly consistent: rather than to drop everything and go to some outlying camp to collect a seasonally abundant resource, which then might be preserved by smoking, drying, or fermentation, it was preferable to maintain a steady work pattern involving wage labor and the collection of resources closer to home (I. Large 1905:591–92). This was a more temporally and physically disciplined pattern, in which the food one consumed and the work one did remained more uniform over the course of a year. It was also preferable that women especially remain under the watchful eyes of the missionary, his wife, and the community of the faithful. Persons used to living in a temporally lax manner were unfit to receive the benefits of civilization. One early missionary teacher decries the "roving habits" of her charges, who were used to coming and going as they pleased (A. Knight 1885–87:15).

Reform operated on the body of the individual and the "body" of society through the eradication of "backward" forms of social relations and practices (see Foucault 1975:33). Large, writing his annual report in 1904, observed: "We find it difficult to make two distinct reports—one spiritual and the other medical. The work done is medical and missionary, and our ideal should be, we believe, to make a perfect blending of both." Spiritual progress was marked in terms of corporeal states and signs. Thus, Large goes on to give a positive assessment of the year's success by citing the marked "industriousness" of the people in building new houses and facilities (ARMCC 1903–4:51–52).

The problems of health and hygiene, spiritual as well as physical, were seen as being in direct correspondence to the material condition of the village, in particular the houses. Traditional housing was condemned from the first as being unhealthful, cold, damp, and—surprisingly, coming from worldly ascetics—uncomfortable (Charles M. Tate 1929). Large notes the "unsanitary conditions" of "old time Indian houses" in which one found "crowds of men, women and children with their portable property about them" (R. W. Large 1904:131). This contrasts with the ideal house, wherein "everything is scrupulously clean, where there are blinds and curtains on the windows, paper on the walls, oilcloth on the floor, a well-polished stove, and neat furniture in the room" (I. Large 1905:591).

Although the metaphor is one of hygiene, the objective condition of "cleanliness" is in fact order and discipline, in particular under the authority of the missionary-doctor and his wife (Foucault 1980a:175). "Neat furniture" is contrasted with "portable property" placed higgledy-piggledy.[15] The former is doubly a sign of grace; "neatness" and "furniture" are both condensed forms of systematic labor, and thus of bodily discipline. The social unit has also become more orderly and disciplined. The new European-style houses provided a suitably partitioned living space and were generally inhabited by a single nuclear family (R. W. Large 1909:8-10).[16] The organization of the nuclear family, unlike traditional social organization, was transparent to the missionary and thus more susceptible to control. The missionary controlled its very existence and legitimacy. The family itself became the object of medical and moral control, with the focus particularly on the children, who held a privileged position in the estimation of both the doctor and the minister, although for rather different reasons (E. Darby 1922; Foucault 1980a:172; Thompson 1980:412).[17] The house, as the primary extension of symbolic space, became an expression of new principles of spatial and social organization based on the overarching principles of discipline and moral authority. For the Heiltsuks, of course, the equation of house and body meant that the new house symbolized a new concept of the body.

If the house was a space relatively susceptible to the authoritarian discipline of the medical missionary, the hospital was the embodiment of that discipline. The first Bella Bella hospital was completed in 1902, the product of organized, free native labor (ARMCC 1901-2:39-40). The hospital is the privileged space of disease, and thus of medical control (Foucault 1980a: 176). A patient is circumscribed by what Foucault calls a "tertiary spatialization": a controlled space marked off by the gaze of the physician, in which the patient is transformed into a pure object (Foucault 1975:16).

That gaze here resembles the divine gaze of Judgment, insofar as it was an assessment of the moral as well as the physical condition of the patient. Thus, if a patient were found to harbor a residual "heathenism," especially in the form of lingering "superstitions" concerning sickness and healing, he was made to feel "ashamed" (R. W. Large 1903a:229). The time spent in convalescence, although lost to the possibility of physical labor, could be fruitfully employed in the edifying task of religious study. Nurses provided patients with Bibles, discussed religious matters with them, and reported numerous sickbed conversions.

Not surprisingly, the medical authorities had some difficulty attracting native patients to the hospital and keeping them once they were there. Large complained of the "many disadvantages" involved in home treatment, where the patient was outside the immediate authority of the doctor (ARMCC 1903-4). Likewise, patients left the hospital on their own volition for a variety of reasons related to the regimen (R. W. Large 1903a:228; ARMCC 1903–4). Often the patient would then turn to a native healer or attempt to treat himself, with a technique such as emesis or bathing (R. W. Large 1903b:416).

The Heiltsuks subtly rebelled against medical authority, even as their dependence on it became greater. This was manifested in a passive disagreement with certain medical techniques and a preference for traditional methods. One telling example is a Heiltsuk oral tradition stating that a certain wise woman started using oolichan grease to treat influenza, as the postwar epidemic reached its peak. She administered two tablespoons to patients, who then recovered. According to this account, Dr. George Darby, a long-tenured medical missionary to the Heiltsuks, himself then began to administer it and even ordered forty four-gallon cans of it from the Nass River to be sent to Vancouver. In his own reminiscences, Darby recalls using beef tea to similar, if more muted, effect (G. Darby 1959; McKervill 1964:87).

The Heiltsuk account is cast partly in terms of a traditional narrative describing the acquisition and use of supernatural power. Thus, the ritual number four describes the quantity of grease, which is brought in from the outside in containers. This power, once internalized, is projected outward to Vancouver, which stands for white society in general. The narrative also includes new elements. In particular, the method of administering the grease has a quasi-medical quality: it is administered in equal quantities (that is, doses) measured in tablespoons, to everyone who is ill. The parallels with Darby's story are interesting as well; Darby, in the face of an untreatable illness, reverts to the para-scientific level of Anglo-Protestant ethnomethodological "common sense."

The Heiltsuk account represents an attempt to maintain and assert control over the process of bodily reform, as against the increasing hegemony of the white medical-missionary discourse. Like the incidents of opting out of the white medical system by self-treatment, this represents an assertion of some aspect of the Heiltsuk concept of the body. What is more, the narrative asserts that the white medical system in fact borrowed from the Heiltsuks; this claim is echoed by several consultants. These attempts to reassert Heiltsuk categories were noted by white authorities and tolerated to a certain degree. The missionary authority attempted, and probably succeeded, at least in the confines of the village of Bella Bella, to circumscribe them with the overarching monologue of authority.

The model for this circumscribed dialogue is the relationship of parent and child. Images of childishness permeate the missionary discourse. Thus, natives are described in turn as foolish, willful, amusingly sententious, naive, disobedient, slovenly—but ultimately educable. Missionary history depicts a protracted racial childhood, which provided a pseudonatural, bodily based metaphor for the missionaries' project of reform. In this respect the most telling aspect of missionary discourse is the concept of shame. All attempts to seriously assert a dialogic or reciprocal relationship (for example, an attempt to include some Heiltsuk songs in a Christmas program) were dismissed as examples of willful disobedience that inevitably led to shame and reconciliation to the parental-authority figure (R. W. Large 1901).

This focus on shame suggests the primary object of authority to be the body, specifically the guilt-associated areas that constitute the foci of stages of development (Freud 1924:329–47). Thus, the early and continuing concern on the part of the missionaries with sanitation reflects an authoritarian interest in organizing excretion, which was traditionally performed in the open (see Thompson 1980:414). Likewise, the attention to the "discipline" of children, especially girls, had as its sometimes explicit object the prevention of juvenile sexuality. Indian parents, it was thought, could not provide proper discipline for their children, and so the latter should be taken out of the home (E. Darby 1922). How, after all, could "children" discipline children?

For the goal was indeed to impose a parental discipline on the Heiltsuks, which meant primarily a corporeal discipline. I have shown how most aspects of missionary reform had a corporeal component. By the end of the period I am considering, the Methodist conception of the body was in ascendence, although not uncontested. As early as the first decade of the twentieth century, the Heiltsuks were no longer looking upon the missionary hospital as an unalloyed good. Their increasing refusal to provide free labor for hospital construction or maintenance was noted by a nurse stationed there (Bruce 1912). Indeed, open conflicts occasionally arose. One such incident occurred in the 1930s. Dr. Darby brought back from the Rivers Inlet hospital the corpse of a Heiltsuk man and refused to release it to the kin, allowing them only five minutes alone with the body, in order to prevent "heathenish" mortuary rites. The kinsmen acquiesced in the matter and let Darby do as he wished. They then returned to the grave site, retrieved the body, and performed the necessary mourning (Olson 1949, 4:35). This grim tale provides a fitting symbol of Heiltsuk resistance to colonial hegemony.

In the next chapter I address the evangelical concept of the soul; here I would simply point out its relevance to corporeal discipline. According to Foucault, the soul itself is the product of a body over which power has been exercised: it is "born . . . out of methods of punishment, supervision and constraint" (1979:29). The soul inhabits the subjected person as an internalization of the power of authority, as discipline; that is why the Methodist becomes "his own slave driver." Bodily discipline releases this soul and gives it its own being: work will make you free. As Foucault states, "The soul is the prison of the body" (1979:30). The process of bodily reform of the Heiltsuks can be seen in this sense as a construction project, in which structures of power are established and maintained.

Bodily Power, Bodily Resistance

I have argued that the body is a primary field of transformation and contestation in the Heiltsuk experience of colonialism. Older models of cultural and religious change, such as "revitalization" and syncretism, emphasize only the ideological aspects of the two (or more) systems in conflict (Worsley 1968; Wallace 1970). The Heiltsuk case has illustrated the centrality of corporeal practices, beliefs, and ways of being, allied with hegemonic ideologies, in the experience of and response to colonialism.

Corporeal power, therapeutic in its positive form, constituting witchcraft in its malevolent deployment, is a basic fact of social life. The value, status, and survival of individuals and groups depend upon it. Potlatches, for instance, are at one level a contest of such powers.

During the colonial period the Heiltsuks, as individuals and as a group, were placed in a marginal position, becoming open to the operations of a superior power. Heiltsuk society was in a position formally identical to that of the victim of witchcraft. Narratives that explain pandemics as products of witchcraft have metaphorical as well as literal meanings. That is, the specific disease episodes epitomized larger processes of subjugation in which the "body" of society was brought under the control of a total ideology focused on the individual body. The encapsulation of Heiltsuk society within the Canadian state was achieved simultaneously.

Just as the victim of witchcraft is at the mercy not only of his tormentor but of his doctor, the Heiltsuks suffered profoundly from both the sickness and the cure. Pandemic disease and Western theories of the body, including biomedicine, were elements in a hegemonic strategy.

Colonial agents were successful, but their success was never total. Resistance to the disciplinary regimen was always present. Although the concept of resistance has been used loosely by some scholars (e.g., Said 1978), elements of it remain useful. As Kaplan and Kelly argue, resistance is never a simple matter, because the hegemony to which it stands opposed is always partly implicit and even unconscious. A dialogic approach, in which those dominated contribute to the reshaping of public discourse in diverse ways, is preferable (Kaplan and Kelly 1994:127, 128). As we read through Heiltsuk history, we find various "countertexts" that suggest ways in which this dialogic resistance was carried out and are themselves instances of resistance against a hegemonic history. In the present day we see a continuation of attempts, both subtle and overt, to play off dominant ideological structures, to deflect them, to reinterpret them, rarely simply to oppose them.

The body is not the contested field that it once was, but the display of a distinctively Heiltsuk body is an important element in the assertion of collective identity and rights. The Heiltsuks have maintained a distinctive identity, as seen in language and cultural practices. Bodily displays and practices that recapture or reinvent Heiltsuk tradition, such as dances and therapies, are a statement of a distinctively Heiltsuk bodily aesthetic and ethic, standing in contrast to the Eurocanadian view of the body. They emphasize that the Heiltsuk world has not collapsed into the Eurocanadian world around it.

On a more overt political level, the Heiltsuks have taken up land claims and other political-legal defenses of their rights. This is not unconnected with bodily display. In 1986, when Vancouver hosted a World's Fair, a group of young Heiltsuk men paddled a native-built traditional war canoe the 400 miles between Bella Bella and the Expo '86 site. In doing so, they emphasized the aboriginal claim to the territories through which they passed. The image of healthy bodies in native dress, cooperatively working toward a common goal, was central to the semiotics of the event. In contrast to the northward canoe journey that spread smallpox, marking progressive death and suffering, this southward journey represents a state of vitality and power in the larger world.

7

Souls

Ethnohistorians have long been interested in missionization. This is not surprising because in the evangelical dialogue we see the most sustained and intensive exchange of ideas, stories, material goods, practices, technologies, and ways of being. As we find in studies of missionization in Africa (Beidelman 1982; Jean Comaroff and John L. Comaroff 1991), the most quotidian practices—perhaps especially those—of European missionaries had profound and far-reaching effects on the subject peoples. It is the missionaries' unexamined assumptions as much as or more than their specific doctrine that exercise this inordinate influence. Although European traders, government agents, and other secular officials may come and go (among the Heiltsuks, for instance, the Indian agent usually made only annual or semiannual visits), the missionaries stay, often for most of a lifetime.

Their missionaries' language, conversational style, technology, gender relations, and so forth are the lens through which the colonial subjects view whites and, arguably, come to view themselves as well. Thus, the concept of Bella Bella as a self-conscious group arose only after the Methodist mission was established among them. This is not uncommon. Peel (1989) points to the crucial role of Anglican missionaries in Yoruba ethnogenesis, and the Comaroffs show something similar for the Tswanas. Nor is it simply that missionaries and colonial agents construct or advance higher-level units, based on linguistic or geographic affinity, than had existed before. Rather, they, especially the missionaries, are the initiators of a dialogue in which identity arises as cultural practices are reified (Jean Comaroff and John L. Comaroff 1991:18). As missionaries present a "package" of their own culture, in explicit contradistinction to the natives' culture, so the natives begin to think consciously about their own culture and, later, construct a concept of tradition (G. G. Brown 1944). As culture reaches the higher echelons of consciousness, it becomes both a symbol and an arena for meaningful action.

As we saw in the previous chapter, the cultural domination of subject peoples is carried out through the emergence of hegemony, in which a dominant conception of the world becomes subtly imposed through everyday actions. This conception of the world is manifest in all aspects of "individual and collective life" (Gramsci 1971:321). Thus, new ideas about disease etiology diffused to Heiltsuk culture via the missionary. These ideas had little to do with official medical discourse, because they touched on issues such as the arrangement of Heiltsuk houses or their gender roles, but they were very influential. Similarly, missionaries made a connection between the wearing of "appropriate" European clothes and achieving a state of grace; although that was not part of official church dogma, it was an important association nonetheless. These underlying assumptions about what was appropriate and proper, as opposed to "uncouth," "dark," or even "savage," were the true content of the missionary message.

Although it is important to recognize the operation of hegemony, it would be mistaken to see the process of missionization as simply one of the imposition of Eurocanadian conceptions in place of Heiltsuk ones. Rather, the Heiltsuks maintained (and in some ways invented) a strong sense of themselves and their tradition in opposition to definitions imposed by missionaries. Perhaps more important, novel practices were integrated into Heiltsuk culture and given specifically Heiltsuk readings. As Morrison (1990) has demonstrated for the seventeenth-century Montagnais, syncretism provides a symbolic mediation between tradition and change, inside and outside, in a collective attempt to deal with serious stress (Wallace 1956; see Peel 1968).

The dialogue between missionaries and the Heiltsuks opened up to question things that "go without saying" (Bourdieu 1977:167; Jean Comaroff and John L. Comaroff 1991:23–24). Both Heiltsuk and Anglo-Canadian assumptions about the world were relativized in their juxtaposition. Resistance to dominant conceptions cropped up constantly, in the seemingly trivial affairs of everyday life. Small disagreements between missionary and Heiltsuk (as well as between Heiltsuk and Heiltsuk) over dress, gift exchange, and the like, revealed the underlying contestation of meaning that characterizes Heiltsuk postcontact history.

The Methodists

The mission among the Heiltsuks was carried out by the Methodists, who in the 1880s retained the working-class ethos that had characterized their roots in urban English slums of the Industrial Revolution. A particularly vigorous offshoot of Dissent, Methodism preached values of self-reliance and especially self-discipline appropriate to factory work. Indeed, its adherents referred to their entire belief system synecdochically as "the Discipline." Submission to the authority of God was the primary duty of the Methodist. However, submission to the lesser but no less real temporal authorities, especially one's employer, was integral to the practice of Methodism. Methodist clergy stressed the iconicity between the two relationships of subordination (Thompson 1967:399). One of the objects of the Discipline was to create of its adherents the good working men and women (and children) required by new industrial modes of production. Possibilities for material and social advancement in the factory system were extremely limited, no matter how hard one worked. The rewards of Methodism, even more than those of other forms of Protestantism, were deferred until death; only the simple satisfaction of carrying out God's plan provided comfort and motivation in the here and now.

The Methodism of the Manchester slums was transplanted to British Columbia during the colonial period. Men such as Charles M. Tate, who would become the first missionary to the Heiltsuks, emigrated from England to British Columbia in the 1860s and later, to work in mines and on wharves, bringing with them working-class values and ardent faith (Charles M. Tate 1929). Victoria, the only real city in British Columbia at the time, was a natural milieu for storefront chapels and street-corner proselytizing and later provided a staging point for missions to "the wilderness." Among their early converts were Indians of various ethnicities who found themselves in Victoria, pursuing employment and vices available only in cities. With the success of the Discipline among such converts, interest was piqued in establishing missions in the home territories of the Indians, where it was hoped conditions could be created that would allow for the conversion of entire peoples, and where the ill influence of unreformed whites would be relatively absent.

Of course, the Methodists were far from being the first in the field, and they were constrained by the established missions in their choice of sites. In the south and in the interior, Oblates and other Roman Catholic groups were predominant. In many of the larger and more accessible communities on the northern coast, the Anglican church had placed missions. The Canadian Methodists, arriving in British Columbia in response to the 1859 Fraser River gold rush, at first attended to their natural constituency, the miners and other working-class white settlers (Grant 1984:132-33). However, the enthusiasm of the Methodist revival soon spread to native people, who were beginning to suffer seriously from white contact. Disease, alcoholism, economic exploitation, and cultural dislocation all predisposed many native people to accept this latest and most emotionally charged version of Christianity.

Most influential of the Methodists in spreading the Gospel to natives was a lay preacher from Ontario, Thomas Crosby. Like his English counterparts, Crosby was thoroughly a man of the working class and combined a love of discipline in all its forms with a spiritual emotionalism (T. Crosby 1914; Thompson 1968:402). This uniquely Wesleyan combination appealed to native people, and Crosby made the most of its appeal by recruiting not only converts but lay preachers from among coastal tribes (Grant 1984:133). With the help of these native preachers, and often under their direction, revivals or camp meetings were offered in communities up and down the coast. The large-scale gathering of people at these meetings, in this respect similar to a potlatch, conferred status among native people on the evangelical message and its messengers.

The Evangelical Dialogue

By *evangelical dialogue* I mean the dialogic relationship between the Heiltsuks and the Methodist missionaries referring to the notion of the soul. It is important to keep in mind the etymology of the word *evangelical;* its noun form means 'good news' in ecclesiastical Greek and 'payment or sacrifice made upon receiving good news' in classical Greek. Evangelism is above all a type of centered discourse; it involves the broadcasting of good news from a central space. The classical undercurrent of dialogue and sacrifice or payment is particularly appropriate here. The evangelical dialogue involves an exchange of what Foucault calls "bio-power"—control of the productivity and reproductivity of disciplined bodies—for "news" concerning the Christian soul (Foucault 1980a:143; Dreyfus and Rabinow 1983:133-42).

The Christian idea of the soul constituted the primary focus of disciplinary technology. The soul was, to the Methodists, a divine essence. The body was an evanescent and yet dangerous aspect of the person. Methodists believed the body to be a temporary prison of the soul. Bodily discipline was to release this soul and give it its own being.

Foucault argues that the concept of the soul is itself the product of a body over which power has been exercised: it is "born . . . out of methods of punishment, supervision and constraint" (Foucault 1979:29). The soul inhabits the subjected person as an internalization of the power of authority, as discipline.

The missionaries wished to "free" Heiltsuk souls, that is, to impose a Methodist notion of the soul on the Heiltsuks. They placed their efforts within a teleological-developmental temporal framework (cf. Berkhofer 1965:14). In this discourse the Heiltsuks were considered as spiritual children; and for the Methodists, that assumption meant that the Indians were in a state of original sin rather than of innocence. The belief in the evilness of children produced unimaginably harsh treatment of children of the English working class, designed to "break their will" (Thompson 1968:414). Because the Heiltsuks were themselves like children, every effort must be made to destroy their "pride" and make them humbly dependent on the missionaries (see Axtell 1985).

The missionaries spoke of a new "liberty" of the soul as opposed to the "old-time freedom" in which a man was "able to change his wife when he got tired of her" and whose economic life consisted in a free-ranging pursuit of resources rather than in a steady job or "calling" (R. W. Large 1901). Methodism stressed the importance of humility and subjection to authority, to "follow the meek and lowly Jesus" (Charles M. Tate 1883; Thompson 1968:399). This obviously was antithetical to the "proud" demeanor of a chief, or even the relative independence of a commoner.

There are several paradoxes evident in this set of ideas. Although for the Methodists earthly authority was unquestionable and, in Luther's words, "even if those in authority are evil or without faith, nevertheless the authority and its power are good and from God," the authority of the chief was illegitimate precisely because it was not a Christian authority (quoted in Thompson 1968:399). Moreover, there is ambiguity in the missionary ideology with respect to whether the commoner Indian was the subject of a cruel and unreasonable authority or rather the epitome of the natural libertine, in an inversion of the Noble Savage (see, e.g., ARMCC 1880-81; Charles M. Tate 1884a; Cuyler 1885). It is equally ambiguous whether the evangelical reform represented a "liberation" or a "humbling." This is not resolved but is maintained within the paradoxical ideology of the liberation of the soul through bodily discipline. Indeed, the state of the soul becomes inscribed on the body itself; as one early missionary commented: "If a company of Christian Indians and heathen Indians were mixed up I could separate every one—the expression of their faces being my only guide" (Caroline Tate 1881).

The soul's liberation provided the opportunity for a temporal transcendence at death, when it would finally be released from the bonds of the body. Thus, the condition of the soul at death was crucially important (Weber 1976:141). Missionary reporting, especially in the early years, was permeated with accounts of good deaths, such as this maudlin one recounting a young Heiltsuk girl's death in the measles epidemic of 1882 to 1883:

> The most interesting of any was Jane, who died February 12th. She was about thirteen years of age, had attended school very regularly, was foremost in her class in day school, and could read the Bible remarkably well. Early last fall she told her mother that she would not be long here, said she loved Jesus very much, and thought He would soon call her to live with Him. She frequently urged her mother to LEAVE HER OLD WAYS, and to think of "Jesus' way." She often spoke of death, telling her mother not to grieve, but to seek Jesus, then she would meet her in heaven. On one occasion her mother expressed her regret that she was so poorly clad. Never mind, mother, she replied, Jesus will give me a beautiful dress by and by. Early in the winter she suffered from the epidemic that was then sweeping over us; she recovered and was back in her place at school, yet she never fully recovered her strength. In January she accompanied her friends to their hunting grounds. While there, THE "CALL" CAME. They brought her home, and, seeing she was seriously ill, we brought her to the Mission House; tried all within our power to restore her to health. But delirium rapidly set in, and after three nights and days of watching all that was mortal of Jane lay with folded hands in the sitting-room of the house, there to await Christian burial. One of her last conscious acts was to take her Bible from under her pillow, and kissing it lovingly she exclaimed, "Oh how I love Jesus." [Caroline Tate 1883, emphasis in original]

This morbid tale represents a genre of narrative that varies little among many examples. Several diagnostic elements appear, the most significant of which is the fact that the victims are children.[1] There are two aspects to this. First, the child is the utterly dependent being, reflecting the state of humans vis-à-vis God. This childishness is doubly true for the Heiltsuks, who were viewed as childlike by the missionary; the dying child is an exemplar for the Heiltsuks as a whole. Her ability to disdain utterly the concerns of the body and actually to welcome death is a key symbol for the missionary program for the Heiltsuks, the goal of which is to discipline the body until it becomes merely a passive and temporary receptacle for the newly liberated soul.

The second point concerns the nature of death as a temporal transcendence. The Christian evangel of course offers the promise of a temporally infinite life with Christ. In the case of the death of children, that temporal transcendence replaces rather than complements the wholeness and finitude of physical life; one sign of this in the narrative is the use of prophecy on the part of the child to predict her own death. This mastery of the directionality of time is exactly an awareness of the telos of the divine plan for the individual. The ideology of progress, perceived in "The First Schooner" and carried out in the missionary project, may be seen as merely the by-product of the deeper understanding of God's plan.

The fullness and finitude of physical life directed toward the divine telos is expressed for the Protestant in terms of a "calling" (Weber 1976:79–92). Children do not have a calling but can be "called," that is, can die without having undertaken the self-discipline entailed in a calling. For this reason the death is a cause for rejoicing (despite the inherent pathos and bathos); it is, as it were, a spiritual windfall. This is connected with another point: the victims were always from among the worthiest children. Those who "attended school . . . regularly" and "could read the Bible remarkably well" were those who might receive the call.

This view contrasts radically with Heiltsuk concepts of death. The Heiltsuk person may be viewed as a complex compound of elements—body, life force, and persona—which dissolves at death (see Harkin 1990a). The life force survives in a parallel world for a time and then reenters the world of the living via reincarnation. The persona, on the other hand, is a complex aspect of the social person that endures in the perpetuation of the name and, in the case of chiefs, in an ultimate identification with the mythical ancestor.

The Heiltsuks deal with death in metaphysical rather than specific terms. The details of a death, in particular of a person's final suffering, are entirely suppressed, and it would be considered insulting to discuss them during the mourning period. The Methodist obsession with precisely these details would have appeared as utterly alien.

From the Heiltsuk perspective the death of a child is not a "good death," but rather is often the consequence of witchcraft and represents a constricting, rather than a transcendence, of time. One possible attraction of Christianity is that it did in fact provide an explanation of sorts for anomalous deaths that did not involve witchcraft. In the face of widespread death, a new method for coping with its consequences was clearly required.

There is, however, abundant evidence that these issues were vigorously contested. Mortuary practices and eschatological beliefs were among the foremost arenas of conflict between Heiltsuk and Methodist cultures. The example given in chapter 6 of the dying girl attests to this contestation of mortuary practices. More than this, the contestation was over ideas of life, death, and the person. For the Heiltsuk, life ends when a person's animating force, $p\acute{k}^{w}a\acute{\imath}$, leaves the body. The mortuary process is essential for the state of the community and the deceased. It ensures the deceased a reasonably pleasant sojourn in the underworld and possible reincarnation as well. These goals are in stark contrast to the Christian aspiration of living "with Jesus," which requires a "proper Christian burial" in an oblong box in the ground. The struggle over the disposition of the girl's body was a struggle between two cultural systems.

There is one point of contact between these two systems, which in fact constitutes the initial foundation of the dialogue. The Heiltsuks viewed the Christian evangel as a type of supernatural power. At first it was an esoteric form of power, which bore a resemblance to the acquired power that forms the basis of the dances of the Winter Ceremonial. Several of the Heiltsuk dances involved the resurrection from the dead by virtue of a relationship with a distant source of power. The paradoxical claim that the dead are actually alive is characteristic of both Winter Ceremonial and Christian evangel.

The Establishment of the Bella Bella Mission: The Consolidation of the Heiltsuks

One of the first Heiltsuk converts, Bella Bella Jack, baptized Arthur Ebbstone, received the evangel in Victoria in the aftermath of an alcoholic binge. He attended services at a storefront church (actually a rented barroom) established in 1870 by a lay preacher named William McKay (Grant 1984:133). Ebbstone became (in accordance with the genre of conversion narrative) immediately and enthusiastically converted (Charles M. Tate 1916; see Weber 1976:140-41).[2] He then returned to Bella Bella armed with a Bible and preached, basing his discourse (perhaps) on bits of remembered sermons, excoriating people for their "heathenish" way of life. He wore European clothes and erected a flagpole (in contrast to a carved pole) in front of his house, on which a Union Jack was raised on Sundays (Charles M. Tate 1917).

This act in itself represents a new temporal mode, the beginning of "public time"—very important to the Methodist temporal discipline and to the Victorians generally—which would be developed much further by the introduction of clocks and bells, publicly to mark off hours, quarter hours, and minutes (Buckley 1966:5; Thompson 1967:90). Thus began a process that had its logical conclusion in the "micro-penalty" of time deployed in the carceral institutions: the school, especially of the residential and "industrial" varieties, the hospital, the salmon cannery, and the prison itself (Foucault 1979:149–69; see Haig-Brown 1988). The measurement of time, time's alliance with a moral/teleological program, and its deployment within a disciplinary grid introduce an entirely novel mode of power relation, "panoptical" in the sense that all members of the community (which would come to be defined formally as a Christian community) participate in this temporality, both as observers and as observed (Foucault 1979:195–228, 1980b).

Arthur Ebbstone spoke of the power of Jesus, how he could heal the sick: "Jesus never lost a patient." He "took away disease from their bodies" and "sin from their heart" (Charles M. Tate 1917). According to a modern consultant, he urged people to give up alcohol and guns. He found his message at first unpopular among the local chiefs and so went alone up into the hills to pray (T. Crosby 1914:143). He carried a Bible and pondered over it, without the benefit of literacy. He tried to read the words and began to pray for a white missionary to come (Charles M. Tate 1917).

This pattern contains elements both of Heiltsuk acquisition of power and of Methodist evangelism. In structure it parallels the former. Thus the convert or initiate ventures out, obtains a type of power, and then reveals it to the community. Outward signs of the new power are the change in attire and the erection of a pole.[3] In addition, conversion, like initiation, gives one a new name. A name is an identity; to change one's name is to change not only status but social identity. To claim a name, one must have knowledge of and rights to a validating narrative. The validating narrative of the Christian convert is the evangel itself.

A second movement to the outside is required in this case; this was characteristic of shamanic healing powers. Here, the holder of the power retreats to the woods above the village to practice his power. This phase involves an attempt at spatiotemporal expansion: Ebbstone tries to communicate with God (vertically) and with white missionaries (horizontally). Moreover, he predicts the coming of the white missionaries, who do indeed come; thus he achieves a type of temporal extension of the self in the mode of prophecy.

The content of the message is, however, characteristically evangelical. Of course, insofar as the story was reported by missionaries, it is impossible to know how much to rely on the reported details of the message; it is likely that some aspects were made by them more generic. However, much rings true: in particular, the focus on disease and healing. This is characteristic of *revitalization movements,* which are attempts to achieve a more satisfactory relationship between a culture and its changing context (Wallace 1956).

Ebbstone comes down from the mountain in anticipation of the missionaries who do arrive shortly thereafter, in the late spring of 1880 (Charles M. Tate 1917). According to the first missionary, the mission was "enthusiastically received by the people" (Charles M. Tate 1877–83). With the help of Ebbstone and other converts, a church and parsonage were built within a month (Charles M. Tate 1900). This began a period of radical reform of Heiltsuk society, including the banning of the Winter Ceremonial (Canada 1882; Charles M. Tate 1917; see Olson 1955:343).[4] There was also full-scale adoption of European dress (Canada 1882; see G. G. Brown 1944:216). As Tate said, "at the end of four years the blanket and the paint, symbols of the uncivilized life, had disappeared, and many were living in comfortable cottages" (Charles M. Tate 1900:3). One reason given for this sudden abandonment of important Heiltsuk bodily practices was the "terror" in which the Cannibal Dancers were held by the people; one cannibal chief was said to bite too savagely (ARMCC 1880–81; Charles M. Tate 1929; Olson 1955:343).

Certainly, the inability of shamanic healers to treat the various new diseases lessened their authority (Charles M. Tate 1917). It is clear that the state of bodily "dis-ease," in which the body provides a discursive field for the representation of cosmological and sociological disorder, prepared the way for missionary reform (Jean Comaroff 1981:369, 1985:211). That is, things that go wrong with bodies are connected with things going wrong in the larger world. A failure to rectify bodily affliction indicates an ineffectualness on other levels as well.

The limits of shamanistic power were tacitly admitted by shamans themselves. One man, Késina, said to be the most powerful Heiltsuk shaman, was unable to treat his brother's (unspecified) illness. Késina took his brother to a Kwagul shaman for treatment. In addition to being a shaman, Késina was a "Christian Indian" (Curtis 1915:87). This syncretism is striking but not surprising. Shamans were persons who were extremely sensitive to the spirit world and were always desirous of obtaining new forms of power. In the face of their failure to treat the new diseases, it is logical that Christianity would be included among outside powers sought.

In light of the sudden change to a missionary-led ethos, it is clear that the premissionary activities on the part of Ebbstone and others were syncretistic, but they also were along the lines of a successful prophecy. Although initially accommodated as a form of supernatural power, the evangel of Ebbstone appears as a turning point at which the Heiltsuk lifeworld is radically changed and the direction of possible future events is constrained.

Politics of the Bella Bella Mission

Factors other than disease and witchcraft allegations contributed to the adoption of the evangelistic message. The political situation was unstable. At the village of Bella Bella the head chief of the *uyalitx̌ʷ* (in whose territory the village was located), *haémzit* (anglicized as Humchitt), was the most powerful, although Heiltsuks from other tribal groups lived there as well.[5] In particular, a young chief of the *q̓ʷúqʷayaitx̌ʷ*, called by the missionaries "Wockite," "Kokite," or "Krite,"[6] was challenging Humchitt. This rivalry benefited the missionaries because it was transformed into an economic rivalry, with Wockite attempting to establish his position by donating a large sum of money toward the establishment of a mission. Tate used his donation as a means of gaining an even greater contribution from Humchitt. After seeing the head chiefs contribute so much to the building of a church, the people (probably those of the noble class) contributed as well (T. Crosby 1914: 184–85).

The acceptance of the mission was, however, not yet complete. Native lay preacher William H. Pierce arrived in Bella Bella in the spring of 1880,[7] soon after the initial establishment of the mission, and was using the house of one of the chiefs as a church (Tod 1924; Pierce 1933:39–40). The entire summer of that year went by without any large-scale enthusiasm for the mission, which had been set up in an unused Hudson's Bay Company warehouse; most people were at the fish camps (Tod 1924). By fall a meeting of the council of chiefs[8] was called to hear the question of allowing the Christian mission to be established in the village. Pierce relates that a signal was agreed upon to let him know if the decision was positive: two gunshots would be fired by midnight, none if negative. After he waited for hours, two gunshots were indeed heard around midnight. Pierce then preached a sermon to a full house; many prominent persons professed their intention to become Christians (Pierce 1933:41–42).

This event marked a new degree of unification of many of the Heiltsuks in Bella Bella. Modern consultants point to it as the beginning of modern Heiltsuk history. The increasing consolidation that followed is said to have been the direct result of the establishment of the mission. People moved to Bella Bella because of the mission, to be close to this new form of power (including, of course, medical power). Further, the establishment of the mission is said to have allowed for peaceful coexistence of Heiltsuk tribal groups by putting an end to intertribal fighting (see Storie and Gould 1973:193–95). Tribal divisions came increasingly to be officially suppressed by the chiefs in the name of Bella Bella unity and replaced by divisions between converts and nonconverts (ARMCC 1895–96; see Berkhofer 1965:134).

The immediate effect of the establishment of the mission was the baptism of some ten children in late 1880. Also, a sum of $321.50 was raised, mostly among the Heiltsuks, for the construction of a school house. They had already contributed toward the building of a church (Tod 1924). These two facts together indicate a characteristic willingness on the part of British Columbia Indians during this period to allow their children to be brought up as Christians (Rumley 1973:86–87). Indian parents correctly saw the symbolic forms in which the evangel was cast, the written word and mathematics, as important modes of power.[9] The majority of Heiltsuk adults, although they were curious about the evangel, were themselves, especially at first, unwilling to make the commitment required by the missionaries (ARMCC 1882–83). Rather, they viewed it as a new form of power, most appropriately acquired by the young (see Rumley 1973:86–87). Children and youths were of course the age groups that primarily participated in the acquisition of power in the Winter Ceremonial.

The new discipline involved esoteric forms of bodily display. At the beginning of the mission a group of ten young men was recruited to act as ushers and acolytes in the church. This involved not only the performing of minor duties, such as seating people, but also enforcing the code concerning deportment and dress. On the most general level, European clothes were considered appropriate, whereas blankets were not. After "a little drilling" these functionaries learned to distinguish items of clothing that must be removed upon entering church, those that must not be removed, and those, such as women's hats, for which the matter was optional (Charles M. Tate 1888). Even such recondite matters as what to do with a woman wearing a man's hat were addressed (she was finally asked to remove it). Moreover, norms of physical behavior were maintained, such as sitting erect in the pews, not talking, and so forth. Arguably, this specific code of bodily representation was more readily and completely adopted by the Heiltsuks of this period than the religious aspects of Methodist ideology. In fact, it seems to have been the most important criterion used by the missionary himself in evaluating the spiritual state of a person, the soul being a product of submission to a bodily discipline, in this case an arbitrary code of bodily representation.

It was not the case, at least judging by somewhat later missionary correspondence, that this mode of dress was strongly formally tied to the religious ideology, as, for instance, Puritan dress was. Rather, it reflected a slightly modified version of fashionable clothes, as they were worn in Victoria and Toronto, and thus was bound up with the class consciousness of the missionaries. The missionaries were part of a particular subculture of Anglo-Canadian society, the cultural code of which was transmitted as a package, although not unchanged, to the missionized Heiltsuks, both consciously and inadvertently (G. G. Brown 1944:214-15).

The steady increase of children, and some adults, on the church membership rolls continued. In 1881 a "conversion class" was held, in which three people enrolled, including Ebbstone and his wife (Tod 1924). By the summer of that year, some 90 people had enrolled, and 80 children were enrolled in the new missionary school (Caroline Tate 1881). Within four years the Bella Bella church had 112 members, approximately half the village, including those members who were "on trial." The number of adults and even senior individuals enrolling in the church greatly increased by 1882.[10] In addition, the church drew a considerable attendance of the nonconverted (ARMCC 1882-83; Tod 1924).

The religious festivities surrounding Christmas were immediately popular among the entire village. The Christmas Eve caroling by young men was the focus. This aspect of public performance of songs related to forms of power was reminiscent of the Winter Ceremonial, as were other aspects of the Christmas celebration: the time of year it was held, the giving of gifts, the erection of a tree (not unlike the erection of a pole), and the use of "trimmings" of coniferous greenery, which characterized as well the most powerful Winter Ceremonial dances. Even the "magic lantern" show that was traditionally given at the missionary house recalled the display of magical tricks in some of the lower dances (Charles M. Tate 1882a). We see not only a formal continuity with traditional Heiltsuk practices, but also the use of Christian (and more generally European) forms to achieve Heiltsuk goals, in this case political alliance and status.

The success of the mission grew quickly. The missionary was effective in banning from the village remaining "heathen" practices, such as childhood betrothal. New converts came from outside the village. Early in 1881 the head chief of the $\dot{q}^w\acute{u}q^w ayait\check{x}^w$, after talking with the missionary, decided to move to Bella Bella, roughly twelve miles distant. His house and household moved with him, but the majority of the $\dot{q}^w\acute{u}q^w ayait\check{x}^w$ population remained behind. His move led to a heightened degree of friction between himself and his old rival Humchitt, the $uyalit\check{x}^w$ chief (Caroline Tate 1881). This rivalry seems in part to have centered on differing attitudes to the mission. Humchitt, although not a member, supported the mission, as did a majority of the $uyalit\check{x}^w$ people and others living in Bella Bella. Wockite, apart from his initial contribution, did not. Moreover, in his village the Winter Ceremonial and other traditional practices persisted, giving it a dark reputation among the missionaries (and presumably among the converted) (Tod 1924).

Jealousies also existed between Humchitt and another $uyalit\check{x}^w$ chief known as "Chief Charley," although both supported the mission. Humchitt offered a feast of reconciliation on Christmas Day 1882, which united the two factions (Charles M. Tate 1882a).[11] Shortly afterward, another chief and his household joined the village and enrolled in the church. One reason he gave for his decision was the fear of sorcery (ARMCC 1883-84). He stated, according to the missionary, that he wished to be free of Satan and heathenish practices. As Kan (1985) has suggested for the Tlingits, the aristocracy used Christianity to shore up its status, under attack from other historical forces, such as the penetration of the wage economy.

The general ethos of the village increasingly came to be dominated by the discipline of the Methodist mission. In January 1884, not long after Humchitt's reconciliation feast, the first sacrament of holy communion was held in the new church and was given to twenty people. This fact is significant because the criteria for receiving communion were to "have been baptized and . . . living Christian lives." One must always, however, be vigilant against backsliding; the Christmas service of that same year was a near disaster, with outsiders from Bella Coola and elsewhere providing unsuitable, that is, traditional, entertainment and nearly causing the church to burn down (Tod 1924). In one sense this undoubtedly strengthened the position of the missionary even further, by bringing into stark contrast the civilized village as opposed to the heathenish outside.

These tensions were exacerbated when in 1891 the entire village of q̓ʷúqʷayaítx̌ʷ converged on Bella Bella in the aftermath of a fire that utterly destroyed the village.[12] The influx of a large non-Christian population evidently created considerable strain, although the missionary record is very spotty for that period. Bella Bella was by then an entirely missionized village, and the move there of the q̓ʷúqʷayaítx̌ʷ was equated, at least by the missionaries, with mass conversion or intention to convert (Hopkins 1891). This apparently was not the case, however.

It is known from oral tradition that on Christmas 1892 Humchitt's heir, who came to be known as Chief Moody Humchitt, sponsored a second feast of reconciliation. The q̓ʷúqʷayaítx̌ʷ chief used the occasion to announce his intention to convert to Christianity and renounce all "heathenism." This paved the way for the reconciliation of the two tribal groups and the ultimate unification of all the Heiltsuk groups in Bella Bella. During the year following the mass conversion of the q̓ʷúqʷayaítx̌ʷ, people from other villages began to arrive in Bella Bella, seeking religious instruction (Hopkins 1893).

Again we see Heiltsuks using syncretistic practices and beliefs to achieve political goals. Traditional feasts, at which gifts are given, are converted to Christmas feasts with relatively little effort. It would be naive to view this as simply a case of trying to accommodate missionary demands, especially in 1882, when the mission was just beginning and had little coercive power. Rather, Christianity provided a potent and useful symbolic system that could be manipulated to achieve personal and communal ends. Especially in its emphasis on the unity of the community of believers, Methodism provided a vehicle for higher-level political solidarity and ultimately a new, more embracing, ethnic identity. In indigenizing Christianity, Heiltsuk actors, especially aristocrats, succeeded in furthering their own individual and collective goals (see Kan 1985).

Material and Spiritual "Progress"

At about this time work was begun on a new church building. Subscriptions were taken to buy lumber, and labor was provided by the Heiltsuks themselves (Hopkins 1892). The church was completed at just about the time of the 1892 feast of reconciliation. By then the importance of the mission had become even greater. It was at this point a center of Methodist missionary activity for the entire central coast, as well as a magnet to those who were interested in becoming Christians (ARMCC 1891-92; T. Crosby 1914:144). The physical appearance of the mission compound as well as of the village bespoke this new role. There were, in addition to a new church with a bell, a mission house and a school building, all enclosed by a picket fence (T. Crosby 1914:193; Tod 1924). In addition, more and more of the houses in the village were of European design. By this time all but one of the houses, a chief's house, were frame cottages.

The village of Bella Bella became an even more potent source of power with the arrival of the first medical missionary in 1897. Dr. J. A. Jackson resided in Bella Bella except for summers, when he accompanied most of the Bella Bella residents to the Rivers Inlet cannery. The Methodist Church established a hospital there, also in 1897, to treat cannery workers (Goodfellow n.d.). Jackson practiced in Bella Bella and outlying areas for the remainder of the year, although there was no hospital.

Jackson was partly responsible for organizing the move to a new village site, two miles north of the old village (Sutherland 1898b; Stephenson 1925: 199–200). Population pressure became a real problem. As the importance of the mission grew, the single village of Bella Bella became the physical center of the Heiltsuk world, its centripetal force pulling in people from distant places. Space for expansion at the old location was very limited (Sutherland 1898c).

The initial plan for the move probably came from the Heiltsuks themselves, because it was a great inconvenience and expense for the mission, which had only relatively recently completed its mission complex (Sutherland 1898c). In any case, Jackson soon got behind the project in the name of progress and helped to lay out the village. In particular, he was interested in establishing a hospital, for which there was not sufficient space in the old village. Heiltsuk oral tradition maintains, no doubt correctly, that the Heiltsuks themselves were the ones to plan the exact locations of the houses. As in other Heiltsuk villages, the line of houses was symmetrical, with centrality marking status. The church occupied a central position, alongside chiefly houses. In addition, houses were built along a straight line, with no house fronts allowed to jut out, iconic of order within a pervasively hierarchic structure.

However, this common cause of a large, modern, and (at least in layout) relatively disciplined village was opposed by one of the chiefs. Chief Charley, the sometime rival of Humchitt, refused to go along with the plan and went so far as to rip up marker posts at the site (Sutherland 1898a, 1898b). This was attributed by the missionaries to an economic interest he was believed to have had in land at the old site (Sutherland 1898b). It is likely that his motivation was more complex, reflecting a resistance in the face of profound social change and a desire to assert his own power, as against that of Chief Moody Humchitt. In fact, his attempt was futile, as apparently the people of the village were strongly behind the move. The missionaries successfully placated him (Sutherland 1898b; 1898c).

The move was begun in 1898, with the village of Bella Bella in a spatially divided state for a number of years. Public works were carried out using labor organized by the missionary and the council of chiefs. In this way a hospital was built and opened in 1902. Other works included a very large boardwalk running the length of the village, a wharf, and a church building, completed in 1910 (ARMCC 1903-4; Tod 1924). By 1902 most people were in the new village, including those who had moved there from outside, although the church and the school remained at the old site (ARMCC 1901-2).

Although the Heiltsuk tribal groups had consolidated physically in the new village, there remained problems and jealousies among them and their chiefs. This condition is evident in, among other things, a large number of witchcraft accusations. There was also a fundamental disagreement on whether Bella Bella was to be considered an $uyalit\check{x}^w$ or a pan-Heiltsuk village (E. Darby 1922). This question was particularly pertinent to the issue of public works. The council attempted to address these problems, although it was not always successful. It organized labor parties and fined those who refused to participate (ARMCC 1905-6). It even provided cash subsidies for construction materials for public buildings, such as the hospital, from money received from fines (Stephenson 1925:200).

The council regulated behavior, enforcing with stiff fines bans against drinking, gambling, fighting, and "immorality" (R. W. Large 1902). The council was particularly concerned about accusations of witchcraft and dealt with offenders harshly. On one occasion an accused sorcerer was incarcerated and deprived of food. This exercise of power in the interest of social control was not tolerated, however, by the true authorities, the missionary and the Indian agent. The latter had the council members themselves thrown in jail for illegal arrest (R. W. Large 1904). The council was then dissolved for a period of some twenty years.

The village of Bella Bella was a product of the mission, and the mission was its center of authority. However, the tribal chiefs, in particular Chief Moody Humchitt, retained considerable authority. He was able to organize labor projects and acted as the political figurehead and spokesman for the village as a whole. In spite of this, frictions resulting from tribal divisions remained, with the only stable point of reference the mission itself. The missionaries regretted this fact, interpreting it as a sign of spiritual immaturity. In so doing they missed the point; they misunderstood the consequences of the radical restructuring of Heiltsuk society that had occurred within a period of thirty years (R. W. Large 1912).

Christian Education, Children, and the Discipline

For the Heiltsuks, the attraction of education was the opportunity to gain access to the missionary power. Specifically, power *(náwálak^w)* was thought of as contained in something, as having a particular objective form, which form was indistinguishable from the power itself. The objective form of the missionary power, particularly in the case of Protestant missionaries, was the written word. Thus, when Ebbstone returned from Victoria, he brought with him a Bible and attempted to read the words. He knew that he could not, that he must wait for a missionary to come to teach the people how to read them. Nevertheless, the book remained a highly potent form of power, giving him, among other things, the power of prophecy. Stories abound of missionaries or Indian agents who visit a chief in a traditional village and are shown a Bible and a testimonial, not always favorable, written by another white man concerning the character of the holder (Tod 1924). Moreover, it was known that with enough understanding of this form of power one could become transformed into an evangelist, and thus a master of the power of the logos, as had William H. Pierce and other natives.

For the missionary the question of education of Indian children and youths was paramount: "To educate the children is our only outlook for future permanence and success" (ARMCC 1893-94). In a sense the entire missionary program was considered an educational project; the self-evident truth of the evangel meant that its imposition was in fact an "enlightening," to use the common missionary image. It meant providing the opportunity for the ignorant heathen to recognize the inherent superiority of the package of cultural symbols that was offered by the missionary. In order for this package to be transmitted, or more precisely, for an evangelical dialogue to be established, a certain ground of commonality must be secured. The most efficient way to do this was to set up formal schools, which would transmit not only the explicit cultural codes of language, writing, and simple arithmetic—which were the foundation of the dialogue—but also implicit codes, such as bodily representation. Contemporary consultants' memories of the missionary day schools focus more on the latter, such as the bodily discipline involved in sitting appropriately through a class session or learning turn-taking rules for classroom discourse (see Gladstone 1974).

Formal education began almost with the advent of the mission itself. W. H. Pierce, a "lay teacher," conducted classes on religious matters. With the arrival of the first ordained missionary, Charles M. Tate, in 1880, a day school was established, with his wife as teacher. By the following year they were offering a half-day session, and the average attendance was fifty (Charles M. Tate 1881). Already the load was too great for the missionary's wife, and requests were made to the missionary office for a full-time teacher. In addition to this basic instruction, advanced classes of religious instruction were held for ten young men, who it was thought would become native lay teachers themselves (Charles M. Tate 1882b).

The day school flourished under a full-time instructor, G. F. Hopkins, who arrived in 1883 (T. Crosby 1883). It is impossible to determine the exact curriculum being taught, but it is known that English instruction was foremost (ARMCC 1881–82, 1894–95). By 1883 the day school was so well attended that it was necessary to divide the students into four separate classes (ARMCC 1883–84). In succeeding years the day school continued to attract a large number of pupils and was taught by a full-time female missionary instructor.

However, a major problem for the effectiveness of the school was the seasonal migration pattern of the Heiltsuks. Thus, the school would be heavily attended in the winter and hardly at all during the rest of the year. By this time the seasonal cycle had been commercialized and collectivized to a great degree, with the whole population of the village going west to Goose Island in the spring for fur sealing and south to Rivers Inlet in the summer to work for the canneries (ARMCC 1883–84). That migration was a fact that the missionaries railed against for decades: "Parents take so little interest whether their children attend or not, that it was impossible always to have school open" (ARMCC 1890-91:37; see Thompson 1967:84-85). It threatened not only children's education, but also their very souls; this seasonal absence from the village "militate[d] against their religious stability" (ARMCC 1888-89).

There are several facets of the missionary concern. On the one hand, the season's residence in Rivers Inlet was considered bad for morals, in that it involved close contact with white men of bad character and because gambling, drinking, fighting, and prostitution were prevalent (see, e.g., Pierce 1884; R. W. Large 1900; G. Darby 1914). The ease of access to company stores discouraged the prudent and moral habit of saving (Tod 1924). What is more, the seasonal way of life in itself encouraged backsliding because the people were away from the watchful eye of the missionary and back in a free, undisciplined state of nature, in which days were not closely counted and the Sabbath was often not kept (ARMCC 1903-4). This contradicted the important Wesleyan principle of "husbandry of time" (Thompson 1967:87- 88). However, the cannery itself deployed, for the women, a heightened temporal discipline. As was typical on the Northwest Coast, women worked inside on the production lines, and men worked on the skiffs. Canneries were essentially factories that strictly controlled space and time in the interest of maximum productivity. Women, considered by the missionaries to be the more culturally "conservative," were thus subjected more thoroughly to the disciplinary technologies designed to produce docile and thus productive bodies; that training coincided with the missionaries' own efforts to control and reform women's sexuality and productive labor (Foucault 1979:149-69).

Nevertheless, missionaries feared the influence of those Heiltsuks who were not themselves thorough Christians. They were a bad influence on their own children, who could not be expected to become any better than nominal Christians:

> The standard of morality among the people, as a whole, is low and the conditions one meets in first coming among them seem absolutely appalling. You can understand, then, how anxious we are that these little ones should be taken out of their present surroundings and given a good spiritual and industrial training. [I. Large 1905:593]

Interestingly, this sort of statement tends to contradict what is more commonly said about the "standard of morality" of the Heiltsuks, statements that are generally closer to the ground and more specific. This is part of a larger rhetoric concerning the proper methods for disciplining Indian children and thus of placing Indian cultures fully within the teleological scheme of the missionary (see Fisher 1977:139). All aspects of Heiltsuk culture, simply because they had been, as it were, metonymically connected with heathenism, were themselves fertile ground for heathenism (see LaViolette 1973:18-31). At the very least, they stood in the way of the Discipline. Even in England the Methodists had been famous for their enthusiastic uprooting of local pre-industrial traditions, which were thought to impede the achievement of a disciplined and morally upright life, and hence of the divine telos (Thompson 1967:75-80, 1980:449).

The more "modest proposal" to combat this problem was to make attendance at school mandatory, somehow (ARMCC 1905-6). The great problem was that the parents' way of life required them to move seasonally. One possible solution was to create a dormitory in the village for the children, who would then remain behind. Such an institution could serve children in outlying areas as well (who then would scarcely ever see their families) (ARMCC 1892-93). The more radical solution—and the one that was implemented—was to take "the promising ones" out of the homes altogether and ship them off to "industrial schools" in Port Simpson and Chilliwack, and later Alert Bay, hundreds of miles from Bella Bella (G. Darby 1914). These schools were founded by missionaries and were then supported and overseen by the Indian Department, although they maintained their denominational affiliation.

The industrial schools were intended as replacements of, not complements to, a child's home life. They were creating an ideal disciplined Christian environment, in which the child would be entirely enveloped. The regimen was very strict, with one of the prime objects being the erasure of Indian cultural identity. The most basic and encompassing regulation was a complete ban on the use of any Indian language. Even contemporary middle-aged informants stress the psychological trauma involved in being unable to speak one's own language and then, even worse, to return home having mostly forgotten it. The schools were, in Grant's phrase, "agents of alienation" (Grant 1984:178-79, 179, 181; Haig-Brown 1988).

The industrial schools were arranged according to the harshest principles of physical discipline. In addition to the rudimentary education provided, pupils spent half their time performing agricultural labor and other heavy tasks in support of the school (Grant 1984:180). They rose early in the morning, performed tasks before school began at eight, and then spent a long afternoon in continuous labor. Food was meager, and any nonconformity led not only to beatings but also to deprivation of food (Ford 1941:89–91). Mortality rates at many of the industrial schools were, not surprisingly, scandalously high (Grant 1984:180). One telling comment comes from the director of the Crosby Girls' Home in Port Simpson, who worried about the high ratio of young girls to older girls in her incoming class; she feared that the student body might find the work "too heavy for their growing strength, yet there is the weekly routine" (Hudson 1910).

This Dickensian routine was the end rather than the means of the industrial school education. The skills taught were rudimentary, essentially limited to the "three Rs" and some vocational training. The idea was to create persons capable of functioning in subservient but useful economic roles in white-dominated society; that is, to "make" a working class in more, or less, than an ideological sense (Grant 1984:178). This of course fitted precisely with the Methodist notion that it was only through such physical denial and discipline that one could free and develop the soul. That ideology masks the function of the system to impose a regimen of bio-power upon the Indian, both during the term of his or her incarceration and as a laborer and consumer fully within the economic organization of white society.

This exploitation was also performed self-consciously by Methodists upon themselves. The taproot of Methodist ideology is the factory system itself. The Methodist sought to create out of himself, as the highest spiritual good, a human counterpart to the machine (Thompson 1980:397–98). Discipline comes from within, as an adaptation to the exigencies of a production system based on endless repetition of a single task. And yet this discipline always points beyond itself to a permanently deferred reward, which is obtainable only when the body itself ceases to function and is of no more use to the system of production.

Body and Soul

What is extraordinary about the nineteenth-century Methodist theology of discipline is the degree to which it conformed to the disciplines that were being deployed in praxis in various contexts in an industrializing society such as British Columbia. Here I have spoken especially about contexts such as factories and industrial schools, institutions designed to produce docile and thus productive bodies. Arguably, the telos of the Methodist evangel was to infuse every social context with disciplinary technologies, to achieve absolute conformity between the organization of private life, to the degree that such a thing continued to exist, and public forms of collective discipline.

Technologies of discipline—private and self-directed as well as public and other-directed—were dependent upon control of both time and space. Thus, the creation of public time that is marked off, measured, imbued with a moral cathexis, and inscribed upon public surfaces—bodies, houses, pay packets—makes possible the final control of the individual. This deployment of time is of course an aspect of the teleological metatime of salvation, of which individual discipline and progress is a microcosmic instantiation. Ultimately, such distinctions collapse in the identity of the Divine Watcher, who is clearly imminent in the world, to be found there in many guises.

Similarly, the control of space within a disciplinary grid, at once hierarchic and uniform, is central to the Methodist project. The new architecture of evangelism made possible the articulation of public and private spaces as units of observation and control. If entering a traditional house was to be transformed and made subject to a particularistic moral order, the new frame houses offered no such possibility. They were instead placed within a grid of public space and constituted formally identical units within that grid (Foucault 1980b:149).

As the house plans varied little, so too did the occupants, who increasingly approximated working-class nuclear families. Comings and goings among these minimal units were easily observed, as were the activities within, thanks to large and prominent windows designed to let light in where once there had been only darkness. Thus, the extension of reciprocities outside the household was subject to missionary and community control. Feasts and even Christmas parties, although persisting in the new village, were tolerated only up to a point. On Christmas 1900 the choir danced "with painted faces and fantastic costumes," which was not tolerated by the missionary (R. W. Large 1901:54). Potlatches, which continued to operate surreptitiously and on a reduced scale, were simply forbidden. Alliances between groups were especially discouraged. Of course, an important part of the Methodist ideology was to erase particularistic status within the community of believers. More important, perhaps, was the overall deployment of "bio-power," which involved control of populations as well as of individuals (Foucault 1980a: 140–44).

The gendering of missionary control, the particular focus on the woman and the child (especially the female child), can be seen in this light. Thus, the "deployment of sexuality," as opposed to sex or alliance, signifies the control of reproductive as well as productive capacities (Foucault 1980a:106). Women were not only "darker," that is, more savage, but they were also agents for the perpetuation of "darkness" by means of illicit and hence "unhygienic" sexuality, which led to racial degeneration. Serial monogamy—the primary source of women's power within the traditional system—was not hygienic, nor was childhood betrothal. The "salvation" of women was always on shaky ground because they were the prime candidates for "backsliding" when in the relative freedom of the resource camps. Thus, it was women, as workers and worshipers, patients and inmates, housewives and mothers, who must be most closely observed and disciplined within ever more controlled spaces.

The extension of the Methodist hegemony to most of Heiltsuk society, its coming to appear ever more as "common sense" in relation to the industrial capitalism of the outside world, reformed Heiltsuk society radically and irrevocably. By offering little space or time for competing practices and beliefs, Methodism and missionary control achieved relative, but not unchallenged, dominion. The pandemic disease that marked the beginning of the missionary period signified the dislocation of self from society and of society from the larger world. The missionary period is characterized by a reorientation of the subject within a new social and meaningful context: a series of homologous disciplinary structures that exercised control over all aspects of life.

8

Goods

The first documented contact between the Heiltsuks and Europeans occurred in May 1793, when George Vancouver passed through Heiltsuk territories:

> In the evening we passed close to the rock on which the village last mentioned is situated; it appeared to be about half a mile in circuit, and interely [*sic*] occupied by the habitations of the natives. These appeared to be well constructed; the boards forming the sides of the houses were well fitted, and the roofs rose from each side with sufficient inclination to throw off the rain. The gable ends were decorated with curious painting, and near one or two of the most conspicuous mansions were carved figures in large logs of timber, representing a gigantic human form, with strange and uncommonly distorted features. Some of our former visitors again came off, and conducted themselves as before with great civility; but these, as well as those on shore, had great objections to our landing at their village; the latter making signs for us to keep off, and the former giving us to understand, that our company was not desired at their habitations. Their numbers, I should imagine, amounted at least to three hundred. After gratifying our friends with some presents, they returned to their rock, and we continued our route homewards. [Vancouver 1967: 272]

The Heiltsuks displayed a dual attitude with respect to the Europeans. They were interested in obtaining material goods, but they did not want the European ship to land. Whether this unwillingness was due to fear of the Europeans as possible supernatural beings or simply a wariness toward such socially distant strangers is not known. Perhaps the Heiltsuks feared the strangers as potential taboo violators, who would cause fish to disappear at this crucial time of resource gathering. In any case it is very interesting that the Heiltsuks, who, forty years later, would heartily welcome Europeans to set up a trading fort in their territory, made such reluctant partners early on. The material dialogue thus began with the demand to be left alone, a refusal of dialogism itself. Such refusals would be repeated at several junctures in subsequent Heiltsuk history, acting as a counterpoint to the dominant mode of dialogism.

The purpose of Vancouver's journey was primarily scientific, but with an eye toward opening up trade relations with natives. After Vancouver, Europeans were interested primarily in trade. Relations between the Heiltsuks and Europeans came increasingly to focus on the exchange of material goods. However, this relationship was not, from the Heiltsuk perspective, economic in the initial stages. Indeed, material relations within traditional Heiltsuk society, before hegemonic culture change, were not economic, at least not in the sense that assumes maximizing strategies, "rational actors," a "law of supply and demand," and so forth. However, the process of culture change under colonialism and missionization *did* result in a fully commercial economy, in something approaching the neoclassical sense. That transformation is the subject of the current chapter. To burden this analysis with the ready-made explanatory frameworks of neoclassical or Marxist economics is to conflate strategies of ethnographic representation with ethnohistorical processes. We are faced with the very real semantic problem of discussing the coming into existence of capitalism without being able to use the concepts of *capital* or *labor* to do so (Roseberry 1989:162).

Similarly, ethnological concepts drawn from the neoclassical tradition, with its stated and implicit assumptions about human nature and social organization, are of questionable value in discussing the material dialogue of cultures. The model of potlatch as a competitive investment in prestige, held widely in ethnographic literature, is not so much wrong as infelicitous (see Drucker and Heizer 1967). The very terms *prestige* and even *potlatch* are reifications, so that their use constitutes an imposition of Western categories upon native cultures (see Goldman 1975:133).

Conscious of these problems, I will present data on traditional Heiltsuk exchange and production as much in Heiltsuk terms as possible, rejecting social science concepts such as potlatch. Although it may seem that this is merely a rhetorical strategy that unnecessarily distances my analysis from established scholarship, in fact I draw on the insight of previous scholars that the potlatch is historically constituted (Kan 1989). It was Helen Codere who demonstrated that Kwakiutl ceremonial exchange underwent significant transformations in response to colonialism, producing the institution we know as the potlatch (Codere 1950). However careful one is not to reproduce the mental structures of social science, one is nevertheless left with the extremely difficult task of reconstructing an aboriginal past with data drawn from later periods.

The Heiltsuks and the World System

On the macro level, the transformation of the Heiltsuk culture of exchange and production can be seen as a process of articulation with the world system (Rey 1973; Wolf 1982:158–94; Roseberry 1989:145–74; MacDonald 1994). This process has involved the reorganization under capitalism of the relations of production, the alienation of the Heiltsuks from their own resources, the commoditization of production, and the commercialization of exchange. In short, Heiltsuk men and women became laborers under a capitalist system of production and consumers in a commercial commodity market. They were no longer central actors in a circumscribed universe of goods; rather, they were located on the distant periphery of a universal capitalist system.

Although undeniable, the value of this insight is limited. One limitation is the very universalizing quality of the underlying model. To say that the Heiltsuks and the Hawaiians, or the Zulus and the Zunis, have undergone the *same* political-economic transformation is to ignore or misread what is specific about the history of each (Taussig 1987). In assimilating many different forms of material organization to the Procrustean bed of "modes of production," we ignore the fact that material relations are embedded in other social relations (Jean Comaroff 1985:154)

In applying this sort of analysis to the transformation of local societies, we run a serious risk of missing what, to those peoples themselves, may be the driving force behind that transformation.[1] What is more, the world system theorist sides, intellectually if not politically, with the Europeans. For it is always they who act according to the self-evident logic of the system, never the natives. The latter are reduced to mere objects of exploitation, passively waiting to be absorbed into "history," which, like capital, can be produced only in the West or its colonies.

What is of central interest to the ethnohistorian—how cultures do in fact produce history independent of the West; how they resist the political, economic, and cultural hegemony of the world system; how they represent this resistance to themselves and others—is obscured by a focus on the dynamics of the world system. For the Heiltsuks, the economically motivated appearance of the whites was seen as an opportunity for empowerment more than enrichment. When the terms of exchange were altered to the great advantage of the whites, the Heiltsuks resisted these changes by attempting to reassert both balanced reciprocity of material and symbolic values and the overall dialogism of the historical discourse.

Types of Prestation in Aboriginal Culture

Although it is impossible to gain a truly emic perspective on Heiltsuk exchange practices of the precontact period, linguistic and cultural data drawn from later periods allow us to construct a typology of exchange types, or prestations. By *prestation* I mean any marked material giving, which is to say giving that is formally counted and recorded and occurs within a ceremonial context.[2]

The potlatch, even in the colonial period, was not really an institution sui generis. *Potlatch* is a term derived from Chinook jargon, which gained currency during the fur trade period. There exists no word for potlatch in Heiltsuk, and the general term that might be taken as referring to a large ceremonial distribution, *λiála,* means simply 'to invite'. Other relevant terms also refer to actions that take place in a potlatch, not to the event itself. Thus, *yáqʷa* means 'to distribute gifts', whereas the cognate *yáxa* means 'to give away gifts at a potlatch'. Specific kinds of gifts are marked linguistically, such as a gift of containers (e.g., feast dishes), *λúqʷa,* or bridewealth, *ngʷúlém.* In the present-day community, the word *potlatch* is used in English to describe large distributions of goods, and *feast* describes smaller, although sometimes still rather sizable, distributions (Harkin 1985–87).

Marked forms of giving are part of the "grammar" of Heiltsuk culture and are implicated in all forms of symbolic, that is, meaningful and effective, action. I propose an analytic division of historic prestations into four basic forms, reflecting the different functions of prestation in Heiltsuk society; they also coincide with specific types of publicly attested action. Two forms of prestation refer to the hierarchical-segmentary social structure, the conical clan, and its transformations.

The first form corresponds to the formal feasts held at the house of a chief, to which members of his own village were invited. This act constitutes the social unit asymmetrically by incorporation. That is, it defines individuals with respect to the group, embodied in the founding ancestor and his instantiation, the chief. On the personal level, this form of prestation constitutes a positive value transformation of the host, as embodiment of the social group. We could say that the chief gains in prestige, but it would be misleading to think of this as a zero-sum game. That is, prestige in the sense required here could not be viewed as a scarce quality. The act of hosting (or attending) such a feast therefore cannot be understood by an economic logic. Rather, notions of responsibility to one's group and "respect" (in modern Heiltsuk English) for one's position are the motivation for hosting such a feast.

The second form of prestation corresponds to intervillage feasts as well as to any occasion on which two comparable chiefs, or "rivals," face each other, as for instance in the grease feast. This type of prestation constitutes the social group symmetrically in opposition to other social groups. The partner in this agonistic prestation, in which one chief attempts to overcome the other within the incorporative metaphor of bodily transformation, is an allied group on the same relative structural level (see Strathern 1971:130). That is, the dominant social group through its chief temporarily encompasses the other, primarily by giving more material goods.[3] This differs from the first type of prestation in that the host entertains someone with a comparable degree of power, and therefore any incorporation is normally only metaphorical and temporary; the guest leaves the host's house as a member of an independent social unit, defined in opposition to the other.[4] Here an economic logic is not altogether inappropriate, as the gains of one are the other's losses.

The third form of prestation is the exchange of generalized containers for named ones. By generalized container I mean especially animal skins and, at a later period, Hudson's Bay Company blankets (see Goldman 1975). As the embodiment of the principle of incorporation on the most general level, the animal skin constituted in aboriginal society a "generalized medium of social interaction" (V. Turner 1968). An abundance of pelts was the direct correlate of supernatural power (see Boas 1897:349–53). The ability to place a large volume of pelts into circulation relates to other types of circulation between human and nonhuman worlds, the mastery of which is the essential characteristic of supernatural power. Pelts were generalized exactly inasmuch as they were not named. In contrast to containers such as houses or feast dishes, they were the only type of container that was not named, and thus the only possible medium among specified containers and contained beings (i.e., persons or groups).[5]

As unnamed containers, pelts were countable and thus provided a measure, or better, a quantifiable material expression of the value of named containers (including the personal name), themselves unique and incommensurable (Drucker 1936–37). Coppers,[6] canoes, houses, boxes, masks, feast dishes, and crest carvings were all named containers; of these, only coppers could circulate outside the social group, except in marriage. Coppers were thus doubly generalized media. They mediated between named entities, as for instance when a copper was given to another group. They also mediated between named and non-named containers, as when sold for pelts (Drucker 1936–37; see Boas 1897:344–53; Goldman 1975:178). There were instances in which otherwise inalienable property was alienated, but these appear to be related to late-nineteenth-century social displacements. One instance involved the giving away of rights to build a house, but this brought misfortune on the recipients (Olson 1935, 5:21–23). In the case of the other named containers, pelts were used to pay for their construction according to an inherited design (Olson 1935, 5:21). In order to have carved objects made, such as masks and feast dishes, the owner of a named design went to a carver outside his own social group to perform the work (Harkin 1985–87).

The fourth type of prestation I will call *sacrifice*. It involves the distribution or destruction (or both) of material goods, namely coppers and pelts. Sacrifice is the act of "redressing equilibriums that have been upset" (Mauss and Hubert 1964:102). Thus, in the mortuary potlatch the heir broke a copper and distributed the pieces, called "the bones of the deceased" (Drucker 1950:292). Less explicitly, accidents or bad feelings between individuals could be redressed only by prestation, which has this sacrificial function. Similarly, the contradiction involved in liminality, when an initiate is between statuses, was resolved by this type of prestation (see Walens 1981:65). Healing, or "setting right," was achieved through the proper channeling of generalized life force and specific forms of power between realms of being, iconically represented by the transfer of generalized media across sociological boundaries (Mauss and Hubert 1964; Bloch 1982:227). Both this type of prestation and the third type occurred within the context of the potlatch, as it evolved in the middle to late nineteenth century. It is not clear to what degree these modes of exchange may have been intermixed in the precontact period; certainly, a good deal less than in historic or modern periods.

These four categories describe the entire range of marked distribution and exchange of material goods in Heiltsuk culture. Marked circulation was primarily associated with the ceremonial context of the winter village and was subsumed entirely within the ceremonial nexus of exchange. Transfers of material goods taking place outside the ceremonial nexus, and outside the marked sociological space of the winter village, were generally unmarked. This is not to say that such exchange was unimportant, only that it was not registered and remembered within a ceremonial context. Some food exchange, reflecting ecological variation, took place, primarily with the Bella Coolas (McIlwraith 1948, 1:17–40). The one item of luxury exchange was oolichan oil, which was imported from the Nass River, in exchange for herring eggs, a product of the deep water area the Heiltsuks inhabit. Trips were made periodically to the Nass to carry out this trade (Tolmie 1963:275). The gathering and consumption of food from an abundant resource base were unmarked, except when food accompanied prestations; as such, it became a substance contained in named containers.[7] Its function as subsistence was in this case subsumed by the necessary connection between food and power in the cycle of ceremonial exchange.[8]

Currency and Economic Exchange in the Fur Trade Period

Animal skins were a generalized medium approaching the functions of money in monetized economic systems. They constituted a "class of objects possessing generalized exchange value for goods and services" (Nash 1966:26),[9] but they did not therefore constitute a type of money, which would have required a different set of social relations. In what could be termed a *ceremonial-altruistic* system of material relations, based on abundance of resources and the exigencies of supernatural power and chiefly office, the function of a generalized medium was entirely embedded in the ceremonial context. Both reciprocity and redistribution were the prerogative of the chief and high-ranking nobles (see Sahlins 1972:209). Those who held no high office thus by definition did not engage in marked prestation. They contributed to prestations by working for a chief (Drucker 1936–37; see Boas 1925:137).

The movement to an economic system of exchange—by which I mean one in which the cash nexus is fairly generalized and in which maximizing strategies come into play—is then not to be found simply in the appearance of a type of currency, but rather in a fundamental change in society itself, resulting from the introduction of new types of material relations, of production, and of exchange. The famous Hudson's Bay Company blankets constituted a generalized medium of exchange that included relative divisibility and stability of value among its qualities. But the opening up of a monetized sphere of exchange was the result of two factors: the introduction of objects that could possibly circulate in an unrestricted manner—that is, something that could be purchased with Hudson's Bay Company blankets— and, more important, the appearance of a class of persons with whom unrestricted but marked exchange could possibly occur. Thus, in narratives of contact, one outcome of the initial encounter with whites is the obtaining of novel objects that, viewed in retrospect, are trade items. The constitution of the whites as a group over and against the Heiltsuks made possible the opening of new exchange relationships not already embedded in the existing ceremonial system.

The maritime fur trade of the late eighteenth century introduced a type of exchange analogous to the third prestation in my typology. Thus, animal skins were traded for more particular manifestations of power. These items were particularized not in being named, but in being unique, rare, or at least novel. This partly explains the extremely sudden shifts in "fashion" in goods that Northwest Coast Indians were willing to accept in the early days of the maritime fur trade (Wike 1951:37–38). The possession of such particularized items constituted a form of power insofar as it implied a specific relationship with an outside source of power. Thus, in the early maritime fur trade period (before ca. 1800) the greatest demand was for items of adornment and various sorts of "trinkets" that had the dual quality of great variability—in clothing, often in step with Continental fashion of the day—and ease with which they could be displayed on the body (Wike 1951:46–48; see Sahlins 1981:31).

Early trade among the Heiltsuks followed this basic pattern. When the Boston-based schooner *Columbia Rediviva* called in 1789, those aboard found that they were able to obtain a great number of furs for a few iron chisels (Howay 1941:86–87; see Pethick 1976). Vancouver arrived in 1793 to find that Heiltsuk chiefs were willing to part with great stores of furs in return for trinkets and small pieces of iron and copper (Vancouver 1967:273–79). Iron and copper were at first used largely, perhaps primarily, as personal adornment, in particular taking the form of metal "collars" (Howay 1923; Wike 1951:33, 46).[10] Also, elk hides were popular trade items in the early 1790s (Wike 1951:ix). During this period the exchange with white traders was essentially ceremonial, as is evident in the frequency with which names were acquired in this trade. One Heiltsuk chief took the name Boston, presumably from one of the American fur-trading expeditions; American traders were known as "Boston men," a name that was still in use in the 1830s (Tolmie 1963). Perhaps other personal names derived from this early contact as well.[11]

The ceremonial nature of Heiltsuk trade in the late 1700s is seen most clearly in the use of these items of adornment in the *λúeɫáẋa*. Thus, thimbles reportedly received from George Vancouver were sewn into a dancing apron worn in a *λúeɫáẋa* performance observed by Tolmie in 1834. In that performance the master of ceremonies wore a "suit of blue cloths [*sic*], braided with yellow gartering, and with a piece of looking glass frame in each hand" (Tolmie 1963:295). That this trade was ceremonial can also be inferred from the early reluctance of the Heiltsuks to include food as an item for direct exchange, although it was on occasion freely offered as a gift. Vancouver attributed this to a dearth of halibut, for which he was trying to bargain. The Heiltsuks liberally gave the English other food on the same trip (Vancouver 1967: 273–82).

The Heiltsuks' ceremonial exchange is characterized by *schismogenesis,* or positive feedback (Bateson 1972:68–72). That is, the greater the variety of items of personal adornment offered in trade by the Europeans, the greater the demand for new items. Although the material dialogue was given momentum by that pattern of ceremonial exchange, clearly it could not continue. If goods were to define social categories, they could no longer do so as unique signs referring to individual persons and powers, but instead must have been considered as classes of signs referring to classes of persons. Thus, by the nineteenth century, trade items had become important elements in ceremonial distribution, but *as commodities* (Boas 1897). Expensive trade goods such as sewing machines were presented at potlatches in lieu of blankets or furs; they largely replaced blankets as vehicles of material value and markers of social status.

By the early nineteenth century, trade on the entire Northwest Coast had shifted from primarily ceremonial to primarily luxury-oriented exchange, with inroads into the subsistence nexus. Accordingly, items of food such as molasses, pilot biscuits, tea, rice, and alcohol, along with commodities such as firearms and ammunition, tobacco, metal tools, blankets, and bolts of cloth, were major items of exchange (Wike 1951:51). It was not merely the nature of the goods that had changed, but the nature of the uses to which they were put and the implications of those changes for material relations. Although items of personal adornment were prominent in the trade of both periods, in the later period these constituted basic clothing for most people. Indeed, by the 1880s the Heiltsuks wore wool blankets to such a degree that the missionaries considered them to be traditional attire (Charles M. Tate 1888).

Relations between the Heiltsuks and the fur traders obviously had, from the Heiltsuk perspective, changed fundamentally. No longer was the trade between named beings possessing complementary properties—analogous to the relationship between chiefs in a ceremonial context, or between a donor and a receiver of supernatural power—but rather between mutual markets. The initial demand created by the first European goods was augmented by the creation of dependencies. The attitude of the Heiltsuks toward the fur traders shifted accordingly, from the serene goodwill encountered in the early 1790s to an attitude of structural antagonism more appropriate to capitalist relations (Vancouver 1967:279). I do not mean to imply that there were stirrings of class consciousness among the Heiltsuks at this point, but rather that relations with Europeans had reverted to the "default" condition of underlying hostility relieved by intermittent mutually beneficial trade, characteristic of aboriginal intergroup exchange (Lévi-Strauss 1969:67). This antagonism characterized the most notable events to take place in the later maritime and land-based fur trade.

In 1805 the American trading vessel *Atahualpa*[12] was attacked while anchored in Millbanke Sound trading with the Heiltsuks. The ship's captain, Oliver Porter, was killed, as were ten crew members, with nine wounded, out of a total crew of twenty-three (Walbran 1971:153–55). Unlike the superficially similar case of Captain Cook, there is no evidence that would allow us to see the attack as a stage of ceremonial exchange (Sahlins 1981; Obeyesekere 1992). Rather, the white[13] traders came to be viewed as an alien and hostile tribe, part of the Hobbesian world that was beyond the pale of ritual alliances, or that resulted from failed alliances (Lévi-Strauss 1969:67; Sahlins 1972:302–3).

The land-based fur trade continued this relation of uneasy accommodation. According to one Hudson's Bay Company employee at Fort McLoughlin, the relations between the traders and the Heiltsuks were characterized by suspicion: "They are ever ready to believe our inquiries are directed by improper motives. Owing to this they view with much mistrust all questions relative to their numbers" (Ross 1842). As mentioned in chapter 6, another fatal encounter occurred in 1833, very soon after the establishment of Fort

McLoughlin (Wilson 1833; Anderson 1878). The incident centered on the practice of taking hostages, itself indicative of the state of relations between the two groups. The Hudson's Bay Company maintained the practice of taking several hostages whenever one of its men went to an Indian village (Tolmie 1963:293). The custom was extended to the taking of a chiefly hostage in order to produce the return of a runaway servant—a practice not recognized by the Heiltsuks—and led to a significant loss of life (Wilson 1833; Anderson 1878).

The increasing dependency and antagonism of this phase of the material dialogue is seen particularly clearly in the introduction of two types of trade goods: guns and rum. Each created new dependencies that fed back into the trade relationship. The introduction of rum produced, most obviously, physical and psychological dependence on the substance itself. In addition, it came to mark temporary cooperation with the fur traders; thus, in the aftermath of the attack on Fort McLoughlin, peace was restored by the payment and drinking of rum (Wilson 1833:4). The transcultural practice of drinking together as a sign of goodwill became established between the traders and the Indians. The very need to mark periods of goodwill signifies that these were considered a temporary departure from the norm.

The introduction of guns had even more far-reaching effects. Of course, their presence exacerbated the tensions between Indians and whites in incidents such as the attacks on the *Atahualpa* and Fort McLoughlin (both involving guns), as well as making matters worse among Indian groups. The introduction of guns also changed the mode of production of pelts by greatly improving the available technology. The hunting of sea otters and certain other types of fur-bearing game was made much more efficient for the time being. This fact in turn made the traders as well as the Indians economically dependent on the Indians having guns; sea otter pelts were the key to the riches of China for the traders (Wike 1951:3, 93).[14]

This equivalence between the gun and wealth is made explicit in Heiltsuk oral tradition, which maintains that the price of a musket or a rifle was equivalent to the number of pelts that could be stacked up to the height of the gun when it was stood upright (Harkin 1985–87). This image contains an implicit connection not only between the gun and its efficacy (that is, the gun as an instrument of causality from afar, as discussed in chapter 6), but between the gun and the power and status of the owner. The image of pelts or blankets piled up and measured vertically is the archetypal display of wealth in Heiltsuk as well as in Kwagul culture (see Boas 1925:213).

Guns constituted an important element of the internal native economy. Heiltsuks were known to rent muskets to groups who wished to use them for raids against other groups. The Heiltsuks were the first group on the central coast to gain access to large numbers of guns, which added to their wealth and prestige. On one occasion a Kwagul group procured guns, powder, and ammunition from the Heiltsuks at exorbitant terms; one slave was the price for each of the following: a single charge of powder, a single ball, a single charge of priming powder, and a single use of the musket. This event must have occurred at the beginning of the nineteenth century, for by the 1840s the Heiltsuks were no better supplied with guns than were many Kwagul groups (Curtis 1915:114–15, 303).

The gun was not only the main form of capital for the Heiltsuks but constituted a symbolic medium as well. It was widely circulated as a commodity with a definite equivalence in money, as Hudson's Bay Company blankets came to be. It was a commodity in the sense that it circulated freely and was not destined for a particular person (Marx 1967:41). Further, it mediated between traditional Heiltsuk notions of causality and strictly economic material relations (see Wike 1951:69). It was with the appearance of a *second* medium of generalized exchange that the possibility for the fundamental economic relationship between money and commodity could exist. This became true as guns gained wide circulation, by the early 1830s, the result of American traders flooding the market (Hudson's Bay Company 1834). Once this relationship—of money, commodity, and capital—was established, it became possible for other objects to fill these roles (see Marx 1967:146–55).

The appearance of the gun was a watershed event insofar as it constituted a new type of material relationship. The new relationship with the European was conceived initially in terms of Heiltsuk culture itself: the complex relationship of wealth, animal skins, verticality, personal power, and causality. The practical logic of commercial exchange, however, exerted a powerful disruptive force.

The Heiltsuks first perceived the fur-trading Europeans in Heiltsuk terms as akin to supernaturals, who initiated particularized exchange.[15] Later they were seen as something like an alien tribe, who participated in a generalized exchange. Over time the generalized exchange developed its own logic and instrumentalities that in turn fed back into Heiltsuk culture itself. What began as a reproduction of key structures of Heiltsuk culture ended with a radical and decisive transformation of that culture (see Sahlins 1981:33).

Consumption and Production of Commodities

At the beginning of the material dialogue, Europeans perceived the Heiltsuks as producers of commodities. However, the Heiltsuks did not view themselves as such until they became consumers of commodities as well. At that point they were fully drawn into the commercial system and had two essential concerns: (1) the price of their commodity in relation to the price of other commodities and (2) their access to markets.

This is not to say, however, that the individual Heiltsuk producer is to be taken as a utilitarian monad. Rather, commodity production was organized along traditional lines of domestic production, with members of a house working for a chief, under his authority and organization (see Wike 1951:54). Resources belonged to the house itself and were thus exploited by, or with the consent of, the house under the authority of the chief. Moreover, certain types of commodity production were necessarily group efforts that required cooperation. In particular, sea otter hunting required a minimum of four men, with greater efficiency obtaining with larger parties. The same was true of the labor-intensive process of preparing the pelts (Wike 1951:65–68; Fisher 1977:19).

Another process of commodity production with built-in economies of scale was the provision of fuel wood to passing steamships. By the mid-nineteenth century Heiltsuk men were regularly supplying ships with fuel (Hudson's Bay Company 1850–52; Bancroft 1887:189). This was a simple transformation of the cutting of wood for houses, canoes, poles, and so forth, a collective undertaking traditionally directed by the chief. Initially, the mode of production was unchanged, with the key difference being the commoditization of exchange. However, the lucrative trade made it possible for individuals to profit by organizing production along innovative lines.

Another new area of commodity production was the provision of food for the Hudson's Bay Company Fort McLoughlin and passing trading ships. The Heiltsuks provided most of the basic food needs of Fort McLoughlin, such as "deer, halibut, salmon, and wild fowl." The Hudson's Bay Company men also attempted to grow vegetables, which effort met with mixed success (Dunn 1844:263, 265). The fur traders thus depended on the Heiltsuks for basic subsistence (Finlayson 1941; see Fisher 1977:34). The production of food was for the most part a complex collective undertaking, the epitome of the domestic mode of production.[16] For example, collectively managed salmon weirs provided large quantities of the fish, which then had to be dried or roasted and packaged in boxes—a multistage process involving several types of expertise and virtually every member of the social group. Women in particular, but not exclusively, processed and prepared food.

Other types of food production, such as deer or fowl hunting, were not inherently collective operations but were subsumed under the traditional domestic mode of production. Such items were often procured prior to a feast or a potlatch by a chief's *own man* under his orders. That the individual Heiltsuk producer was not an economic free agent at this stage is evident in the structure of the commercial trade relationship itself. The Hudson's Bay Company traders dealt for the most part only with the chief, who acted as a "delegate of a network of producers" (Wike 1951:54). This structural fact was expressed spatially in the layout of the fort itself. There was an outer gate, through which only a few people were admitted at one time, to be allowed into the Indian Hall, where they waited to trade at the Indian store. This area was walled off from the interior square of the fort and sealed with a gate through which only chiefs were allowed to pass. Within this square lay the sanctum sanctorum of the "Governor's house," to which the chiefs were occasionally admitted for "some biscuits and molasses and a little weak spirits" (Dunn 1844:264).[17]

Although commercial trade was for the most part carried out as a relationship between groups rather than individuals—fur traders were themselves representatives of a corporate entity—this does not vitiate the economizing logic of the trade. The coastal Indians were known as shrewd traders, with justification. One particularly effective development was the creation of trade domains around the Hudson's Bay Company forts. The domains were controlled by a local chief or chiefs. The most famous case was on the Skeena River around Fort Simpson, where the local Coast Tsimshians, under a series of chiefs named Legaix, tightly controlled trade and acted as middlemen to the interior Gitksans (Fisher 1977:31–32).[18]

A similar situation developed around Fort McLoughlin, where several local chiefs, especially of the *uyalitx̌ʷ* and *q̓ʷúqʷayaítx̌ʷ* tribal groups, dominated the trade with Fort McLoughlin, at the expense of the Bella Coolas, the Carriers, and other interior groups, from whom came the majority of the furs (Hudson's Bay Company 1834; Anderson 1845). The same few names appear throughout the record as the primary actors in the trade around Fort McLoughlin: *wákas*, Boston, *q̓a'aít, haémzit* (Humchitt), and *waúyala* (Hudson's Bay Company 1834; Tolmie 1963).

Not only did these chiefs act as middlemen, but among themselves they formed a cartel. Thus, on occasion furs were withheld when the price was not considered high enough (Hudson's Bay Company 1834; Tolmie 1963; Fisher 1977:27). They used the presence or the rumor of American or Russian trading vessels to drive fur prices up at the fort. On one occasion the chiefs reported a veritable fleet of trading ships in a nearby cove, which led to an immediate increase in prices at the fort. The presence of the ships was a fact, but the Indians had exaggerated the prices that were being offered (Tolmie 1963:312).

This situation was quite favorable to the Heiltsuks economically. Although the dependency cut both ways, the Heiltsuks had the clear upper hand. The fort was dependent on the Heiltsuks for its very existence, whereas for the Heiltsuks the fort's presence was simply a very efficient means of obtaining external commodities. This asymmetry was unsettling to the Hudson's Bay Company authorities. Gov. George Simpson proposed the termination of northern outposts in favor of a return to maritime trade (Rich 1943: xv). The local factor remarked that the removal would be "a sad blow" to the Heiltsuks (Ross 1843). The abandonment of the fort in the spring of 1843 was "managed very quickly. The greater part of the Indians of Millbank were absent at their fisheries when the event took place" (Ross 1844).

The termination of this favorable trading relationship did not, of course, mean the end of the Heiltsuk involvement in the commodity nexus. However, it did signal their increasing marginalization. For the next quarter century the main contact points with the commodity market were trading vessels, such as the Hudson's Bay Company's SS *Beaver.* Its ship's log for 1850–52 reports the purchase of wood from the Heiltsuks on dozens of occasions, as well as the frequent trading of fur. The Heiltsuks also on occasion supplied provisions of food to passing ships (Hudson's Bay Company 1850–52, 1858). In addition to these opportunities for trade, individuals made the long trip to Victoria and later to Vancouver by canoe, especially in preparation for potlatches, which required the accumulation of blankets or the purchase of a commodity such as rum (see Charles M. Tate 1929).

In 1866 an independent trader opened a small trading post on the site of Fort McLoughlin, thus altering the trade situation significantly (Bissett 1870). The post was taken over four years later as a Hudson's Bay Company outpost of the regional trading post at Bella Coola. The purpose of the company's reappearance was not to trade furs, because the number and quality of furs brought in did not justify a post; the Heiltsuks no longer had control over furs coming from the interior (Bissett 1870). Rather, the company maintained the post to prevent it from being taken over by a competitor. Its profits came entirely from the trade in commodities, including fabric and clothing and a variety of foodstuffs, sold to the Heiltsuks (Hudson's Bay Company 1876–77). Some trading was done with passing ships as well (Bissett 1870).

Capitalism

The most significant aspect of the reestablishment of a local point of access to the commodity markets was the effect it had on Heiltsuk consumption of commodities and the medium of exchange employed. The trade in the early to middle 1870s consisted primarily of foodstuffs, especially potatoes, rice, flour, salt, and molasses, as well as guns and gunpowder, fuel oil, tobacco, and hardware (Hudson's Bay Company 1876–77). But by 1877 the goods listed in bills of lading increase in quantity and diversity. Items such as lanterns, candlesticks, and men's cotton shirts appear (Hudson's Bay Company 1877–82). By early 1880 the quantity of goods had increased tremendously, and novel items such as refined sugar, men's "regatta shirts," suspenders, tweed suits, and bed quilts were being imported in volume. Later that same year there was an explosion in the importation of household items, such as cups and saucers, plates, silverware, glasses, ornamental items, stoves, and lamps; new foodstuffs such as mustard, butter, and corned beef appeared (Hudson's Bay Company 1877–82). In addition, finished building materials, such as siding and shingles, were beginning to appear in the lists, indicating the construction of European-style houses. Not surprisingly, the following year saw the arrival of door and chest locks (Hudson's Bay Company 1877–82). The first missionaries also arrived that year.

A development of equal importance in this period was the penetration of the cash economy. Previously, wool blankets, especially of Hudson's Bay Company manufacture, had functioned as currency, but by the late 1870s blankets had retreated into the ceremonial realm. In 1877, under direction from the Hudson's Bay Company administration in Victoria, the trading post stopped accepting blankets in payment for goods. Previously they had been taken as currency and then "sold" back to Indians in exchange for furs (Charles 1877). This action limited the possible media of payment to cash and furs. Because the latter were available for only part of the year, the possession of cash was essential; it became the only actual form of currency.

The record of donations collected in 1880 for the construction of a church and schoolhouse indicates that the economy of Bella Bella had become based on cash. The donations consisted entirely in cash, and a fairly large amount of it, considering the size and location of the village (Tod 1924). Of course, the missionaries no doubt asked the Heiltsuks for cash, because they associated blankets with "heathenism." The Heiltsuks probably considered cash more appropriate as well. In any case, the fact that more than three hundred dollars was raised among the small group supporting the church at that stage is significant (Tod 1924).

I have argued that the appearance of a new medium of exchange is not itself the primary fact, but that it reflects changes in the material relations of society. The introduction of cash coincided with the appearance of capitalist employment—in the most general sense of work done by an individual for payment, either as a seller of labor or an individual producer—and a much more individualized system of material relations. It is impossible to state exactly when capitalist employment first appeared. Certainly by 1860 a major reason for making the trip to Victoria was to obtain cash. A large party of Heiltsuks appeared there on one occasion in order to sell carved items (*Victoria Colonist,* 28 Feb. 1860, PABC). The Heiltsuks created a small industry making items such as carved boxes and canoes, which were sold to other Indian groups as well as to whites (T. Crosby 1914; Tolmie 1963:308; Holm 1983:68–71). In addition, "tourist" pieces were made for sale in Victoria and to visiting collectors (*Victoria Colonist,* 28 Feb. 1860, PABC; *Vancouver Daily World,* 16 May 1891, PABC).

Direct wage labor was an increasingly important source of cash income. Certain individuals earned wages by performing odd jobs for the local trader. The trader also organized the supply of fuel wood to steamships as a cash-based operation, employing the Indians for wages (taking a considerable profit out for the company, of course) (Hudson's Bay Company 1876-77).

The most important development along these lines was the opening of a fish cannery at Rivers Inlet in 1883, representing an investment of $35,000 in capital, with the capacity to employ 275 women and men (T. Crosby 1883; R. Knight 1978:78). Canneries employed men, primarily Indian and Japanese, to operate two-man oar and sail skiffs; the salmon were caught by gill nets. In the nineteenth century the fishermen were generally hired as direct wage laborers, although later they operated the boats under contract to the cannery (R. Knight 1978:79, 82).[19] Women were employed inside as cutters and packers on the assembly line. In the first year of operation, the Rivers Inlet cannery employed approximately two hundred Indians, a large percentage of whom were Heiltsuks from Bella Bella (T. Crosby 1883). By the early 1890s virtually the entire Heiltsuk population living in the vicinity of Bella Bella spent summers employed in the cannery (Hopkins 1891). By 1909 there were seven canneries operating in the vicinity of Bella Bella, each employing an average of 335 workers (Preston 1909).

This pattern of seasonal employment bore a certain resemblance to the traditional pattern of seasonal resource gathering. The essential type of production, the catching and preserving of salmon, remained the same, but virtually every aspect of the mode of production had changed. People were no longer working in their traditional territories. Nor were they working as part of a corporate group within which the distribution of food was unmarked. Instead, they worked as individuals with at most one other person; in the case of the inside workers, they worked alone as appendages of the machinery. The cannery was above all a factory (R. Knight 1978:87–91).

This development, combined with other opportunities for individual wage labor, in particular, hand logging, created fundamental changes in Heiltsuk culture (Codere 1961; R. Knight 1978:116–23). Individuals worked for themselves and their nuclear families, rather than laboring within a complex collective production process under the direction of a chief. Chiefs maintained some authority, but in a more limited and formalized sphere. The council of chiefs controlled public affairs in the village of Bella Bella, which was increasingly separated from summer activities. This is not to say that previously chiefs had actively dominated others during the summer, which does not seem to have been the case, but rather that the entire domestic system of production was predicated on, and in turn reinforced, the material relations of the corporate group. These relations, by the very nature of the corporate group itself, its organizing principles and phenomenology, were focused on the chief as the personal embodiment of the group. When material relations became divorced from the ideology of the corporate group, the latter became ossified within a formal public code.

The issue of social mobility is interesting from several standpoints. In the most obvious sense, the influx of money in the form of blankets, and later cash, as well as commodities, led to new opportunities for ceremonial display and social advancement (see Codere 1961). This is especially true because of the astronomical mortality rates from smallpox and other diseases that created vacancies in the social structure (see Suttles 1954:45). There is no doubt that a greater flexibility was created. This is seen particularly among the Oowekeenos, who had higher mortality rates than did the Heiltsuks. Olson reports practices such as the "borrowing" of vacant names and finally the creation of a "black market" in names and prerogatives (Olson 1935, 2:91-92; 1966). By the early twentieth century the right to perform the Cannibal Dance had for the first time been passed to women, owing to the lack of men to inherit it (Stevenson n.d.:88).

A similar situation arose among the Heiltsuks, reflected in greater flexibility of succession and inheritance patterns in the late nineteenth and twentieth centuries (Olson 1935, 5:24-29, 91; Drucker 1936-37). In this type of kinship system commoners were lineally related to chiefs, making most persons capable of presenting a good claim to chiefly office within their own house, should the occasion arise.[20] The increasing wealth in the society made more people able to live up to an office thus obtained.

More interesting than the individual jockeying for hereditary offices is the type of social mobility that sociologists term *horizontal,* that is, a movement in social position that does not entail an upward or downward movement within a hierarchical order. The very possibility of such horizontal movement constitutes a radical change in the social structure. By becoming wage earners or independent producers, individuals to a certain degree opted out of the matrix of roles that constituted the traditional social group. This fact is seen most clearly in the creation of new domestic units that came with the building of European-style houses. As mentioned above, in the twenty years following the establishment of the mission in Bella Bella, virtually everyone moved to such houses. The building of a house was one of the most important symbolic acts in Heiltsuk culture. In mythology a house was built as the result of the acquisition of supernatural power and was one of its material forms. This act signified the founding of a lineage, or of society itself. Similarly, when a chief died, his house was burned and rebuilt by his successor.

To build a European-style house was therefore to establish a new social unit, a household, predicated on a radically different set of material relations. When Tolmie took a census of local villages in 1835, he found an average of twenty-five or more residents per house. By the early twentieth century the average number of occupants was four (Tolmie 1963:306). The household was the essential economic unit of production and consumption. Most, if not all, houses were headed by an adult male wage earner (R. W. Large 1907). Women were connected with the more collective aspects of food preservation and preparation—involving pooled labor among related households—which perhaps was one reason for missionaries' complaints that women were too culturally conservative (I. Large 1905).

The introduction of outside money had a multiplier effect within Bella Bella, stimulating a great deal of local commerce. A native-owned trading company took over the post vacated by the Hudson's Bay Company in 1883. By the early twentieth century there were five stores run by individual Heiltsuks, and there was one local loan shark (R. W. Large 1907). A large number of men owned gasoline-powered boats (I. Large 1905). By the turn of the century Bella Bella was, from an economic standpoint, more similar to European settlements in British Columbia than to a traditional native village.

Public Works and the Idea of Material Progress

The radical change in the material life of the Heiltsuks cannot be explained in purely economic terms—that is, in terms of economizing behavior on the part of individuals or small domestic units. Rather, it depended in large part on a notion of material progress and a means of effecting it that was a unique combination of an imported ideology, transmitted mainly by Methodist missionaries, and the bricolage of traditional Heiltsuk social organization.

As we saw in the narrative "The First Schooner," the concept of material progress, an accelerating rate of material change within a linear and teleological conception of time, was the result of a collective relationship with white forms of power. This notion was forwarded by Chief Humchitt in 1881, in an address to Dr. Israel Wood Powell, the superintendent of Indian affairs, who visited Bella Bella in 1881:

> We hope our chief, Dr. Powell, will see that there is a change among the people of Bella Bella. We have given up the potlatch and the dance. We have no more gambling nor whiskey drinking. All our people want to become better and do what's right. . . . As we have given up all our bad practices we want to give up our houses too. This is why we ask for a saw-mill. We would also like the Queen to send us a large flag for our village. [Canada 1882]

Humchitt stresses the ways in which the Heiltsuks have changed, that is, have internalized certain white forms that were part of an ideology centered on the notion of progress. Significantly, he asks for a Union Jack, which for the Heiltsuks symbolized this ideology. Arthur Ebbstone and other early converts, in a simple but essential transformation of the Heiltsuk pole, ran Union Jacks up newly erected flagpoles on Sundays to remember the Sabbath. This is connected with the possibility of obtaining an item of material wealth—a sawmill, which is an excellent item of capital—in the traditional equation between forms of power and wealth. Thus, by accepting the white's religion of Methodism, his most explicit formulation of supernatural and indeed material power, the Heiltsuks expected to benefit collectively from the wealth that obviously accrued from it. That was something that British Columbia Methodists objectively *did* do: they owned sawmills and other means of production.

The acceptance of Methodism itself was predicated on a prior acceptance of the material relations of capitalism. This in part explains why Methodism flourished in British Columbia in the late nineteenth century and not earlier. The generic conversion account, of which the story of Arthur Ebbstone is a prominent example, involves a man wandering around in the city alone, drunk or hungover, broke and looking for food. He has earned some money through employment but has spent it primarily on drink (Charles M. Tate 1916, 1929). That is, he has engaged himself fully in capitalist economic relations and has become cut off from traditional sources of support. This was a common occurrence in fact (see Sewid 1969:65). With their emphasis on sobriety, long days, and hard work, the Methodists preached a reformation of the individual that was at its heart economic.

The Indians' reformation must, however, take collective and public forms. This was particularly the case in a social milieu permeated with "heathenism." Thus, the missionaries in Bella Bella actively supported works of material progress organized by the chiefs. The establishment of the council of chiefs represented in some sense a return to a traditional model of collective enterprise that had been made less relevant by the development of the cash economy. Oral testimony states that it was the missionaries who got the various chiefs to suppress their rivalries in the interest of the common good, establishing at the level of the ethnic group a communality that had characterized the house in the traditional social structure.

The new communitarianism had something of the character of an oligarchic commercial enterprise. Its main functions were (1) to promote and organize labor and capital for large projects and (2) to regulate behavior, in particular that which disrupted material progress by creating disharmony. This is why witchcraft was most harshly prosecuted. Not only was it the product and cause of jealousy, but it also represented a serious deviation from the project of material progress, particularly with respect to ideas of causality. By the mid-1890s the council had "done much toward correcting the social and moral evils among the people" (ARMCC 1895-96). To the Indian agents and administrators, Bella Bella in the mid-1890s was a paragon of material and moral progress (Canada 1895).

The council used the system of compulsory free labor to build major public works. A new church was built in 1892 entirely using this system (T. Crosby 1914:193). The major projects involved in moving the village and building up the new site were all done in the same manner. Capital was raised by the imposition of fines for economic crimes such as drunkenness and gambling and was used, for example, to buy building supplies for a new schoolhouse at the new village site (R. W. Large 1902; see Thompson 1967:90). Other major projects in the new village included a wharf and a large boardwalk. In the case of the boardwalk, lumber was purchased using $250 donated by the Good Hope Cannery at Rivers Inlet (Beavis n.d.). The largest capital project was the construction of a steam-powered sawmill, for which more than three thousand dollars of the council's funds was spent. It was built entirely using free labor (R. W. Large 1909).

The new village of Bella Bella attained a level of prosperity and "progressiveness" unparalleled by other coastal villages, a fact commented upon by Indian agents and others (Canada 1907). A boat-building industry had taken off, supplying gasoline-powered boats to other Indians, and by 1909 most Heiltsuk men owned gas boats (Canada 1905; R. W. Large 1909). These were not immediately useful for commercial fishing because regulations prohibited the use of gas boats for this purpose until 1924, but they provided other economic benefits in logging and subsistence fishing; they were also in some cases luxury items (R. W. Large 1909; Stevenson n.d.:76). A cannery founded across the bay from Bella Bella in 1911 provided further opportunities for economic employment (R. W. Large 1912; G. Darby 1914).

The flow of commodities into the village continued to increase after the turn of the century. The advent of Simpson's and Eaton's mail order catalogs greatly improved the access to new commodities. Women were able to maintain a local version of the latest fashion in clothes. A variety of luxury items such as bicycles (truly a luxury, considering the local geography) and gramophones made their way into the village. The missionary viewed this explosion of consumption with an amused acceptance. Missionaries were by then recruited from the middle classes and so demonstrated considerably more tolerance for the enjoyment of the fruits of one's labor than had the earlier, more Wesleyan, ones. As R. W. Large writes, "Their purchases are not always the wisest and best, but they are gaining experience and they must be industrious to earn the money in order to spend it." In fact, the missionaries encouraged consumption for this very reason. Especially in the matter of attire, suitably fashionable clothes were considered a sign of moral maturity (R. W. Large 1909).

And yet there was a limit to the allowable circulation of commodities. Any Heiltsuk practice that recalled the old relationship between the circulation of commodities and the power or status of the donor was vigorously opposed. The infamous potlatch law of 1884 forbade outright the public distribution of wealth. This law was only intermittently enforced, and never actually in Bella Bella (Cole and Chaikan 1990). However, the keen eye of the missionary detected "disguised" forms of the potlatch in Christmas celebrations and the giving of gifts at dinner parties, even in the giving of larger portions of food to chiefs (R. W. Large 1901). If a name was taken at such an event, so much the worse.

The missionaries were essentially correct in their assessment of the functional equivalence between new and old forms of marked distribution. There was a great need for public confirmation of meaning, particularly with respect to liminal events such as marriage, death, and the taking of a name. Indeed, a name is considered even today to have been lost or forfeited if it is not maintained by making a distribution of goods. The floor plans of the houses built in the new village reflect this necessity. Many houses had a large space like a public hall in which to hold such ceremonies.

The public distribution of goods constituted for both the missionary and the political authorities an illegitimate circulation of commodities and money. The vision of the Indian as a productive cog in the provincial economy was quite powerful for the political authorities: "The importance of the tribes, as large consumers and as laborers is understood" (British Columbia 1875:61). For both the government and the missionary, the detour of capital and commodities into the ceremonial nexus was a subversion of the teleological vision of material progress (LaViolette 1973:80).

It was not only the ceremonial exchange of commodities and money that the missionaries objected to, but any aspect of material life that recalled the traditional material life. When both salmon fishing and fur seal hunting failed disastrously in 1900, the missionary believed it was for the best, that the vicissitudes of this sort of economic production made it undesirable in the long run. The Heiltsuks must learn to "trust in the Lord" rather than in the salmon, which is to say they should trust that the telos of the divine plan would lift them from this dependence (Sutherland 1900; R. W. Large 1900). R. W. Large, writing several years later, stated: "Our aim on this coast should be to get the Indians ready for moving away from the reserves in the future, and mingling more with the whites. Hunting, hand logging and fur-sealing will fail them; their land is useless, so they will be forced to do it." What he had in mind was of course industrial employment, for which the children would require "more thorough . . . training" in the form of industrial schools (ARMCC 1905-6). Their land may have been "useless" for agriculture—a factory-like use of land for the production of food—but certainly the resources themselves dictated no such movement. Rather, it was the dictates of the divine teleology in the guise of material progress that created the (ultimately unsuccessful) attempt to alienate the Heiltsuks from their land.

The Question of Land

The Methodist ideology of progress generally supported the colonial project of territorial expropriation. Their idea of the village of Bella Bella ever becoming a thriving, semi-industrialized town, like white communities in northern British Columbia, was always chimerical. However, the vision they articulated of a transformation of the exploitation of northern resources, from an expanded subsistence mode to a thoroughly capitalized and mechanized mode, was an accurate depiction of reality, increasingly so after the turn of the century. This transformation of the underlying mode of production represented a simultaneous transfer of title and usufruct rights from native communities to white-owned enterprises, which possessed the capital and technology necessary to exploit these resources with the grim efficiency required by an international market (MacDonald 1994:160-61).

Because the issue of aboriginal title had never been seriously addressed in British Columbia, much less settled, the Heiltsuks were caught in a legal limbo in which their traditional rights could be alienated by bureaucratic whim. The report of the Royal Commission on Indian Affairs for the Province of British Columbia (McKenna-McBride Commission) of 1913 is a document rich in irony. The inhabitants of the territory are reduced to arguing for the right to use their own resources, while those in authority are unaware of the basic nature of the new economic order that has penetrated into the northern hinterland. Because it is one of the few documents that preserves native voices of the period, I quote from it at length.

Chief Moody Humchitt addressed the commission as follows:

> I would like to say with respect to the Reserves which were set aside for the Bella Bella Indians some time back, that I was with the surveyors at that time, employed by them, and I understood that these Reserves were set aside for the exclusive use of the Indians. I think we ought to enjoy exclusively the fishing privileges, on these reserves and in the vicinity of these reserves, which we do not enjoy at the present time.
>
> THE CHAIRMAN: Do I understand you to say that as these Reserves were set aside for the Indians, the Indians should have exclusive fishing privileges in all the Inlets on the Sea around here?
>
> A: Yes, everywhere. We are more anxious than ever, at present time to have these things put right. It has been a very poor year with us. The Ocean Falls Company for whom many of us had been handlogging, closed down early, and we have also had a poor run of fish. We feel ourselves getting poorer and poorer all the time. We would like to have everything arranged now. There is a part up around the Island here, known as Karamap, although it is not actually an Indian Reserve it has been used for many years by the Indians for a garden and anything else they like to do there, but it still remains Crown land and it has lately been pre-empted. We would like the exclusive fishing rights in all these Rivers in this vicinity, particularly in two, the Kisameet and Tinkey.
>
> Q: Who interferes with you fishing in these Rivers which are situated on the Reserves?
>
> A: Mr. Draney of the Draney Cannery Company has taken the use of the rivers for a long time.
>
> Q: Did you not give the Cannery Company the right to do so?
>
> A: We tried to stop them but have not been successful. We spoke to a former Indian Agent—Mr. Todd—about it, but nothing was done.
>
> Q: Did not the Indians give the Cannery Company permission to take the fish out of these Rivers?
>
> A: No, we did not.
>
> Q: (TO INTERPRETER): Then how did the Cannery Company get that privilege?
>
> A: They applied to the Marine and Fishery Department. [RCIABC 1913: 57]

Minor bureaucrats were able to do what a royal commission could never undo: award fishing rights that had traditionally been the very basis of Heiltsuk subsistence to a white-owned cannery company. The awarding of fishing licenses and the setting forth of fishing regulations have been a major way of divesting the Heiltsuks of their economic patrimony. As there had never been treaties, nor any affirmation of aboriginal title in most of British Columbia, the Heiltsuks were in a hopeless situation.

There is a basic misunderstanding operating here. Although the Heiltsuks understood the granting of reserves to include both land *(wus)* and maritime resources, the Canadian authorities narrowly interpreted the grant to include only dry land. This reflects differing ideas about territorial resources and their ownership. In English common law (and Western law generally), land may be owned individually, but the sea and coastal waters are indisputably federal possessions (Cassidy and Dale 1988:39). For the Heiltsuks and other native groups, maritime resources, ranging from open sea to bays, inlets, and inter-tidal zones, are the more important resource. Such resources were more definitely owned by groups, traditionally, than was land itself (Cove 1982). They were managed and even, in the case of herring roe, "cultivated" (Charles M. Tate 1884b).

By Canadian legal standards, claims to ownership of waters were prima facie inadmissible, since such waters were owned by the province and the Crown. Rather, temporary usufruct could be granted to individuals and com-mercial enterprises, in the form of permits and licenses. Thus, the really important resource rights were not under the jurisdiction of the Royal Com-mission at all, but rather under the federal and especially provincial fishery ministries. For the Heiltsuks, such licenses were at that time available only through the cannery. The irony of being forced to work for the company that usurped native resource rights was not lost on native leaders, who specifically asked for the right to apply for licenses themselves (RCIABC 1913:59). The inability or unwillingness of Canadian authorities to rectify this situation was an element in the larger white strategy of proletarianizing the Heiltsuks and other Indians.

In one of the strongest statements of Heiltsuk ownership, Bob Anderson, a community spokesman, addressed the commission in forceful, eloquent terms:

> We wish to thank you for your kindness in coming to look into our troubles. There are whitemen coming in here and settling on the

land, and we are not able in the first place to tell whether they are
bona-fide settlers or whether they just squat there to help themselves. We don't visit other places and take up land, and we don't
see why other people should come and take up ours. . . . We have
been patiently waiting for this Commission to come along. We have
heard of it for a long time now, and we have no doubt everything
will be settled for us. . . . We are the natives of this Country and we
want all the land we can get. We feel that we own the whole of this
country, every bit of it, and we ought to have something to say about
it. The Government have not bought any land from us so far as we
know and we are simply lending this land to the Government. We
own it all. We will never change our minds in that respect, and after
we are dead, our children will still hold on to the same ideas. It does
not matter how long the Government take to determine this question,
we will remain the same in our ideas about this matter.

THE CHAIRMAN: This Commission takes it for granted that all this land is
"in the Crown" and we have nothing whatever to do with the question of Indian Title. [RCIABC 1913:60]

The commission, in other words, although undertaken with the intention
of seriously addressing land and other economic issues important to British
Columbia Indians, was constitutionally incapable of addressing the two most
important issues: aboriginal title and fisheries policies. The latter was primarily the jurisdiction of the provincial ministry, over which the commission
had no authority. The former involved a principle so profound that its resolution would have implications for the entire British Empire.[21] As mere representatives of the federal government in Ottawa, the commission was relatively powerless.

The frustration of this situation and the increasing awareness that they
were being used in a process that intended to validate territorial expropriation
as a fait accompli can be seen in the changing attitudes of Heiltsuk leaders.
They were willing to cooperate by stating carefully their view of the situation,
but they had less patience with a quasi-judicial process that failed to address
any of the issues of importance to the Heiltsuks themselves. Their frustration
led to a new strategy: rather than trying to influence events through the
dialogic process of Royal Commission hearings, the Heiltsuk paramount chief
closed off the dialogue completely:

Chief Moody Humchitt was then sworn, and examined by Mr. Young:

Q: You are the Chief of the Bella Bella Indians?

A: Yes.

Q: Also of the Kokyet Indians?

A: Yes.

Q: Now, take this big Reserve, No. 1, where the village is, that is 1625 acres, what use do you make of this Reserve?

A: We use it, but it is not enough.

Q: The village is on this Reserve and all of your houses are here?

A: Yes.

Q: Is there any land on it, fit for gardens or for cultivation of any kind?

A: Yes, there is some on here that is good enough, but not enough.

Q: How much land is there on this Reserve which is good enough for gardens or cultivation in other respects?

A: NO ANSWER

Q: How many acres of gardens on this Reserve have you?

A: NO ANSWER

Q: Show me the village on this plan, Chief: where are the houses?

A: NO ANSWER

THE CHAIRMAN (indicating on plan): That is the old village, is it not?

A: Yes.

Q: And the new village is just down about that point (indicating on plan) is it not?

A: Yes.

MR. YOUNG: The Reserve has timber all over it, has it?

A: Yes.

Q: Is it good timber?

A: NO ANSWER

THE CHIEF DID NOT APPEAR TO HAVE ANY WISH TO ASSIST THE COMMISSION IN IT'S [*sic*] INVESTIGATION, AND WAS IMMEDIATELY ASKED TO STEP DOWN. [RCIABC 1913:31]

Chief Moody Humchitt's unresponsiveness was itself a powerful statement. Although he was willing to express the point that the Heiltsuks required more territory and resources than they currently had, he was unwilling to "assist the commission" in its task of documenting specific resources still held by the Heiltsuks. This line of questioning must have seemed especially impertinent and, given the context of land-grabs, dubiously motivated. Chief Moody Humchitt undoubtedly interpreted it as representing a threat of further expropriation. Rarely in Heiltsuk history do we see such outright resistance to colonial agents.

In the end the Royal Commission had very little impact upon the Heiltsuks. In its final report the commission "awarded" the Heiltsuks approximately 15 acres of land, in addition to the 2,636.5 acres already set aside as reserves (RCIABC 1916:298–300). The final report did not address questions of aboriginal title or fishing rights.

The Use and Abuse of Time

Methodist missionaries acted as advocates for the Heiltsuks in their land claims. Charles M. Tate, founder of the Bella Bella Mission, wrote a sort of amicus brief for the Royal Commission (RCIABC 1913:30). This is characteristic of the actions of the Methodist missionaries in general; they usually toiled with the best of intentions and believed their work to be in the interests of their "charges." These efforts on behalf of the Heiltsuks notwithstanding, the missionaries supported an ideological system that presupposed the disappearance of traditional Heiltsuk lifeways and, with them, the need for extensive collective land holdings. The reason the Heiltsuks were in the position of being dependent upon canneries for employment, no longer economically independent, was in large part because the missionaries preferred cannery and other routine employment over the traditional seasonal pattern of resource gathering.

The fundamental nature of the missionary objection to the seasonal, resource-based mode of production was temporal. Thus, as pointed out above, the missionaries believed that the temporal informality of the resource camps led to a corresponding moral and spiritual laxity. If one does not count days, one does not even know when the Sabbath comes (ARMCC 1903–4; see Hallowell 1955:218–19). Much less is a strict discipline possible in the absence of clocks and public bells (Buckley 1966:2–5; Thompson 1967:90). The preferred type of employment is direct wage labor, ideally in a factory.

The factory setting is the perfect means for temporal discipline, where every moment is counted as a subdivision of the value of the product and all workers are closely watched (in the multiple senses of that word) (Thompson 1967:90). For Marx, as well as the for the Methodist industrialist, the necessity for a total accounting of every possible division of labor time is implicit in the conception of value itself (Marx 1967:35–41; Thompson 1980: 393–96). This minute accounting of time differs fundamentally from the seasonal cycle of the Northwest Coast Indians, where the point of division between summer and winter, secular and sacred seasons, was determined by the dryness of the salmon or, for the Oowekeenos, the approach of the snow down from the mountaintops (Olson 1935, 3:106). Even the most distant remnant of this temporal orientation represented an impossible freedom. The inner life of the Methodist was a moral Panopticon, in which time was divided down to the most infinitesimal instant (see Foucault 1979:195–228). The factory mode of production produced, in Edward P. Thompson's words: "new discipline, new incentives, and a new human nature upon which these incentives could bite effectively" (1967:57). Capitalist time is identical to divine time; both posit an omniscient minder of the clock.

Saint Augustine discussed the paradox of time in terms of its divisibility, down to the smallest temporal constituent of consciousness (Augustine 1961: 253–80; see Ricoeur 1983:22–23). This smallest subdivision is permeated with the omniscient other who created time itself, an internalized, transcendent other. For the Heiltsuks as well as for Augustine, consciousness becomes filled with the demands of this other.

The three ethnohistorical dialogues we have examined merge in the image of the clock. Bodies, souls, and goods are regimented within its demanding temporality. The Heiltsuk submission to the mastery of the clock was the crucial step in acceding to the larger demands of living in a colonial society. Clock time was the building block of a Western historical time, in which the Heiltsuk believed themselves to be tethered to the engine of progress.

Conclusion:

Worlds in Collision

Opposition and Mediation

Two very different themes are emerging to dominate the ethnohistory of North America in the period after the Columbian quincentenary. On the one hand, the theme of genocide, the absolute opposition to and lack of comprehension of the Indian by European invaders, is stressed, especially in works on the Spanish conquest (e.g., Sale 1990). In this version America is a "paradise" to be cruelly conquered, its inhabitants wiped out and rendered powerless. Even the ecosystem is conquered by the European, reformed in his own image (Crosby 1986). Our increasing appreciation of the scope of the mortality that occurred in the wake of contact has lent a poignancy to our understanding of these issues. We can hardly imagine the inhuman scale of the death of perhaps eight million people in fifteen years, as apparently occurred in Hispaniola around the turn of the fifteenth century (Sale 1990: 161). Not just disease, but cruel treatment, wanton murder, and forced starvation contributed to this mortality, lending justification to the use of the word *genocide.*

Another theme, in many ways opposed to the theme of genocide, centers on the concept of a *middle ground* (R. White 1991). The middle ground is a metaphor for mutual reinvention by Indians and Europeans in the process of exchanging goods, genes, and ideas. In the Pays d'en Haut (what is now the American upper Midwest) in the eighteenth century, the French and the

154

English came together with the Algonkians and other Indian groups for trade, alliance, mutual protection, and enrichment. Europeans drew on native technology and knowledge and formed social, sexual, and economic unions with Indian groups. Indians borrowed extensively from European culture to deal with the devastations of epidemic disease and the cultural and spatial dislocations of the postcontact era (Wallace 1970; R. White 1991:1–49).

Middle grounds, for all their multicultural vibrancy, are fleeting things. They represent a stage in the power relations between ethnic groups at which no side can dominate—and so it was in the interest of everyone not only to "get along," but to gain what could be had in the way of material wealth, local knowledge, useful ideas, and technology (this exchange clearly cut both ways: Indians learned to use plows and Europeans learned to use canoes, for example). As the balance of power erodes, exchange gives way to cultural and military domination, defense and resistance, and even genocide. As the League of the Iroquois lost its hold on the Anglo-French rivalry in the Great Lakes region, they became increasingly marginalized and their western cousins were slaughtered and removed, to the point where *Indiana* was devoid of Indians (R. White 1991:515–17). Middle grounds are a moment in the larger, fundamentally asymmetrical relationship between Indian and European—certainly not a useful way of understanding this relationship as a whole.

Hegemony and Resistance

It is clear that both theoretical approaches (or tropes) contain important elements of truth. Mediation is circumscribed, but it is a central process in both European and aboriginal adaptation to new environments. Genocide is a legitimate theme in far too many cases to be ignored or dismissed: in the "Black Legend" of Spanish Conquest, in Jacksonian federal Indian policy, in the California Gold Rush. On the Northwest Coast the combination of catastrophic disease mortality and a callous ethnocentrism on the part of most European colonists may have constituted a form of genocide, although this is a question for ethicists and native peoples themselves to decide. Certainly, *ethno*cide was the intentional policy of governments and churches dealing with Northwest Coast Indians until very recently.

The ethnohistorical truth does not, I think, lie somewhere in the middle, in some interpretive Middle Ground, but rather eludes capture altogether by such totalizing metaphors. As Obeyesekere (1992) has recently argued, individual motivations and voices must be taken into account, in addition to cultural and historical structures, when we consider the nexus of ethnohistorical events. This multiplicity of voices, always culturally, socially, and historically situated, that is to say this state of *heteroglossia,* undermines the structuring of history by both scholars and actors. The writing of history is always an act of rhetoric, an imposition of tropes upon "the data," which goes beyond an "interpretation" of "the facts" and is deeply embedded in social praxis (H. White 1973; de Certeau 1988:29–30). The present study is no exception. I have used a metaphor of communication, dialogue, to address the historical processes of contact, trade, colonialism, and missionization. Obviously, this bears a certain affinity to Richard White's mediation model of ethnohistory, with its emphasis on cultural exchange. The acknowledgment of dialogue does not, however, presuppose an interpretation of the process as more or less benign. Conversations may be hostile as well as amicable, Machiavellian as well as forthright. The things gained in this trade may be, at best, of dubious value.

All scholars of culture, even (especially) those who claim otherwise, have some idea of what is at the heart of things, what is "really real." Such a foundationalism provides a needed philosophical anchor and is better revealed than masked (cf. Geertz 1973:3–32). In the present work it should be clear that it is not only communication, but discursive and coercive modes of power that drive my analysis of Heiltsuk ethnohistory, especially in the missionary period. Like Richard White, I am interested in intercultural communication, but I see in it a fundamentally negative process of the suffusion of techniques of power throughout the Heiltsuk lifeworld. Under the guise of humanitarianism, the bonds of discipline were imposed and strengthened.

In small matters and large, the thrust of European actions during the missionary period was to impose hegemonic conceptions of the person and the body in relation to society and the cosmos. It is difficult to view this project as anything but successful. Heiltsuk society became encapsulated within multiple disciplinary structures. And yet, we have seen how that hegemony was contested, especially with respect to the body. We have also seen how the Heiltsuks adapted and used European and Methodist concepts and practices for their own ends. Especially, we see that the fragmented world of the Heiltsuks after contact was fertile ground for new ideas that promised to help them make sense of and improve their lives.

The coming of the missionary and other agents of "civilization" was neither unforeseen nor unwelcome. It was for many a possible resolution to the lethal and chaotic state of affairs in which the Heiltsuks found themselves during the colonial period. At first, evangelical and other hegemonic discourse was apprehended as a type of supernatural power, akin to the powers of shamans and the Winter Ceremonial. Later, as the cultural specificity of these discourses became apparent, their elements were adopted, adapted, or resisted in accordance with the needs and pragmatic interests of the Heiltsuk actors. Thus, biomedicine, in addition to providing effective therapy for European diseases, constituted an ideology of the body that was useful to Heiltsuk chiefs. Its monologic qualities suppressed competing sources of power employing witchcraft and shamanism, which were still seen as an active threat into the 1940s.

Similarly, Christianity as an ideology of universal solidarity allowed local chiefs to extend their influence by constituting the social group at a higher structural level than had previously existed. This new social unit was the vehicle through which the Heiltsuks were absorbed into colonial society. Access to the cash economy, medical services, and education was dependent upon the existence of a Christian and "civilized" town. The achievement of this project of self-civilization conferred upon the Heiltsuks a new status and an ability to present themselves more effectively on the new stage of colonial and provincial society. They gained limited autonomy within the encapsulating institutions (see Kan 1985). Each of these institutions required, however, a new person, one based on concepts such as individual (rather than collective) responsibility, contractual obligation, and submission to the law (Mauss 1985). The Methodist doctrine of discipline was an especially effective means of achieving this transformation.

Heteroglossia, inherent in all dialogic discourse, is especially evident here. A diversity of discourses was present at all times. Important counterdiscourses arose even in the face of an imposed hegemony. It was through these counterdiscourses that the Heiltsuks and other missionized groups constructed an identity distinct from that allowed by the dominant groups. These counterdiscourses in turn fed back into hegemonic discourse.

This is very much tied to the historical consciousness of the group, which is to say its sense of identity temporalized. For the Methodists, as for virtually all missionaries everywhere, events and actions are viewed in the context of a teleological history. Such histories are profoundly imperialistic, imposing their meanings on the smaller histories of subject peoples (cf. Martin 1992). And yet these more modest histories persist, adapting even to the telos of divine ordination. If "progress" and "discipline" were the key elements of that telos, these elements could be adopted and reinterpreted without surrendering the collective identity and destiny of the Heiltsuk people. As in Northwest Coast myth and ritual practice, powers brought in from the outside may have surprising and threatening qualities but may nonetheless ultimately be possessed, controlled, and displayed. Missionaries and other colonial agents eventually accepted the Heiltsuk reinterpretation of colonial ideologies, as long as certain minimal standards of adherence to the Protestant, capitalist ethos were met.

The idea, then, of the Heiltsuks as a "progressive" people, which is central to their identity, may ironically be seen as part of the contestation of European cultural domination. This has always been the syncretist's dream: to adapt the best, most effective concepts and techniques of each world in the creation of something new that transcends both. However, the nineteenth-century Heiltsuks seem unique in their ability to perceive what is at the heart of European power: the linked ideas of progress and discipline. The Heiltsuks, by harnessing this power themselves, and for their own ends, could perhaps escape the fate then promised to other Indian groups: cultural and even physical extinction.

The key remaining question is, of course, whether their progressivism is entirely a false consciousness and the Heiltsuks have been betrayed by their own history, or whether they have strategically made the best of a difficult situation. Ultimately these are questions for the Heiltsuks themselves to answer.

Notes

Chapter 1

1. I use the term *Cannibal Dance* despite Hilton and Rath's objections (1982) to the translation. Partly this is conventional. Moreover, it seems that, whatever the legitimate linguistic objections to such a gloss, there can be no doubt that the theme of anthropophagy was richly represented in the *hámáċa* performance.

2. In addition to the specific documented instances of diffusion, evidence for a Heiltsuk invention of the Winter Ceremonial is speculative but intriguing. Only in the Heiltsuk case do we find a strong and clear example of a dialectical opposition between two dance series, in which the forces of chaos are subdued and appropriated by forces of structure.

3. Basic clan affiliation was apparently matrilineal. The major exception was adoption. In the case of such adoption, the adoptee retained ties with the natal (by most accounts maternal) clan (Olson 1935, 5:38).

4. The word *gáláẋa* means 'first down' (i.e., from heaven) and contrasts with *λúeḷáẋa,* meaning 'second down'. Thus, the position of chief is quite explicitly tied to the Winter Ceremonial.

5. Olson (1954:242–49) gives an apparently complete list of dances for the Oowekeenos. His list is of considerable interest but cannot be assumed to be identical to that of the Heiltsuks. Indeed, it seems to be a general principle of dance forms on the Northwest Coast that they differ significantly among groups. Nevertheless, Olson's list is worth mentioning.

159

For the *čaíqa,* beginning with the highest, he lists Cannibal Dance, Fool Dance, Grizzly Bear Dance, Skull Dance, and Ghost Dance as the most important. Lesser dances include the Ak!la'k!em 'taken into the woods', Sleep Dance, Salmon Dance, Bird Dance, Hai'liktsakstah (judging by the name, a healing dance), Thieving Dance, and Rat Dance. For the *λúeḷáx̌a,* beginning with the highest, he lists War Dance, Healing Dance (Hai'likila), Land Otter Dance, Urinating Dance, Eagle Dance, Raven Dance, Humanoid Monster Dance (Pu'kus, called Man of the Woods [*pk̓ʷs*] Dance by the Heiltsuks), Sea Monster (K!u'magwa) Dance, Monster-Who-Swallows-Canoes Dance, Blackfish Dance, Whale Dance, and Echo Dance. Minor *λúeḷáx̌a* dances included Beaver Dance, Kitxanis and Xwa'niah (Tsimshian dances), Weather-Spirit Dance, U'makamL Dance, Brant Dance, and Crow Dance. The Heiltsuks had many of these dances and probably had a full complement of dances similar to this.

6. The phrase *possession drama* is carefully chosen. Although Bourguignon classifies the Kwagul Winter Ceremonial as a "possession trance" (1976: 44), it is debatable whether a state of trance is present or whether some lesser form of ecstatic experience is involved, as would be suggested by the common English gloss that the Cannibal Dancer is "excited" by the Cannibal Spirit. A related issue is the high degree of dramatic staging and artifice involved in the Winter Ceremonial. I retain the word *possession,* with the recognition that it means something different here than in, say, Haitian *voudoun.* In doing so I am responding to the ideology of the *čaíqa* itself, which is conceived as an imitation of shamanistic trance states.

7. Here, the ranked order of the dances is especially uncertain; the order of the War Dance and *mítla* are reversed by Kolstee (1988:93). This is perhaps explained by the fact that his main consultant was of Oowekeeno origin.

8. These two dances—the *λúgwela* and the *hailíkila*—are the two highest-ranking ones in the *λúeḷáx̌a* series, although I am not sure which should be ranked first. Drucker ranks the former first, and Kolstee, who worked with an Oowekeeno consultant in the 1970s, ranks the latter first (Drucker 1940:210; Kolstee 1988:93).

9. This figure is given as the second-ranking dance in Drucker's Oowe-keeno list but is omitted as a dance from the Bella Bella list.

10. The Cannibal Dancer is also called *tanis,* which refers to his state of possession.

11. Clearly, a great deal of theatrical staging was used to create the terrifying effects of the *ċaíqa* dances. Whether the Cannibal actually engaged in necrophagy has been much disputed. What seems clear is that people believed that he did. In precontact times slaves were perhaps killed during the Cannibal Dance (Curtis 1915:221-22). The evidence for actual arm biting seems incontrovertible (T. Crosby 1914:191).

12. These birds include the *hoxhoq,* which Boas (1897:395) describes for the Kwaguls as a close associate of *báxʷbakʷáláḣusiwa,* and the *qulus,* a type of eagle (Curtis 1915:157). I was not able to obtain a complete list of these, however, from contemporary Heiltsuk consultants (Olson 1954: 245; Harkin 1985-87).

13. The Northwest Coast Ghost Dance bears no resemblance to the famous religious movement of the same name of the Plains and Great Basin.

14. This word is probably semantically related to the notion of illness. Clearly, that would be in keeping with the character of the *ċaíqa* as dealing with dangerous elemental forces.

15. If my analysis of the name of this dance is correct, it seems likely that the dance had something to do with the supernatural power of paralysis. Paralytics were both feared and revered as possessors of considerable *náwálakʷ,* as even contemporary consultants have attested (Harkin 1985-87). In particular, paralytics were associated with destructive power and war. A Tlingit war helmet thus depicts a paralytic (Boas 1955:184).

16. The *maqaẍsúklaxi* dance is perhaps related to the Oowekeeno k!ya'Lkya-Lamas 'sleep causing', ranked seventh in the series, as reported by Olson. It is possible that these were distinct, because there appear to have been several similar performances, judging by the presence of masks with closing eyes in museum collections (Black 1988:149).

17. This artifact is held by the University of British Columbia Museum of Anthropology, accession number A7877.

18. The root meaning 'black' is also contained in the word for the sacred winter season.

19. For a full account of traditional Heiltsuk mortuary practices, see Harkin (1990a). Although the past tense is used throughout, many of the beliefs and some of the practices described are still maintained in some form. For instance, property is still burned, and the mortuary potlatch still follows roughly the form described.

20. Taboos were stronger and in force longer for widows than for widowers. I speak of widows in the following passage because my data is gender

specific. There is a sense in Heiltsuk culture, as elsewhere, that women bear the brunt of pollution associated with death (Harkin 1990a).

21. *híkelá* is etymologically related to *hailíkila* and can refer similarly to shamanistic healing and the taming of the *hámáċa* (Boas 1923:247). Clearly, there is an equivalence among possession, death pollution, and menstrual pollution (see Douglas 1966:94–113).

22. Ten months was the culturally recognized length of human gestation; the mortuary potlatch thus represented a social "rebirth" both for the widow and for the heir, as well as a more complete transportation of the deceased into the underworld.

Chapter 2

1. Since this writing, a New Democratic Party (social democratic) government led by former Vancouver mayor Mike Harcourt has taken power in British Columbia. An agreement reached in 1993 with the Clayoquot First Nation over resource management defused one of the most controversial land-use cases in Canada. Nevertheless, the issue of aboriginal title remains under the purview of the provincial courts; no real progress has been made on this front.

2. Thus, elders frequently cite ways in which the traditional forms are not completely adhered to, as, for instance, in the omnibus character of modern potlatches, or the status of individuals participating in feasts and potlatches.

Chapter 3

1. This situation may not pertain to the postmodern epoch, in which change occurs too rapidly to be assimilated and representational practices borrow haphazardly from the styles of different historical periods. The "metanarratives" of the past are replaced by radically superficial "hypertexts."

2. In practice, the relationship between being and its negation, which is essentially temporal, is viewed as primarily a spatial and functional relationship.

3. *Episodic* here refers to the Aristotelian notion of plot with "neither probability nor necessity in the sequence of its episodes" (Aristotle 1920: 45).

4. It should be clear that my sense of the term *symbolic* is modeled on language, which has pragmatic as well as syntactic and semantic dimensions. I do not think this general philosophy of history is correctly termed *idealistic,* although I have been accused of this (Krech 1991).

Chapter 4

1. This narrative was told to me in English by Heiltsuk elder Gordon Reid, Sr., in 1985 and 1986. I am grateful to Dell Hymes, who helped me organize this narrative into verse lines and gave good advice on several points of interpretation.
2. The speaker indicates himself.
3. *q̓élc'* or Old Town, three miles south of the present village of Bella Bella, was the location of the Hudson's Bay Company Fort McLoughlin, which operated from 1833 to 1839. Later it was the site of a Methodist mission.
4. By the early twentieth century a large boat-building industry had arisen in Bella Bella, providing rowboats, sailboats, and gas boats to other native villages (Canada 1907:218).
5. This agrees with Goldman's view (1975:113; cf. Kobrinsky 1979:164) that the *hámáċa* is an agent of entropy. Like the syntagmatic series of hunting, in which species difference is temporarily effaced through consumption of one by the other, the *hámáċa* "consumes" the social order. However, it is important to recognize that any movement toward entropy—that is, lack of differentiation—is also a movement back in the direction of potentiality, from the point of view of a cosmology of progressive differentiation. Thus the *hámáċa* recaptures the potentiality of precultural days. This is why the acquisition of *náwálak^w* is associated with the founding of a new social order. Eliade makes a similar point with respect to the notion of eternal return (1954:88).
6. The two episodes correspond in a specific sense to two thematic types of Heiltsuk narrative, one involving encounter with a supernatural being, the other with the display of names and privileges (compare Boas 1932:155 with Olson 1955:330–33).

Chapter 5

1. Feasts and potlatches were held during the secular (*bák^wenx̌*) season in
    the case of death or perhaps other unforeseeable events, such as acci-
    dents. These were of course held in the village, in "structured" space.
2. Spatially, villages were two-dimensional, with houses ranged along a
    beach. The central space was the most valued and was the place where
    the greatest house was located. If there was a separate dance house (or
    later, community hall), it occupied this central space.
3. A common theme in Heiltsuk mythology is that of the (potential) chief
    who goes out from a starving village to encounter a supernatural crea-
    ture. The creature gives him the power that enables him to obtain a
    wealth of food with which to feed his people (Boas 1916:886–88).
4. Of course, the incidence of raiding was greatly increased by the intro-
    duction of firearms, alcohol, and other banes by the Europeans.
5. In one case the Fort Rupert Kwaguls obtained the rights to the Cannibal
    Dance in the 1840s after killing some Heiltsuk chiefs (Curtis 1915:220–
    21; Boas 1966:258, 402).
6. Of course, the economic practice of the Heiltsuks and other coastal
    groups required a much larger territory than that required for agriculture
    or husbandry, and certainly more than the territory actually resided in,
    which was used as the basis for the drawing up of reserve boundaries.

Chapter 6

1. The concept of hegemony is borrowed from the work of Antonio
    Gramsci (1971). An ideology imposed by an elite is hegemonic if it ac-
    quires the appearance of common sense.
2. Recent scholarly debate has centered on the question of precontact
    aboriginal population levels and subsequent mortality rates. Although
    disagreeing on methodology, most scholars agree that both population
    levels and mortality rates were considerably higher than previously
    thought (see Dobyns 1966, 1983, 1989; Thornton and Marsh-Thornton
    1981).
3. The mortality rate could have been worse than even these figures
    indicate. Tolmie records only the population of three tribal groups; the
    isdaítx^w moved from their inland home to join the people living around

Bella Bella after smallpox decimated their population (Olson 1935, 5:52). An 1889 census places the population at 188, but this figure may be vitiated by a failure to count those away at resource camps and those who were not baptized (Canada 1889). These early government census figures fluctuate somewhat; however, this could perhaps be the true picture, in which case mortality would be nearly 85 percent.

4. The narrator refers to land officially designated as Bella Bella Indian Reserve number 8.

5. Colonists, as opposed to the older fur trade interests, had little use for Indians and less for their cultures. Although the Hudson's Bay Company depended upon relatively healthy and intact groups to produce and consume commodities, the colonists, who gained political ascendancy at midcentury, were interested in natives, if at all, only as a humbled and docile proletariat (*Colonist,* 26 Oct. 1860). Missionaries were often viewed suspiciously, but their programs were supported by the more "progressive" colonists as the best means to achieve the progressives' goals. The colonial position is expressed most fervently and most relentlessly by the bizarrely misnamed Amor de Cosmos, whose Victoria newspaper, the *Colonist,* explicitly equated pandemic disease with colonial interests (*Colonist,* 6 Sept. 1861).

6. I follow Allen Young's definition of sickness, as opposed to disease and illness, as the social process of creating meaning out of corporeal signs and placing them in a healing context, one in which these symbols can be manipulated with respect to desired outcomes (Young 1982:270).

7. Gunshot wounds were a frequent complaint treated by the missionary hospital at Bella Bella. On more than one occasion the white doctor found himself in competition with a native healer over the removal of a bullet from a patient (G. Darby 1915:406). Some healers were renowned for being able to suck a large ball out of a patient (Boas 1923:18).

8. On 10 October 1833, just several months after the establishment of Fort McLoughlin, one of the Hudson's Bay Company's indentured servants, a French Canadian, escaped. The Hudson's Bay Company officers responded by accusing the local Indians of harboring him. The latter denied any knowledge of the escape. The traders refused to believe this and took Boston, the friendly chief of a local village, hostage. He was put in irons and paraded about in view of the Indians outside the fort. This led to an attempt on the part of the local Heiltsuks to free him by attacking the fort. Many of the Heiltsuks had muskets, but they were repulsed, and

many were felled by gunfire. At least one Heiltsuk was killed, and dozens were injured. Peace was soon made, aided by payments of rum and tobacco. The Hudson's Bay Company officers allowed the wounded to be treated by their physician, Dr. William Fraser Tolmie (Wilson 1833; Tolmie 1963:264).

9. It seems very likely that the introduction of liquor was indeed related to the increase in violent death and injury, but there is no direct evidence for it specifically for the Heiltsuks; this equation was, however, important in the ideology both of the missionary and of the anti-Indian colonial press (*Colonist,* 12 July 1862, p. 2; Fisher 1977:112; Gough 1984).

10. This was the first *documented* epidemic. Boyd (1985) suggests a small-pox epidemic of 1775, although the extent of such a disease event and whether it affected the Heiltsuks are not known.

11. Of course, the primary message of the Methodists was not their ability to overcome sickness, although this notion was deeply embedded in their rhetoric, but rather to overcome death itself, perhaps a more potent message in this context.

12. Missionary attitudes toward the Heiltsuks oscillated between imputations of "savagery"—which, especially for the earlier missionaries, implied the active presence of Satan—and the view that they were simply childlike, and thus guilty only of original sin. Missionary reforms thus employed two modalities, retributive and paternalistic.

13. Caroline Tate's account of this struggle between the forces of light and the forces of darkness is followed by several accounts of children's "good deaths" in the same epidemic. "Holy dying" was an important aspect of Methodist belief, as death was the only worthy goal of a Christian; this was a theme of which the nineteenth-century Methodist missionaries were particularly fond (Thompson 1980:409–10; see Weber 1976:141). It reaches back to Chaucer's *Prioress's Tale* and therefore into the Middle Ages. The contrast with the native view of death could not be more extreme (see Kan 1989; Harkin 1990a).

14. Epworth Leagues were local organizations devoted to supporting Methodist missions. The use of black in the uniforms corresponds to the Heiltsuk color symbolism, according to which black is associated with contact with the supernatural.

15. Things were not really arranged higgledy-piggledy in traditional houses; space was in fact highly organized.

16. The average number of people inhabiting a house in Bella Bella in 1914 was 4.3 (Fougner 1914-15).

17. The doctor was concerned with children as the main victims of epidemic diseases; the missionary was concerned with them because of what he believed to be their innate sinfulness. The two concerns were united, as were the two roles before the First World War, in the technique of removing children from their homes and placing them in "industrial schools" or girls' homes. The need for these institutions in Bella Bella was constantly being harped upon by missionaries in reports home (ARMCC 1905-6:60-64).

Chapter 7

1. There are accounts dealing with adult deaths, but these are not so formulaic and tend to be much more ambiguous; that is, they are probably more accurate.

2. According to the Bella Bella missionary during the 1890s, Ebbstone remained "a constant Christian and watchman" in his later years. His duties as watchman included monitoring the behavior of villagers, always watching out for signs of immorality (Beavis n.d.).

3. The pole is iconic of the vertical communication, with heaven and the underworld, and thus of the spatiotemporal expansion characteristic of *náwálak^w*.

4. This of course applied only to the village of Bella Bella itself, and not to other Heiltsuk villages. Moreover, forms of power not dependent on the Winter Ceremonial persisted even in Bella Bella well into the twentieth century. It was nonetheless an extremely important event.

5. Humchitt had his own village also, near Bella Bella.

6. These appear to be crude transcriptions of the name of the village itself, *q̓^{w}úqvayaítx^w*, rather than a personal name. The head chief of the village was named *waúyala*. He was the heir of a chief who had refused Christianity and shortly thereafter was drowned.

7. Inexplicably, he recalled the year as 1883, which was certainly not the case, making his other recollections suspect.

8. The council of chiefs was an institution consisting of the head chiefs of the local tribal groups, which probably dates back at least to the 1830s, when joint action with respect to fur traders was required and achieved.

Extraordinary councils to plan raids seem to be an aboriginal institution (Barbeau n.d.). In the early 1890s the council was reorganized under the auspices of the Indian agent and headed by the missionary. It had legal authority on petty matters (Beavis n.d.). The council was abandoned around the turn of the century, to be reinstated as an elected body in the 1920s (E. Darby 1922).

9. The importance of the written word to Christianity is obvious. Mathematics was, arguably, almost equally integral to the particular Methodist evangel. Certainly, the knowledge taught in the day school cannot be absolutely separated from the doctrine taught by the missionary. It is not merely a question of form and content; both the written word and mathematics were taken as good in themselves, and the latter had a strong influence on Wesley's theology.

10. The missionary, in keeping with the Discipline, was not hesitant to drop from membership those who did not live up to it. Even in these early years, almost as many names were dropped from the rolls as were admitted to full membership.

11. According to the cultural logic of hospitality, to act as host in such a feast indicated that Humchitt was ascendant. This is borne out in later history, when he became the overall chief of all the tribes that gathered in Bella Bella.

12. The fire occurred during the summer, when the people were away at the camps; only one old woman was left behind. All the masks and ritual property were destroyed. According to oral tradition, one factor in the destructiveness of the fire was the large quantity of oolichan grease that was being stored for use in the winter. The fire was thus both partly the result of the cultural conservatism of the village and the cause of the village's abandonment of tradition.

Chapter 8

1. Even on its own terms, Wolf's mode of production typology (1982:73–100) cannot accommodate Northwest Coast cultures, which are organized along neither purely kinship, nor purely tributary, lines. Although the existence of marginal cases does not invalidate a model, the preponderance of marginal cases here, along with the fact that the closer one looks at any specific case the more marginal it appears, suggests that Wolf's

model may hinder ethnohistorical understanding.

2. Formal counting was done by a hereditary counter using tally sticks. A precise mental record was kept of all such transactions (Drucker 1936–37; see Boas 1897). This required, obviously, a countable medium.

3. Generally it was the host who gave more, except in the extraordinary circumstance of the grease feast. The role of donor and incorporator was implicit in the role of host.

4. Of course, both in myth and in longer-term history, the repeated dominance of one person or group over another group led to incorporation (see Suttles 1960).

5. There were instances of utilitarian canoes, boxes, and dishes that were unnamed, but in general such objects were named. Thus they could not as a class constitute a medium of exchange.

6. In speaking of coppers, one is not speaking of precisely aboriginal culture, because these copper shields were made of copper sheeting that was used to line the hulls of European ships (Keithahn 1964; Lévi-Strauss 1982:132). However, native copper was an important wealth item before contact.

7. Although it may be the case that mass starvation occurred once every generation in the Salish culture area, there is no evidence of any sort that such a condition existed among the Heiltsuks (Piddocke 1965; Suttles 1968). On the contrary, all oral testimony on the subject stresses the extreme abundance of food available when resources were gathered in the traditional manner; archaeological evidence also suggests stability of resources (Pomeroy 1980:223). Moreover, even if local variation in resources did produce pockets of deprivation, this would have been corrected by unmarked transfer of food; oral testimony suggests an altruistic concept of land use, whereby friendly groups—even other ethnic groups, such as the Bella Coolas—were allowed to use certain resource areas.

8. Food was the most contained and thus the least specific entity. It was contained in boxes and feast dishes and, when consumed, was contained within the body, which was not only a container but was in turn contained, to several degrees.

9. Einzig (1948:321) lists seven requisite functions of money: utility and value, portability, indestructibility, homogeneity, divisibility, stability of value, and "cognizability." Furs satisfy five of these seven, excluding divisibility and stability of value. However, such substantive definitions

miss the point. What is important is how pervasive the "cash nexus" is within society (Nash 1966:27).

10. Thus, according to oral tradition, the ax heads that were received in trade were worn as pendants; this is one interpretation of the comment in "The First Schooner" that the Heiltsuks did not know what axes were used for. Using metal for collars is obviously very close to the use of cedar bark rings in the *čaíqa*.

11. In Bella Coola the name Schooner was taken and still exists as a surname. In the 1940s at Rivers Inlet, the names of famous Europeans and Americans were taken as chiefly names, for instance Theodore Roosevelt and Margot Asquith, as happened in late-eighteenth-century Hawaii (Olson 1949, 4:58; Sahlins 1981).

12. In an interesting irony, the ship's name was taken from the Quecha name for the last Inca, defeated by the Spaniards; it refers also to the general notion of defeat in the Spanish conquest, the overturning of a world order, and the chicken, which was an imported and important subsistence item (Seligmann 1987).

13. The term *white,* with reference to the fur trade, is merely a shorthand. The Hudson's Bay Company and the maritime fur traders employed a variety of ethnic groups. The Fort McLoughlin contingent, for instance, contained, in addition to the requisite Scots, French Canadians, Iroquois, and Hawaiians, among others. One evening's entertainment saw the Iroquois singing war songs, the Canadians singing voyageur ballads, and the Hawaiians singing "Rule Britannia" (Tolmie 1963:300).

14. With the outbreak of attacks by Indians on white traders on the northern coast in the 1830s, there was an interest in restricting the firepower of the Indians. John McLoughlin, chief factor of the Hudson's Bay Company, wanted to ban the sale of arms and ammunition to the Indians outright. A compromise was reached, by which the price of gunpowder was quadrupled. Obviously, Indians without guns would be of much less commercial value than Indians paying four times the normal price for gunpowder (Bancroft 1887:639).

15. The connection between a particularized other and a particularized object and sphere of exchange, in the context of the fur trade, can be seen in the *λúeḷáx̌a* dancing apron mentioned above. The thimbles sewn into it were particular thimbles given by a particular named being, Vancouver. By 1834 the thimble as a class of object had lost this particularized value.

16. On the Northwest Coast the domestic mode of production was rather

different from what Sahlins (1972) describes. There are two reasons: the superabundance of resources and the overproduction that resulted from the demands of the ceremonial system (Sahlins 1972:87-92).

17. Dunn, not a very accurate reporter, means the factor's house.

18. Legaix was a Heiltsuk title. The original holder was Heiltsuk, and the qualities embodied in the title were thought to be characteristically Heiltsuk (Garfield 1939:184).

19. The government issued licenses almost exclusively to the canneries, meaning that Indian commercial fishermen had to work as cannery employees (R. Knight 1978:82).

20. The claim to a title was validated primarily by a knowledge of the narrative behind the name, which would have been, by the definition of *núyemgíwa* itself ('carrying forth a narrative'), known to some degree by all named members.

21. The question of aboriginal title was not addressed in Canadian law until 1992, when aboriginal title was recognized in principle by the federal and provincial governments. However, with the recent *Delgamuukw* decision in British Columbia, denying the Gitksan and Wet'suwet'en land claim, clearly the principle has not yet been applied in concrete terms in the province of British Columbia (Burns 1992).

References

Abbreviations

ARMCC   Annual Reports of the Methodist Church of Canada
HBCA   Hudson's Bay Company Archives, Winnipeg, Manitoba
NAC   National Archives of Canada. Ottawa, Ontario
PABC   Provincial Archives of British Columbia, Victoria, B.C.
RCIABC   Royal Commission on Indian Affairs for the Province of British Columbia
UCA   United Church Archives, Toronto, Ontario
UCABC   United Church Archives, British Columbia Conference, Vancouver, B.C.

Primary Sources

Anderson, Alexander C.
    1845   Letter to Gov. George Simpson, 5 March. HBCA, D5/13.
    1878   History of the Northwest Coast. PABC, add. mss. 559.
ARMCC
    1880-1906 Annual Reports of the Methodist Church of Canada. UCA.
Barbeau, C. Marius
    n.d.   Notes from Alert Bay. Barbeau Papers, BF 270.15. National Museum of Civilization, Hull, Que.
Beavis, R. B.
    n.d.   Bella Bella. Goodfellow Papers. PABC, add. mss 2714.
Bissett, James
    1870   Report to Chief Factor James Graham, 12 Oct. HBCA, A.11/85, fols. 466-466d.
Boas, Franz
    1923   Bella Bella field notes. Boas collection, 372, reel 1. American Philosophical Society. Philadelphia.

British Columbia
    1875   Report on Indian Reserves. Sessional Papers for the Province of British
            Columbia. Robarts Library, University of Toronto.
Brown, Robert
    1866   Journal of the Goldstream Voyage. PABC, add. mss 0794.
Bruce, Edith
    1912   Correspondence to T. Edgerton Shore, 20 July. T. Edgerton Shore
            Papers, 78.093C, box 6, file 122. UCA.
Calvert, James
    1888   Correspondence. Missionary Outlook 8:47–48. UCA.
Canada
    1882–95 Reports of the Superintendent of Indian Affairs for British Columbia.
            Parliament of Canada, Sessional Papers.
    1905   Reports of Superintendents and Agents. Department of Indian Affairs.
            Parliament of Canada, Sessional Papers.
    1907   Reports of Superintendents and Agents. Department of Indian Affairs.
            Parliament of Canada, Sessional Papers.
    1916   Royal Commission on Indian Affairs for the Province of British Co-
            lumbia. Evidence. Bella Coola Agency (McKenna-McBride Commis-
            sion). NAC, RG10, v. 1044:T-1461.
Charles, William
    1877–78 Correspondence outward. PABC, AD 20/BB2.
Crosby, Thomas
    1883   Correspondence. Missionary Outlook 3:159. UCA.
Cuyler, W. B.
    1885   Correspondence. Missionary Outlook 6:14–15. UCA.
Darby, Edna (Mrs. George)
    1922   The Problem of the Indian Girl. Missionary Bulletin 17:109–12. UCA.
Darby, George
    1914   Correspondence. Missionary Bulletin 11:131–34. UCA.
    1915   Correspondence. Missionary Bulletin 21:401–6. UCA.
    1919   Correspondence. Missionary Outlook 39:53. UCA.
    1922   Correspondence. Missionary Bulletin 17:449–54. UCA.
    1959   Farewell address. CBC Radio, audio recording. UCA.
Drucker, Philip
    1936–37 Fieldnotes taken at Bella Bella. Smithsonian Institution, National
            Anthropological Archives, Bureau of American Ethnology Collection
            ms. no. 4516. Washington, D.C.
Finlayson, Duncan
    1941   Correspondence to Gov. George Simpson, 29 Sept. 1836. *In* The
            Letters of John McLoughlin from Fort Vancouver to the Governor and
            Committee, first series, 1825–38, edited by Edwin E. Rich, 324–25.
            London: Hudson's Bay Record Society.

Fougner, Iver
1914-15 Census of Bella Bella. Internal Correspondence, Office of the Indian
         Commissioner for British Columbia. NAC, RG10, v. 11019, file 504a.
1931   Correspondence from Agent Fougner to Chief Inspector W. E.
         Ditchburn. NAC, RG10, v. 1656.
Gladstone, Lillian, ed. and trans.
1974   Autobiographies of Heiltsuk Elders. Heiltsuk Cultural Education
         Centre, Waglisla, B.C.
Goodfellow, John
n.d.   The Two Bellas. UCABC.
Harkin, Michael
1985-87 Fieldnotes taken at Waglisla (Bella Bella), British Columbia. Manu-
         script and audio tapes in Harkin's possession.
Hopkins, G. F.
1891   Correspondence. Missionary Outlook 11:111. UCA.
1892   Correspondence. Missionary Outlook 12:87. UCA.
1893   Correspondence. Missionary Outlook 13:70-71. UCA.
Hudson, Frances D.
1910   Correspondence. Missionary Outlook 30:238. UCA.
Hudson's Bay Company
1834   Report on Millbank Sound on the Northwest Coast of America. HBCA,
         B.120/e.
1850-52 Ship's log of the SS *Beaver*. HBCA, C.1/208.
1858   Ship's log of the SS *Otter*. HBCA, C.1/220.
1876-77 Fort McLoughlin [*sic*] correspondence inward. HBCA, B.120/c/2.
1877-82 Bills of lading bound for Bella Bella. HBCA, B.120/z/1.
Hunt, George
1933   Field notes from Bella Bella and miscellaneous Kwakiutl notes,
         1897-1933, submitted to Franz Boas. Boas Collection, 372, reel 21.
         American Philosophical Society. Philadelphia.
Kissack, Reba
1903   Correspondence. Missionary Outlook 12:95. UCA.
Knight, Agnes
1885-87 Journal of Miss Agnes Knight, 10 July 1885-23 Oct. 1887. PABC, f7
         W15.
Large, Isabella (Mrs. Richard W.)
1905   Correspondence. Missionary Bulletin 2:591-94. UCA.
Large, Richard W.
1900   Correspondence. Missionary Outlook 19:198. UCA.
1901   Correspondence. Missionary Outlook 20:53-55. UCA.
1902   Correspondence. Missionary Bulletin 1:82-84. UCA.
1903a   Correspondence. Missionary Bulletin 1:227-33. UCA.
1903b   Correspondence. Missionary Bulletin 1:413-18. UCA.
1904   Correspondence. Missionary Bulletin 2:129-37. UCA.
1905   Correspondence. Missionary Bulletin 3:109-20. UCA.

1907   Correspondence. Missionary Outlook 26:6–7. UCA.

1908   Correspondence. Missionary Bulletin 5:17–22. UCA.

1909   Correspondence. Missionary Bulletin 6:7–18. UCA.

1910a   Correspondence. Missionary Bulletin 6:513–18. UCA.

1910b   Correspondence. Missionary Bulletin 6:913–18. UCA.

1912   Correspondence. Missionary Bulletin 8:1297–1301. UCA.

McIlwraith, Thomas F.

1921–24 Bella Coola field notes. McIlwraith Papers, B79-0054, boxes 11, 12. University of Toronto Archives.

Methodist Church of Canada (See ARMCC)

Olson, Ronald

1935, 1949 Field notes from Bella Bella and Rivers Inlet. 6 vols. Bancroft Library, University of California, Berkeley.

Pierce, William H.

1881   Correspondence. Missionary Outlook 1:71. UCA.

1884   Correspondence. Missionary Outlook 4:95. UCA.

Poutlass, Mrs.

1907   Slaughter Ilihee. PABC, add. mss. 199.

Preston, E. A.

1909   Glimpses of Mission Work on the Pacific Coast. Missionary Outlook 29:235. UCA.

RCIABC (Royal Commission on Indian Affairs for the Province of British Columbia)

1913   Transcript and minutes of hearings in Bella Bella, B.C. NAC, RG10, v. 11024, file A2.

1916   Minutes of decision. Bella Coola Agency. NAC, RG10, v. 11026, file SNB-2.

Ross, Charles

1842   Correspondence to Gov. George Simpson, 1 Oct. HBCA, AB 40/R735.

1843   Correspondence to Gov. George Simpson, 13 Apr. HBCA, AB 40/-R735.

1844   Correspondence to Gov. George Simpson, 10 Jan. PABC, AB 40/R735.

Sutherland, Alexander

1898a   Correspondence to Chief Charley of Bella Bella, 10 Oct. UCA.

1898b   Correspondence to Thomas Crosby, 3 Oct. UCA.

1898c   Correspondence to Dr. R. W. Large, 1 Nov., UCA.

1900   Correspondence to Dr. R. W. Large, 15 Aug. UCA.

Tate, Caroline

1881   Correspondence. Missionary Outllook 1:91. UCA.

1883   Correspondence. Missionary Outlook 4:14. UCA.

Tate, Charles M.

1877–83 Diary 1877–83. Tate Family Papers, add.mss 303. PABC.

1881   Correspondence. Missionary Outlook 1:48. UCA.

1882a   Christmas Day at Bella Bella. Missionary Outlook 3:35. UCA.

1882b   Correspondence. Missionary Outlook 3:46. UCA.

1883   Correspondence. Missionary Outlook 4:15. UCA.

1884a   Correspondence. Missionary Outlook 4:110-11. UCA.
1884b   Seal-Hunting in British Columbia. Pleasant Hours. UCA.
1888   Correspondence. Missionary Outlook 8:52-54. UCA.
1900   Correspondence. Western Methodist Recorder 1(5):3-4. UCA.
1916   How Bella-Bella Jack Spent Christmas and What It Meant to His Tribe. Western Methodist Recorder 16(6):4. UCA.
1917   Bella-Bella Jack as a Missionary to His Tribe. Western Methodist Recorder 16(10):10. UCA.
1929   Autosketch. Western Recorder 5. UCA.

Tod, John
1924   Bella Bella Mission Journal, 1880-1924. UCABC.
n.d.   History of New Caledonia and the Northwest Coast. United Church Archives, Vancouver, B.C. PABC.

Vancouver Daily World
1891   16 May. PABC.

Vancouver Sun
1991   4 Dec.

The Colonist
1860-70 28 Feb. 1860-26 Oct. 1870. PABC.

Wilson, [?]
1833   Extracts from the Diary of Fort McLoughlin at Millbank Sound in Relation to an Affair Which Occurred at That Place 10th October 1933. HBCA, B120/a/1.

Secondary Sources

Achard, Pierre
1983   Linguistique et histoire. *In* Histoire et linguistique, edited by Pierre Achard, Max-Peter Gruenais, and Dolores Jaulin, 21-32. Paris: Editions de la Maison des Sciences de l'Homme.

Adams, John W.
1974   Dialectics and Contingency in "The Story of Asdiwal": An Ethnographic Note. *In* The Unconscious in Culture: The Structuralism of Claude Lévi-Strauss in Perspective, edited by Ino Rossi, 170-78. New York: E. P. Dutton.

Aristotle
1920   Poetics. Translated by Ingram Bywater. Oxford: Clarendon.

Augustine
1961   Confessions. Translated by R. S. Pine-Coffin. Harmondsworth, Eng.: Penguin Books.

Axtell, James
1985   "Reduce them to Civility." *In* The Invasion Within: The Contest of Cultures in Colonial North America, 131-78. New York: Oxford University Press.

Bakhtin, Mikhail
1981   The Dialogic Imagination. Translated by Caryl Emerson and Michael Holquist. Austin: University of Texas Press.

Bancroft, Hubert H.
1887   History of British Columbia, 1792–1887. The Works of H. H. Bancroft, vol. 32. San Francisco: History Co.

Barthes, Roland
1986   The Rustle of Language. Translated by Richard Howard. New York: Hill and Wang.

Bateson, Gregoy
1972   Steps to an Ecology of Mind. New York: Ballantine Books.

Beidelman, Thomas O.
1982   Colonial Evangelism. Bloomington: Indiana University Press.

Berkhofer, Robert
1965   Salvation and the Savage. New York: Atheneum.
1978   The White Man's Indian: Images of the American Indian from Columbus to the Present. New York: Vintage.

Berman, Judith
1983   Three Discourse Elements in Boas' Kwakw'ala Texts. Working paper, Eighteenth International Conference on Salish and Neighboring Languages, 1–51. University of Washington, Seattle.
1991   The Seals' Sleeping Cave: The Interpretation of Boas' Kwakw'ala Texts. Ph.D. diss., University of Pennsylvania.

Black, Martha
1988   The R. W. Large Collection: A Bella Bella Document. Master's thesis, York University, Toronto.

Blackman, Margaret
1983   The Haida: A View from 1966. Reviews in Anthropology 10:55–64.

Bloch, Maurice
1982   Death, Women and Power. In Death and the Regeneration of Life, edited by Maurice Bloch and Jonathan Parry, 211–30. Cambridge: Cambridge University Press.

Bloch, Maurice, and Jonathan Parry
1982   Introduction: Death and the Regeneration of Life. In Death and the Regeneration of Life, edited by Maurice Bloch and Jonathan Parry, 1–44. Cambridge: Cambridge University Press.

Blu, Karen I.
1980   The Lumbee Problem: The Making of an American Indian People. Cambridge: Cambridge University Press.

Boas, Franz
1890   First General Report on the Indians of British Columbia. In Fifty-Ninth Report of the British Association for the Advancement of Science for 1889, 801–93. London.

1897   The Social Organization and the Secret Societies of the Kwakiutl Indians. *In* Report of the U.S. National Museum for 1895, 311–738. Washington, D.C.

1916   Tsimshian Mythology. Smithsonian Institution, Thirty-First Annual Report of the Bureau of American Ethnology for the Years 1909–10. Washington, D.C.

1921   Ethnology of the Kwakiutl. 2 vols. Smithsonian Institution, Thirty-Fifth Annual Report of the Bureau of American Ethnology for the Years 1913–14. Washington, D.C.

1925   Contributions to the Ethnology of the Kwakiutl. Columbia University Contributions to Anthropology 3. New York.

1928   Bella Bella Texts. Columbia University Contributions to Anthropology 5. New York.

1932   Bella Bella Tales. Memoirs of the American Folklore Society 52. New York.

1955   Primitive Art. New York: Dover.

1966   Kwakiutl Ethnography. Edited by Helen Codere. Chicago: University of Chicago Press.

Bourdieu, Pierre

1977   Outline of a Theory of Practice. Translated by R. Nice. Cambridge: Cambridge University Press.

Bourguignon, Erica

1976   Possession. Corte Madera, Calif.: Chandler and Sharp.

Boyd, Robert T.

1985   The Introduction of Infectious Diseases among the Indians of the Pacific Northwest, 1774–1874. Ph.D. diss., University of Washington.

1990   Demographic History, 1774–1874. *In* Handbook of North American Indians, edited by William C. Sturtevant. Vol. 7, Northwest Coast, edited by Wayne Suttles, 135–48. Washington, D.C.: Smithsonian Institution.

Braudel, Fernand

1969   Ecrits sur l'histoire. Paris: Flammarion.

Brown, G. Gordon

1944   Missions and Cultural Diffusion. American Journal of Sociology 50:214–19.

Buckley, Jerome H.

1966   The Triumph of Time: A Study of the Victorian Concepts of Time, History, Progress and Decadence. Cambridge: Belknap.

Burns, Peter T.

1992   Delgamuukw: A Summary of the Judgement. *In* Aboriginal Title in British Columbia: Delgamuukw v. The Queen, edited by Frank Cassidy, 21–34. Lantzville, B.C.: Oolichan Books and Institute for Research on Public Policy.

Carr, David

1986   Time, Narrative, and History. Bloomington: Indiana University Press.

Cassidy, Frank, and Norman Dale
    1988   After Native Claims?: The Implications of Comprehensive Claims
              Settlements for Natural Resources in British Columbia. Lantzville,
              B.C.: Oolichan Books and Institute for Research on Public Policy.
Clifford, James, and George E. Marcus, eds.
    1986   Writing Culture: The Poetics and Politics of Ethnography. Berkeley:
              University of California Press.
Codere, Helen
    1950   Fighting with Property: A Study of Kwakiutl Potlatching and Warfare,
              1792–1930. New York: J. J. Augustin.
    1961   Kwakiutl. *In* Perspectives in American Indian Culture Change, edited
              by Edward H. Spicer, 431–516. Chicago: University of Chicago Press.
Cole, Douglas, and Ira Chaikin
    1990   "An Iron Hand upon the People": The Law against the Potlatch on the
              Northwest Coast. Seattle: University of Washington Press.
Comaroff, Jean
    1980   Healing and the Cultural Order: The Case of the Barolong boo Ratshidi
              of Southern Africa. American Ethnologist 7:637–57.
    1981   Healing and Cultural Transformation: The Tswana of Southern Africa.
              Social Science and Medicine 15B:367–78.
    1985   Body of Power, Spirit of Resistance. Chicago: University of Chicago
              Press.
Comaroff, Jean, and John L. Comaroff
    1991   Of Revelation and Revolution: Christianity, Colonialism, and Con-
              sciousness in South Africa. Vol. 1. Chicago: University of Chicago
              Press.
    1992   Ethnography and the Historical Imagination. Boulder, Colo.: Westview.
Comaroff, John L.
    1982   Dialectical Systems, History and Anthropology: Units of Study and
              Questions of Theory. Journal of South African Studies 8:143–72.
Connerton, Paul
    1989   How Societies Remember. Cambridge: Cambridge University Press.
Cove, John
    1982   The Gitksan Traditional Concept of Land Ownership. Anthropologica
              24:3–17.
    1987   Shattered Images: Dialogues and Meditations on Tsimshian Narratives.
              Ottawa: Carleton University Press.
Crapanzano, Vincent
    1980   Tuhami: A Portrait of a Moroccan. Chicago: University of Chicago
              Press.
    1986   Hermes' Dilemma: The Masking of Subversion in Ethnographic De-
              scription. *In* Writing Culture: The Poetics and Politics of Ethnography,
              edited by James Clifford and George E. Marcus, 51–76. Berkeley:
              University of California Press.

1990   On Dialogue. *In* The Interpretation of Dialogue, edited by Tullio Maranhao, 269–91. Chicago: University of Chicago Press.

Crosby, Alfred W.
1986   Ecological Imperialism: The Biological Expansion of Europe, 900–1900. Cambridge: Cambridge University Press.

Crosby, Thomas
1914   Up and Down the North Pacific Coast by Canoe and Mission Ship. Toronto: Missionary Society of the Methodist Church.

Cruikshank, Julie
1990   Life Lived like a Story: Life Stories of Three Yukon Native Elders. Lincoln: University of Nebraska Press.

Curtis, Edward S.
1915   The North American Indian. Vol. 10, The Kwakiutl. Norwood, Mass.: Plimpton Press.

Darby, George
1933   Indian Medicine in British Columbia. Canadian Medical Association Journal 28:433–38.

Davenport, William
1959   Nonunilineal Descent and Descent Groups. American Anthropologist 61:557–69.

De Certeau, Michel
1988   The Writing of History. Translated by Tom Conley. New York: Columbia University Press.

De Laguna, Frederica
1972   Under Mount Saint Elias: The History and Culture of the Yakutat Tlingit. 3 vols. Smithsonian Contributions to Anthropology 7. Washington, D.C.

Dobyns, Henry
1966   Estimating Aboriginal American Population, 1: An Appraisal of Techniques with a New Hemispheric Estimate. Current Anthropology 7: 395–416.

1983   Their Number Became Thinned: Native American Population Dynamics in Eastern North America. Knoxville: University of Tennessee Press.

1989   More Methodological Perspectives on Native American Demography. Ethnohistory 36:285–99.

Douglas, Mary
1966   Purity and Danger. London: Routledge and Kegan Paul.

Dreyfus, Hubert L., and Paul Rabinow
1983   Michel Foucault: Beyond Structuralism and Hermeneutics. Chicago: University of Chicago Press.

Drucker, Philip
1940   Kwakiutl Dancing Societies. University of California Anthropological Records 2(6). Berkeley.

1950   Culture Element Distributions 26: Northwest Coast. University of
            California Anthropological Records 9(3). Berkeley.
Drucker, Philip, and Robert Heizer
1967   To Make My Name Good: A Reexamination of the Southern Kwakiutl
            Potlatch. Berkeley: University of California Press.
Dunn, John D.
1844   History of the Oregon Territory and British North American Fur Trade.
            London: Edwards and Hughes.
Durkheim, Emile
1965   The Elementary Forms of the Religious Life. Translated by Joseph
            Ward Swain. New York: Free Press.
Einzig, Paul
1948   Primitive Money. London: Eyre and Spottiswoode.
Eliade, Mircea
1954   The Myth of the Eternal Return, or Cosmos and History. Translated by
            Willard R. Trask. Princeton, N.J.: Princeton University Press.
Ellen, Roy F.
1977   Anatomical Classification and the Semiotics of the Body. *In* The
            Anthropology of the Body, edited by John Blacking, 343–74. London:
            Academic Press.
Emmons, George T.
1911   Native Account of the Meeting between La Perouse and the Tlingit.
            American Anthropologist 13:294–98.
Fabian, Johannes
1983   Time and the Other: How Anthropology Makes Its Object. New York:
            Columbia University Press.
Fèbvre, Lucien
1942   La Probleme de l'incroyance au 16ᵉ Siecle. Paris: A. Michel.
Fisher, Robin
1977   Contact and Conflict: Indian-European Relations in British Columbia,
            1774–1890. Vancouver: University of British Columbia Press.
Fleisher, Mark S.
1981   The Potlatch: A Symbolic and Psychoanalytic View. Current Anthro-
            pology 22:69–71.
Fogelson, Raymond
1984   Who Were the Aní-Kutáni? An Excursion into Cherokee Historical
            Thought. Ethnohistory 31:255–63.
Fogelson, Raymond, and Richard N. Adams, eds.
1977   The Anthropology of Power. New York: Academic Press.
Ford, Clellan S.
1941   Smoke from Their Fires: The Life of a Kwakiutl Chief. New Haven,
            Conn.: Yale University Press.
Foucault, Michel
1975   The Birth of the Clinic. Translated by A. M. Sheridan Smith. New
            York: Vintage.

1978   The History of Sexuality. Vol. 1, An Introduction. Translated by
            Robert Hurley. New York: Vintage.
1979   Discipline and Punish. Translated by Alan Sheridan. New York: Vin-
            tage.
1980a   The History of Sexuality. Vol. 1, An Introduction. New York: Vintage.
1980b   Power/Knowledge: Selected Interviews and Other Writings, 1972–
            1977. Edited by Colin Gordon. Translated by Colin Gordon, Leo
            Marshall, John Mepham, and Kate Soper. New York: Pantheon.
Freud, Sigmund
1924   General Introduction to Psychoanalysis. Translated by Joan Riviere.
            New York: Washington Square Press.
Furst, Peter T.
1989   The Water of Life: Symbolism and Natural History on the Northwest
            Coast. Dialectical Anthropology 14:95–115.
Gadacz, Rene R.
1981   Understanding and Interpretation in Historical Ethnology. Anthro-
            pologica 23:181–89.
Gadamer, Hans-Georg
1980   Dialogue and Dialectic. New Haven, Conn.: Yale University Press.
1986   Truth and Method. New York: Crossroad.
Garfield, Viola
1939   Tsimshian Clan and Society. University of Washington Publications in
            Anthropology 7(3). Seattle.
Geertz, Clifford
1973   The Interpretation of Cultures. New York: Basic Books.
1988   Works and Lives: The Anthropologist as Author. Stanford: Stanford
            University Press.
Gillespie, Michael Allen
1984   Hegel, Heidegger, and the Ground of History. Chicago: University of
            Chicago Press.
Goldman, Irving
1975   The Mouth of Heaven: An Introduction to Kwakiutl Religious Thought.
            New York: Wiley.
Gough, Barry M.
1984   Gunboat Frontier: British Maritime Authority and Northwest Coast
            Indians, 1846–90. Vancouver: University of British Columbia Press.
Gramsci, Antonio
1971   Selections from the Prison Notebooks. Edited and translated by Quintin
            Hoare and G. Nowell Smith. New York: International Publishers.
Grant, John M.
1984   Moon of Wintertime: Missionaries and the Indians of Canada in
            Encounter since 1534. Toronto: University of Toronto Press.
Haidu, Peter
1982   Semiotics and History. Semiotica 40:187–228.

Haig-Brown, Celia
  1988   Resistance and Renewal: Surviving the Indian Residential School.
            Vancouver, B.C.: Tillacum.
Halbwachs, Maurice
  1992   On Collective Memory. Translated by Lewis A. Coser. Chicago: Uni-
            versity of Chicago Press.
Hallowell, A. Irving
  1955   Culture and Experience. Philadelphia: University of Pennsylvania
            Press.
  1976   Contributions to Anthropology. Chicago: University of Chicago Press.
Harkin, Michael
  1988   History, Temporality, and Narrative: Examples from the Northwest
            Coast. Ethnohistory 35:99-130.
  1990a   Mortuary Practices and the Category of Person among the Heiltsuk.
            Arctic Anthropology 27(1):87-108.
  1990b   Personalistic and Naturalistic Ideologies in Heiltsuk Accounts of Illness
            Events. Paper presented at American Society for Ethnohistory Annual
            Meeting, Toronto, Ontario.
  1993   Power and Progress: The Evangelic Dialogue among the Heiltsuk.
            Ethnohistory 40:1-33.
  1994a   Contested Bodies: Affliction and Power in Heiltsuk Culture and His-
            tory. American Ethnologist 21:586-605.
  1994b   Person, Time, and Being: Northwest Coast Rebirth in Comparative
            Perspective. In Amerindian Rebirth: Reincarnation Belief among North
            American Indians and Inuit, edited by Antonia Mills and Richard Slo-
            bodin, 192-210. Toronto: University of Toronto Press.
  in press Carnival and Authority: Heiltsuk Cultural Models of Power. Ethos 24.
Heidegger, Martin
  1962   Being and Time. Translated by John Macquarrie and Edward Robin-
            son. New York: Harper and Row.
  1972   On Time and Being. Translated by Joan Stambaugh. New York: Harper
            and Row.
  1982   The Basic Problems of Phenomenology. Translated by Albert Hofstad-
            ter. Bloomington: Indiana University Press.
Hertz, Robert
  1960   Death and the Right Hand. Translated by Rodney Needham and
            Claudia Needham. Glencoe, Ill.: Free Press.
Hilton, Susanne F.
  1990   Haihais, Bella Bella, and Oowekeeno. In Handbook of North American
            Indians, edited by William C. Sturtevant. Vol. 7, Northwest Coast,
            edited by Wayne Suttles, 312-22. Washington, D.C.: Smithsonian
            Institution.
Hilton, Susanne F., and John C. Rath
  1982   Objections to Franz Boas' Referring to Eating People in the Translation
            of the Kwakwala Terms of bax^{u}bakwalanux^{u}siwe and hamats!a. Work-

ing paper, Seventeenth International Conference on Salish and Neighboring Languages. Portland State University, Portland, Oreg.

Holm, Bill
1983   Box of Daylight: Northwest Coast Indian Art. Seattle: Seattle Art
          Museum and University of Washington Press.

Howay, Frederic W., ed.
1941   Voyages of the "Columbia" to the Northwest Coast, 1787-1790 and
          1790-1793. Massachusetts Historical Society Collections 79. Boston.

Hoy, David
1978   History, Historicity, and Historiography in Being and Time. *In* Heideg-
          ger and Modern Philosophy, edited by Michael Murray, 329-54. New
          Haven, Conn.: Yale University Press.

Hymes, Dell H.
1981   'In vain I tried to tell you': Essays in Native American Ethnopoetics.
          Philadelphia: University of Pennsylvania Press.

Kan, Sergei
1985   Russian Orthodox Brotherhoods among the Tlingit: Missionary Goals
          and Native Response. Ethnohistory 32:196-223.
1989   Symbolic Immortality: The Tlingit Potlatch of the Nineteenth Century.
          Washington, D.C.: Smithsonian Institution Press.

Kaplan, Martha, and John Kelly
1994   Rethinking Resistance: Dialogics of "Disaffection" in Colonial Fiji.
          American Ethnologist 21:123-51.

Keithahn, Edward L.
1964   Origin of the "Chief's Copper" or "Tinneh." University of Alaska
          Anthropological Papers 12:59-78. College.

Kew, J. E. Michael
1990   History of Coastal British Columbia since 1849. *In* Handbook of North
          American Indians, edited by William C. Sturtevant. Vol. 7, Northwest
          Coast, edited by Wayne Suttles, 159-68. Washington, D.C.: Smith-
          sonian Institution.

Kirchhoff, Paul
1955   The Principles of Clanship in Human Society. Davidson Journal of
          Anthropology 1:1-10.

Knight, Rolf
1978   Indians at Work: An Informal History of Native Indian Labour in
          British Columbia 1858-1930. Vancouver, B.C.: New Star Books.

Kobrinsky, Vernon
1979   The Mouths of the Earth: The Dialectical Allegories of the Kwakiutl
          Indians. Dialectical Anthropology 4:163-77.

Kolstee, Anton
1988   To Impersonate the Supernatural: Music and Ceremony of the Bella
          Bella/Heiltsuk Indians of British Columbia. Ph.D. diss., University of
          Illinois.

Krech, Shepard
  1991   The State of Ethnohistory. *In* Annual Review of Anthropology, vol. 20,
          edited by Bernard J. Siegel, 345-75. Palo Alto, CA.
Lamb, W. Kaye, ed.
  1943   Five Letters of Charles Ross, 1842-1844. British Columbia Historical
          Quarterly 7:103-18.
Large, Richard Geddes
  1968   Drums and Scalpel: From Native Healers to Physicians on the North
          Pacific Coast. Vancouver, B.C.: Mitchell Press.
LaViolette, Forrest E.
  1973   The Struggle for Survival. Toronto: University of Toronto Press.
Leach, Edmund
  1954   Political Systems of Highland Burma. Boston: Beacon Press.
  1961   Two Essays concerning the Symbolic Representation of Time. *In* Re-
          thinking Anthropology, 124-36. London: Athlone Press.
Lévi-Strauss, Claude
  1963a   The Structural Study of Myth. *In* Structural Anthropology, translated
          by Claire Jacobsen and Brooke Grundfest Schoepf, 206-31. New York:
          Basic Books.
  1963b   Totemism. Translated by Rodney Needham. Boston: Beacon.
  1967   The Story of Asdiwal. *In* The Structural Study of Myth and Totemism,
          edited by Edmund Leach, 1-48. A.S.A. Monographs 5. London: Tavi-
          stock.
  1969   The Elementary Structures of Kinship. Translated by James H. Bell and
          John R. von Sturmer. Boston: Beacon Press.
  1977   Tristes Tropiques. Translated by John and Doreen Weightman. New
          York: Washington Square Books.
  1982   The Way of the Masks. Translated by Sylvia Modelski. Seattle: Uni-
          versity of Washington Press.
Lévi-Strauss, Claude, Marc Augé, and Maurice Godelier
  1976   Anthropology, History, and Ideology. Critique of Anthropology (n.s.)
          6:44-55.
Lewis, Oscar
  1966   La Vida. New York: Random House.
Lincoln, Neville J., and John C. Rath
  1980   North Wakashan Comparative Root List. National Museum of Man.
          Mercury Series. Ethnology Service Papers 68. Ottawa.
Loo, Tina
  1992   Dan Cranmer's Potlatch: Law as Coercion, Symbol, and Rhetoric in
          British Columbia, 1884-1951. Canadian Historical Review 73:125-65.
MacDonald, James
  1994   Social Change and the Creation of Underdevelopment: A Northwest
          Coast Case. American Ethnologist 21:152-75.
McFeat, Tom, ed.,
  1966   Indians of the North Pacific Coast. Toronto: McClelland and Stewart.

McIlwraith, Thomas F.
  1948   The Bella Coola Indians. 2 vols. Toronto: University of Toronto Press.
McKervill, Hugh W.
  1964   Darby of Bella Bella: Wo-Ya-La. Toronto: Ryerson Press.
Martin, Calvin
  1992   In the Spirit of the Earth. Baltimore: Johns Hopkins University Press.
Marx, Karl
  1967   Capital. Vol. 1. Translated by Samuel Moore and Edward Aveling.
             New York: International Publishers.
Mauss, Marcel
  1954   The Gift. Translated by Ian Cunnison. London: Cohen and West.
  1979   Seasonal Variations of the Eskimo. Translated by James J. Fox.
             London: Routledge and Kegan Paul.
  1985   A Category of the Human Mind: The Notion of the Person; the Notion
             of the Self, translated by W. D. Halls. *In* The Category of the Person:
             Anthropology, Philosophy, History, edited by Michael Carrithers,
             Steven Collins, and Steven Lukes, 1–25. Cambridge: Cambridge
             University Press.
Mauss, Marcel, and Henri Hubert
  1964   Sacrifice: Its Nature and Function. Translated by W. D. Halls. London:
             Cohen and West.
Medvedev, Pavel N.
  1978   The Formal Method in Literary Scholarship. Translated by Albert J.
             Wehrle. Baltimore: Johns Hopkins University Press.
Miller, Christopher L., and George R. Hamell
  1986   A New Perspective on Indian-White Contact: Cultural Symbols and
             Colonial Trade. Journal of American History 73:311–28.
Mitchell, Donald H.
  1981   Sebassa's Men. *In* The World Is as Sharp as a Knife: An Anthology in
             Honour of Wilson Duff, edited by Donald Abbott, 79–86. Victoria:
             British Columbia Provincial Museum.
Morrison, Kenneth
  1990   Baptism and Alliance: The Symbolic Mediations of Religious Syn-
             cretism. Ethnohistory 37:416–37.
Nash, Manning
  1966   Primitive and Peasant Economic Systems. San Francisco: Chandler
             Press.
Obeyesekere, Gananath
  1992   The Apotheosis of Captain Cook: European Mythmaking in the Pacific.
             Princeton, N.J.: Princeton University Press.
Olson, Ronald
  1954   Social Life of the Owikeno Kwakiutl. University of California Anthro-
             pological Records 14(3). Berkeley.
  1955   Notes on the Bella Bella Kwakiutl. University of California Anthropo-
             logical Records 14. Berkeley.

1966   Black Market in Prerogatives among the Northern Kwakiutl. *In* Indians of the North Pacific Coast, edited by Tom McFeat, 108-11. Toronto: McClelland and Stewart.

Pachter, Henry M.

1974   Defining an Event: Prolegomenon to Any Future Philosophy of History. Social Research 41:439-66.

Patterson, E. Palmer.

1972   The Canadian Indian: A History since 1500. Toronto: Collier McMillan Canada.

Peel, John D. Y.

1968   Syncretism and Religious Change. Comparative Studies in Society and History 15:121-41.

1989   The Cultural Work of Yoruba Ethnogenesis. *In* History and Ethnicity, edited by Elizabeth Tonkin, Maryon McDonald, and Malcolm Chapman, 198-215. London: Routledge.

Pethick, Derek

1976   First Approaches to the Northwest Coast. North Vancouver, B.C.: Douglas and McIntyre.

Piddocke, Stuart

1965   The Potlatch System of the Southern Kwakiutl: A New Perspective. Southwestern Journal of Anthropology 21:244-64.

Pierce, William H.

1933   From Potlatch to Pulpit. Vancouver, B.C.: Vancouver Bindery.

Pomeroy, John A.

1980   Bella Bella Settlement and Subsistence. Ph.D. diss., Simon Fraser University.

Rath, John C.

1981   A Practical Heiltsuk-English Dictionary with a Grammatical Introduction. 2 vols. National Museum of Man. Mercury Series. Ethnology Service Papers 75. Ottawa.

Reid, Katerina Susanne

1976   The Origins of the Tsetseqa in the Baxus: A Study of Kwakiutl Prayers, Myths, and Ritual. Ph.D. diss., University of British Columbia.

Reid, Martine

1981   La cérémonie hamatsa des Kwagul: Approche structuraliste des rapports mythe-rituel. Ph.D. diss., University of British Columbia.

Rey, Pierre-Phillipe

1973   Les alliances des classes: Sur l'articulation des modes de production. Paris: Maspero.

Rich, Edwin E.

1941   The Letters of John McLoughlin from Fort Vancouver to the Governor and Committee. First Series, 1825-1838. London: Hudson's Bay Record Society.

1943   The Letters of John McLoughlin from Fort Vancouver to the Governor and Committee. Second Series, 1839–1844. London: Hudson's Bay Record Society.

Ricoeur, Paul
1983   Temps et recit. Vol. 1. Paris: Editions du Seuil.

Rosaldo, Renato
1980   Doing Oral History. Social Analysis 4:89–99.

Roseberry, William
1989   Anthropologies and Histories. New Brunswick, N.J.: Rutgers University Press.

Rumley, Hilary E.
1973   Reactions to Contact and Colonialization: An Interpretation of Religious and Social Change among Indians of British Columbia. Master's thesis, University of British Columbia.

Sahlins, Marshall
1972   Stone Age Economics. Chicago: Aldine-Atherton.
1981   Historical Metaphors and Mythical Realities. Ann Arbor: University of Michigan Press.
1985   Islands of History. Chicago: University of Chicago Press.

Said, Edward
1978   Orientalism. New York: Vintage.

Sale, Kirkpatrick
1990   The Conquest of Paradise: Christopher Columbus and the Columbian Legacy. New York: Plume.
1991   The Conquest of Paradise: Christopher Columbus and the Columbian Legacy. New York: Plume.

Sapir, Edward
1934   Symbolism. Encyclopedia of the Social Sciences 14:492–95.

Seguin, Margaret
1982   On Symbolic Views of the Potlatch. Current Anthropology 23:333–34.
1985   Interpretive Contexts for Traditional and Current Coast Tsimshian Feasts. National Museum of Man Mercury Series, no. 98. Ottawa.

Seligmann, Linda J.
1987   The Chicken in Andean History and Myth: The Quecha Concept of Wallpa. Ethnohistory 34:139–70.

Sewid, James
1969   Guests Never Leave Hungry: The Autobiography of James Sewid, a Kwakiutl Indian, James P. Spradley, ed. New Haven, Conn.: Yale University Press.

Sheppe, Walter
1962   The First Man West: Alexander Mackenzie's Journal of His Voyage to the Pacific Coast of Canada in 1793. Berkeley: University of California Press.

Stephenson, Annie D.
1925   One Hundred Years of Canadian Methodist Missions. Vol. 1. Toronto:
           Missionary Society of the Methodist Church.
Stevenson, David
n.d.   A Cultural History of the Oowekeeno People. Hull, Que.: National
           Museum of Civilization.
Storie, Susanne, and Jennifer Gould, eds.
1973   Bella Bella Stories. Victoria: British Columbia Indian Advisory Com-
           mittee.
Strathern, Andrew
1971   The Rope of Moka. Cambridge: Cambridge University Press.
Suttles, Wayne
1954   Post-Contact Culture Change among the Lummi Indians. British
           Columbia Historical Quarterly 18:29-102. Vancouver.
1960   Affinal Ties, Subsistence, and Prestige among the Coast Salish. Ameri-
           can Anthropologist 62:296-305.
1968   Variation in Habitat and Culture on the Northwest Coast. In Man in
           Adaptation: The Cultural Present, edited by Yehudi Cohen, 93-106.
           New York: Aldine.
Swanton, John
1905   Contributions to the Ethnology of the Haida. Publications of the Jesup
           North Pacific Expedition 5, Memoirs of the American Museum of
           Natural History 8(1):1-300. New York.
Swearingen, C. Jan
1990   Dialogue and Dialectic: The Logic of Conversation and the Interpre-
           tation of Logic. In The Interpretation of Dialogue, edited by Tullio
           Maranhao, 47-74. Chicago: University of Chicago Press.
Taussig, Michael
1987   History as Commodity in Some Recent American (Anthropological)
           Literature. Food and Foodways 2:151-69.
Thompson, Edward P.
1967   Time, Work-Discipline and Industrial Capitalism: Past and Present 38:
           56-97.
1980   The Making of the English Working Class. Harmondsworth: Penguin
           Books.
Thornton, Russell, and Joan Marsh-Thornton
1981   Estimating Prehistoric American Indian Population Size for United
           States Area: Implications of the Nineteenth Century Population Decline
           and Nadir. American Journal of Physical Anthropology 77:289-94.
Todorov, Tzvetan
1984   Mikhail Bakhtin: The Dialogical Principle. Minneapolis: University of
           Minnesota Press.
Tolmie, William Fraser
1963   The Journals of William Fraser Tolmie, Physician and Fur Trader.
           Vancouver, B.C.: Mitchell Press.

Trigger, Bruce
    1975   Brecht and Ethnohistory. Ethnohistory 22:51-56.
Turner, Terence
    1968   Parson's Concept of "Generalized Media of Social Interaction" and Its
                Relevance for Social Anthropology. Sociological Inquiry 38:121-34.
    1977   Transformation, Hierarchy and Transcendence: A Reformulation of
                Van Gennep's Model of the Structure of Rites de Passage. *In* Secular
                Ritual, edited by Sally Falk Moore and Barbara G. Meyerhoff, 53-72.
                Assen, The Netherlands: Van Gorcum.
Turner, Victor
    1968   The Drums of Affliction: A Study of Religious Processes among the
                Ndembu of Zambia. Oxford: Oxford University Press.
Vancouver, George
    1967   A Voyage of Discovery to the North Pacific and around the World.
                Bibliotheca Australiana 31. New York: Da Capo Press.
Van Gennep, Arnold
    1960   The Rites of Passage. Translated by Monika Vizedom and Gabrielle
                Caffee. Chicago: University of Chicago Press.
Vansina, Jan
    1985   Oral Tradition as History. Madison: University of Wisconsin Press.
Volosinov, Valentin N.
    1973   Marxism and the Philosophy of Language. Translated by Ladislav
                Mateika and Irwin R. Titunik. New York: Seminar Press.
Walbran, John T.
    1971   British Columbia Coast Names, 1592-1906. Vancouver: J. J. Douglas.
Walens, Stanley
    1981   Feasting with Cannibals: An Essay on Kwakiutl Cosmology. Princeton,
                N.J.: Princeton University Press.
Walkus, Simon, Susanne Storie Hilton, Evelyn Walkus Windsor, and John C. Rath
    1982   Oowekeeno Oral Traditions as Told by the Late Chief Simon Walkus,
                Sr. National Museum of Man. Mercury Series, no. 64. Ottawa.
Wallace, Anthony F. C.
    1956   Revitalization Movements. American Anthropologist 58:264-81.
    1970   Death and Rebirth of the Seneca. New York: Knopf.
Weber, Max
    1976   The Protestant Ethic and the Spirit of Capitalism. Translated by Talcott
                Parsons. New York: Scribner's.
White, Hayden
    1973   Metahistory: The Historical Imagination in Nineteenth-Century Europe.
                Baltimore: Johns Hopkins University Press.
White, Richard
    1991   The Middle Ground: Indians, Empires, and Republics in the Great
                Lakes Region, 1650-1815. Cambridge: Cambridge University Press.

Wike, Joyce A.
1951   The Effect of the Maritime Fur Trade on Northwest Coast Indian Society. Ph.D. diss., Columbia University.

Wolf, Eric
1982   Europe and the People without History. Berkeley: University of California Press.

Worsley, Peter
1968   And the Trumpet Shall Sound: A Study of "Cargo" Cults in Melanesia. New York: Shocken.

Young, Allen
1982   The Anthropologies of Illness and Sickness. *In* Annual Review of Anthropology, vol. 11, 257–85.

Index

In *Studies in the Anthropology of North American Indians*

Ceremonies of the Pawnee
By James R. Murie
Edited by Douglas R. Parks

*Archaeology and Ethnohistory
of the Omaha Indians: The Big
Village Site*
By John M. O'Shea and
John Ludwickson

*Traditional Narratives of the
Arikara Indians* (4 vols.)
By Douglas R. Parks